실제 뉴스를 진행하는 '바로그' 아나운서에게 배우는

시사 영어 100

권아나의

27만 구독자

영어 뉴스룸

ENGLISH NEWSROOM

Preface(머리글)

안녕하세요, <권아나의 영어 뉴스룸> 독자 여러분!

시사 영어 학습은 영어 고수 단계로 진입하기 위한 필수코스입니다. 그런 만큼 시사 영어를 익히게 되면 확실히 영어실력이 늘었다는 느낌을 가질 수 있습니다.

'영어 뉴스'는 이러한 시사 영어를 공부하는 학습자들에게는 필수 자료로 여겨집니다. 하지만 대부분은 시사 영어의 높을 벽을 절감하고 포기하고 마는 것이 현실인데요. 이것은 배경지식이 없는 상태에서 영어 뉴스 자료인 CNN이나 BBC를 접하기 때문입니다. 우리나라 뉴스 기사도 배경지식이 없는 상태에서는 한국말로 봐도 이해가 잘 가지 않는 것과 궤를 같이 합니다.

따라서 효율적인 시사 영어 학습을 위해서는 우리가 잘 아는 배경지식이 녹아 있는 영어 뉴스 기사를 학습의 타겟으로 설정하는 것이 좋습니다. 그것이 아리랑 뉴스 기사를 시사 영어의 교재로 활용하는 이유입니다.

이 교재는 최근 1년치 뉴스 중 학습하는 데 도움이 될만한 어휘, 구문, 구조가 골고루 포함된 100개의 기사를 뽑아 구성하였습니다. 이것을 저의 네이버 오디오 클립 강의와 함께 반복 학습하시면 충분하고요. 이 외 다른 뉴스 기사들은 학습의 대상이 아닌 컨텐츠 소비의 대상으로 그냥 들으시면 됩니다.

이제 저와 함께 고급 영어의 정수라고 일컫는 시사 영어를 쉽고 재미있게 정복해 볼까요?

아나운서 권주현

Guide (교재안내)

이 교재의 특징

1

실제 영어 뉴스를 진행하는 아나운서의 강의!

27만 유튜버이자 실제 아리랑 뉴스를 진행하는 아나운서가 최고의
전달력으로 재미있게 설명한다.

2

단 한 권으로 시사 영어 정복!

시사 영어를 이해하는데 필요한 어휘, 구문, 구조가 골고루 포함된
기사들을 뽑아 한권의 반복 학습으로 시사 영어를 정복할 수 있도록
구성하였다.

3

접근하기 쉬운 기사를 통해 학습 능률 향상!

누구나 알고 있는 배경지식이 전제된 100개의 기사를 뽑아 학습에
용이할 수 있도록 구성하였다.

4

최대의 학습효과를 위한 직역과 의역의 절충!

영어를 해석함에 있어서 너무 직역만 하면 어색하고, 너무 의역만 해도
영어 학습에는 도움이 되지 않는다. 따라서 이 교재는 영어뉴스를 체득할
수 있을 정도의 직역과 의역을 절충해서 되도록이면 어색하지 않게,
그러면서도 최대의 학습효과를 낼 수 있을 정도의 텍스트로 해석하였다.

5

영작 연습으로 완벽 마스터!

각 단원 말미에 영작 연습을 할 수 있게 구성하였다.
이 부분은 교재를 2~3회 독 후 도전하는 것을 추천한다.

Contents(목차)

Contents(목차)

Have Fun with the English News Room

BRK 457/3
Today TH

BRK 457/3
457/3
Today TH

영어 뉴스룸 01

English NewsRoom

BREAKING NEWS

S. Korea's car exports up in March, but COVID-19 impact looms in April. Despite the coronavirus pandemic, the South Korean auto industry last month saw an increase in production, domestic demand and exports. According to the trade ministry, auto production rose by around 7 percent on year to nearly 370-thousand units. Domestic consumption surged by 10 percent in part because the government cut the special consumption tax on..

코로나 사태에도 차는 더 잘팔린다고?

코로나 사태로 인한 정부의 자동차 개별소비세 한시적 인하 조치로 자동차 거래량이 증가했다는 내용입니다.

S. Korea's car exports up in March, but COVID-19 impact looms in April

Despite the coronavirus pandemic, the South Korean auto industry last month saw an increase in production, domestic demand and exports.

According to the trade ministry, auto production rose by around 7 percent on year to nearly 370-thousand units.

Domestic consumption surged by 10 percent in part because the government cut the special consumption tax on cars and thanks to discounts given by some dealers.

Exports were up by 1.3 percent on sales of SUVs and eco-friendly cars.

However, a trade ministry official said, "The coronavirus's impact on exports in March was limited, but the figures for April will be worse because of the pandemic's spread in Europe and the U.S."

 스크립트 분석

S. Korea's car exports up in March, but COVID-19 impact looms in April
한국의 차 산업 3월에는 수출증가, 코로나 쇼크는 4월부터 찾아올 듯

　☆loom *(중요하거나 위협적인 일이)* 곧 닥칠 것처럼 보이다

> e.g. In the pandemic, the threat of natural disasters still looms.
> 　　대유행병 가운데, 자연재해의 위험은 여전히 곧 닥칠 것처럼 보인다.

Despite the COVID-19 pandemic, the South Korean auto industry last month saw an increase in production, domestic demand and exports.
코로나19 유행병(여파)에도 불구하고, 지난 달 국내 자동차산업은 생산, 내수, 수출 모두 증가했다.

　☆pandemic 세계적으로 전염병이 대 유행하는 상태, 세계적인 유행병
　☆domestic demand 국내 수요, 내수

According to the trade ministry, auto production rose by around 7 percent on year to nearly 370-thousand units.
산업통상자원부에 따르면 자동차생산은 전년 동월 대비 약 7%가량 증가해 37만 대를 기록했다.

　☆*(year-)* on-year 전년 동월 대비, 전년 동기 대비

Domestic consumption surged by 10 percent in part because the government cut the special consumption tax on cars and thanks to discounts given by some dealers.
내수도 정부의 차에 대한 개별소비세 인하조치와 이를 발판으로 한 일부 업체의 할인 프로모션 덕분에 부분적으로 전년 동월 대비 10프로가 급등했다.

　☆surge 급등하다, 밀려들다

> e.g. Household electricity consumption surged by 22.5 percent.
> 　　가정용 전력 소비량은 22.5퍼센트 급등했다.
> The gates opened and the crowd surged forward.
> 　　문이 열리자 군중들은 앞으로 밀려 들어왔다.

　☆special consumption tax 개별소비세

Exports were up by 1-point-3 percent on sales of SUVs and eco-friendly cars.
수출은 SUV와 친환경차가 전년 동월 대비 1.3% 증가했다.

However, a trade ministry official said, "The coronavirus's impact on exports in March was limited, but the figures for April will be worse because of the pandemic's spread in Europe and the U.S."

그러나 산업통상자원부 관계자는 "3월 수출은 코로나19 영향이 제한적이었으나 미국·유럽지역으로 코로나19가 확산되면서 4월 이후 수출은 더 나빠질 것이다"라고 전망하였다.

☆impact 1. [ˈɪmpækt] *(강력한)* 영향, 충격 | 2. [ɪmˈpækt] 영향을 주다, 충격을 주다

명사, 동사 발음 다름 주의

Writing Exercise

1. 코로나19유행병(여파)에도 불구하고, 지난 달 국내 자동차산업은 생산, 내수, 수출 모두 증가했다.

    Despite

2. 산업통상자원부에 따르면 자동차 생산은 전년 동월 대비 약 7%가량 증가해 37만 대를 기록했다.

    According to

3. 내수도 정부의 차에 대한 개별소비세 인하조치와 이를 발판으로 한 일부 업체의 할인 프로모션 덕분에 부분적으로 전년 동월 대비 10프로가 급등했다.

    Domestic

4. 수출은 SUV와 친환경 차가 전년 동월 대비 1.3% 증가했다.

    Exports

5. 그러나 산업통상자원부 관계자는 "3월 수출은 코로나19 영향이 제한적이었으나 미국·유럽지역으로 코로나19가 확산되면서 4월 이후 수출은 더 나빠질 것이다"라고 전망하였다.

    However,

ⓐ BRK 457/3
457/3
Today TH

영어 뉴스룸 02

English NewsRoom

BREAKING NEWS

How S. Korea can hold up 5 million students in online classes amid COVID-19 pandemic. More than a billion and a half students in 165 countries have been affected by COVID-19 school closures. The world has been deploying distance learning solutions, but finding the right platforms remains a challenge. In some countries, students are having trouble even accessing the Internet. Meanwhile, online classes have gone ahead as scheduled in South Korea.

전세계 유례없는 한국형 온라인 수업이 가능한 이유?

전세계에서 학생 전체가 동시에 온라인 수업을 진행하는 국가는 한국 뿐이라고 합니다.
유례없는 한국형 온라인 수업 가능한 이유에 대한 내용입니다.

 NEWS 전체 스크립트

How S. Korea can hold up 5 million students in online classes amid COVID-19 pandemic

More than a billion and a half students in 165 countries have been affected by COVID-19 school closures.

The world has been deploying distance learning solutions, but finding the right platforms remains a challenge.

In some countries, students are having trouble even accessing the Internet.

Meanwhile, online classes have gone ahead as scheduled in South Korea.

Actual classrooms are empty, but as of Thursday, some 4 million students nationwide are sitting in front of their computers to study online. The country's third-year middle and high schoolers started last week, and from Thursday, so have all grade school students from the 4th grade and up.

An expert on innovative education says this was made possible by a wide range of digital tools and infrastructure.

The transition, he says, was also helped by strong support for it among educators and the fact that young people in the country are so comfortable using smart devices.

How S. Korea can hold up 5 million students in online classes amid COVID-19 pandemic?
어떻게 한국이 COVID-19가 유행 중에 500만 명의 학생들을 온라인 수업으로 수용할 수 있을까?

More than a billion and a half students in 165 countries have been affected by COVID-19 school closures.
165개국에 있는 15억명이상 되는 학생들이 코로나19로 인한 각국의 휴교령에 영향을 받았다.

☆affected by 영향을 받다

e.g. I was affected by her death.
난 그녀의 죽음에 영향을 받았어.

☆closure (공장·학교·병원 등의 영구적인) 폐쇄 (되는 상황)

The world has been deploying distance learning solutions, but finding the right platforms remains a challenge.
세계는 원격 학습 솔루션을 사용해 왔지만, 적절한 플랫폼을 찾는 것은 여전히 과제로 남아 있다.

☆deploy 1. 군대·무기를 배치하다 | 2. 효율적으로 사용하다

☆distance learning 원격 학습

☆remain a challenge (여전히) 해결과제로 남아 있다

e.g. Good network connectivity continues to remain a challenge for people who work at home.
좋은 네트워크 연결상태는 재택근무하는 사람들에게 계속 여전히 해결과제로 남아 있다.

In some countries, students are having trouble even accessing the Internet.
일부 국가에서는, 학생들이 인터넷에 접속하는 것조차 곤란을 겪고 있다.

Meanwhile, online classes have gone ahead as scheduled in South Korea.
한편, 한국에서는 온라인 수업들이 예정대로 진행되었다.

☆go ahead 1. (다른 사람들보다) 앞서 가다[도착하다]
　　　　　2. 일어나다[진행되다]=proceed
　　　　　3. Please do it

e.g. It rained so much that the festival couldn't go ahead as planned.
비가 너무 많이 와서 축제가 계획대로 진행될 수 없었다.

Actual classrooms are empty, but as of Thursday, some 4 million students nationwide are sitting in front of their computers to study online.

실제 교실들은 비어 있지만 목요일부터 전국 400만여 명의 학생들이 온라인으로 공부하기 위해 컴퓨터 앞에 앉아 있다.

The country's third-year middle and high schoolers started last week, and from Thursday, so have all grade school students from the 4th grade and up.

한국의 중·고등학교 3학년 학생들은 지난 주부터 시작했고, 목요일부터 초등학교 4학년과 그 이상의 모든 학생들도 마찬가지로 시작했다.

An expert on innovative education says this was made possible by a wide range of digital tools and infrastructure.

한 혁신교육에 대한 전문가는 이것이 디지털 도구와 인프라의 광범위함에 의해 가능했다고 말한다.

☆innovative 혁신적인 ∣ 영 ['ɪn·ə·və·tɪv], 미 ['ɪn·ə·veɪ·tɪv]
영국, 미국 발음 다름 주의!

The transition, he says, was also helped by strong support for it among educators and the fact that young people in the country are so comfortable using smart devices.

그는, 이 전환은 교육자들 사이 그것에 대한 강한 지지와 한국의 젊은이들이 스마트 기기를 이용하는 것이 매우 편하다는 사실에 의해 또한 도움을 받았다고 말한다.

1. 165개국에 있는 15억명이상 되는 학생들이 코로나19로 인한 각국의 휴교령에 영향을 받았다.

   More than _____

   _____

2. 세계는 원격 학습 솔루션을 사용해 왔지만, 적절한 플랫폼을 찾는 것은 여전히 과제로 남아 있다.

   The world _____

   _____

3. 일부 국가에서는, 학생들이 인터넷에 접속하는 것조차 곤란을 겪고 있다.

   In some _____

   _____

4. 한편, 한국에서는 온라인 수업들이 예정대로 진행되었다.

   Meanwhile, _____

   _____

5. 실제 교실들은 비어 있지만 목요일부터 전국 400만여 명의 학생들이 온라인으로 공부하기 위해 컴퓨터 앞에 앉아 있다.

   Actual _____

   _____

6. 한국의 중·고등학교 3학년 학생들은 지난 주부터 시작했고, 목요일부터 초등학교 4학년과 그 이상의 모든 학생들도 마찬가지로 시작했다.

   The country's _____

   _____

7. 한 혁신교육에 대한 전문가는 이것이 디지털 도구와 인프라의 광범위함에 의해 가능했다고 말한다.

   An expert _____

   _____

8. 그는, 이 전환은 교육자들 사이 그것에 대한 강한 지지와 한국의 젊은이들이 스마트 기기를 이용하는 것이 매우 편하다는 사실에 의해 또한 도움을 받았다고 말한다.

   The transition, _____

   _____

◎ BRK 457/3
457/3
Today TH

영어 뉴스룸 03

English
NewsRoom

BREAKING NEWS

COVID-19 outbreak transforms live performance industry in S. Korea. This sound recording studio is busy ahead of a live streaming on YouTube.Seoul Arts Center has decided to extend its online streaming services, launched as part of its social distancing campaign...after it received positive responses and its highlights of 'The Man Who Laughs' received 150-thousand concurrent views. Seoul Art Center dept. of video culture Shin Tae-yeon said, "It usually...

예술의 전당에 관객이 없다?

코로나19가 가져온 공연계의 큰 변화, 즉 무관중 온라인 공연에 관한 내용입니다.

NEWS 전체 스크립트

COVID-19 outbreak transforms live performance industry in S. Korea

This sound recording studio is busy ahead of a live streaming on YouTube.

Seoul Arts Center has decided to extend its online streaming services, launched as part of its social distancing campaign, after it received positive responses and its highlights of 'The Man Who Laughs' received 150-thousand concurrent views.

Seoul Art Center dept. of video culture Shin Tae-yeon said, "It usually takes more than three days to shoot and more than four to five months for post-production." He added, "Cross-cutting edits of multiple shots heightens realism."

By combining VR technology and high-definition resolution, the live experience can be delivered to some 33 million YouTube users in Korea.

However, online performances have been limited to national art establishments like the Sejong Center for the Performing Arts and Gyeonggi Art Center.

Since building a YouTube channel and filming and editing performances comes with high costs but little to no profit, it's difficult for small production companies to join in.

This shows the need for online performance policies based on distribution networks and profit-making models.

The performing industry has found its way through online performances, but it now needs to discuss ways to turn the crisis into an opportunity by building a competitive platform.

COVID-19 outbreak transforms live performance industry in S. Korea
코로나 사태가 한국의 라이브 공연 산업을 바꾸다

This sound recording studio is busy ahead of a live streaming on YouTube.
이 녹음실은 유튜브 라이브 스트리밍을 앞두고 분주하다.

☆ahead of *(공간·시간상으로)* 앞에

e.g. I finished ahead of schedule.
난 예정보다 일찍 끝냈어.

Seoul Arts Center has decided to extend its online streaming services, launched as part of its social distancing campaign, after it received positive responses and its highlights of 'The Man Who Laughs' received 150-thousand concurrent views.
예술의 전당은 '사회적 거리두기' 캠페인의 일환으로 시작된 온라인 공연이 긍정적인 평가를 받고 뮤지컬 '웃는 남자'의 하이라이트가 동시접속 수 15만건을 기록하자 이를 연장하기로 결정했다.

Seoul Art Center dept. of video culture Shin Tae-yeon said, "It usually takes more than three days to shoot and more than four to five months for post-production." He added, "Cross-cutting edits of multiple shots heightens realism."
예술의 전당 영상문화부 신태연님은 "보통 촬영하는 데 3일 이상 걸리고, 후반 작업만 해도 4~5개월 이상 걸린다"고 말했다. 그는 "여러 촬영본의 교차 편집은 현실감을 고조시킨다"고 덧붙였다.

☆heighten 고조시키다, 강화하다

e.g. COVID-19 pandemic can heighten stress and anxiety.
코로나19 유행병은 스트레스와 불안을 고조시킬 수 있다.

By combining VR technology and high-definition resolution, the live experience can be delivered to some 33 million YouTube users in Korea.
가상현실VR 기술과 고화질 해상도(HDR)를 결합을 통해 국내 3300만 명의 유튜브 사용자에게 생생함을 그대로 전달할 수 있다.

☆combine 결합하다
☆VR Virtual Reality 가상현실

However, online performances have been limited to national art establishments like the Sejong Center for the Performing Arts and Gyeonggi Art Center.

그러나 온라인 공연은 세종문화회관, 경기아트센터와 같은 국가 예술시설로 제한되어 왔다.

☆ establishment 기관, 시설, 설립

Since building a YouTube channel and filming and editing performances comes with high costs but little to no profit, it's difficult for small production companies to join in.

유튜브 채널 구축과 촬영 및 공연 편집은 비용이 많이 들지만 수익은 거의 내지 못하기 때문에 소규모 제작사가 참여하기는 어렵다.

☆ come with 함께 딸려 오다

This shows the need for online performance policies based on distribution networks and profit-making models.

이는 유통망과 수익모델을 기반으로 한 온라인 성과정책의 필요성을 보여 준다.

The performing industry has found its way through online performances, but it now needs to discuss ways to turn the crisis into an opportunity by building a competitive platform.

공연 산업은 온라인 공연을 통해 그 길을 찾았지만, 이제는 경쟁적인 플랫폼을 구축함으로써 위기를 기회로 바꿀 수 있는 방법을 논의해야 할 필요가 있다.

e.g. They turn garbage into fashion.
그들은 쓰레기를 패션으로 바꾼다.

Writing Exercise

1. 이 녹음실은 유튜브 라이브 스트리밍을 앞두고 분주하다.

This sound

2. 예술의 전당은 '사회적 거리두기' 캠페인의 일환으로 시작된 온라인 공연이 긍정적인 평가를 받고 뮤지컬 '웃는남자'의 하이라이트가 동시접속 수 15만건을 기록하자 이를 연장하기로 결정했다.

Seoul

3. 예술의 전당 영상문화부 신태연님은 "보통 촬영하는 데 3일 이상 걸리고, 후반 작업만 해도 4~5개월 이상 걸린다"고 말했다. 그는 "여러 촬영본의 교차 편집은 현실감을 고조시킨다"고 덧붙였다.

Seoul

4. 가상현실VR 기술과 고화질 해상도(HDR)를 결합을 통해 국내 3300만 명의 유튜브 사용자에게 생생함을 그대로 전달할 수 있다.

By combining

5. 그러나 온라인 공연은 세종문화회관, 경기아트센터와 같은 국가 예술시설로 제한되어 왔다.

However,

6. 유튜브 채널 구축과 촬영 및 공연 편집은 비용이 많이 들지만 수익은 거의 내지 못하기 때문에 소규모 제작사가 참여하기는 어렵다.

Since

7. 이는 유통망과 수익모델을 기반으로 한 온라인 성과정책의 필요성을 보여 준다.

This shows

8. 공연 산업은 온라인 공연을 통해 그 길을 찾았지만, 이제는 경쟁적인 플랫폼을 구축함으로써 위기를 기회로 바꿀 수 있는 방법을 논의해야 할 필요가 있다.

The performing

BRK 457/3
457/3
Today TH

영어 뉴스룸 04

English NewsRoom

BREAKING NEWS

Farm produce sold at drive-thru benefits local economy. With no school meals being served, these vegetables were going to waste. So, regional governments have set up drive-thrus in parking lots like this one so people can buy them without having to worry about the coronavirus. People can buy eco-friendly veggies without getting out of their car. This will protect them from making contact with others. These packs include vegetables like sweet...

농산물도 드라이브스루로 판매한다고?

코로나 사태로 학교 개학이 연기되자 학교급식에 농산물을 공급해 오던 농민들이 경제순환을 위해 농산물 드라이브스루를 운영하고 있다는 내용입니다.

NEWS 전체 스크립트

Farm produce sold at drive-thru benefits local economy

With no school meals being served, these vegetables were going to waste.

So, regional governments have set up drive-thrus in parking lots like this one so people can buy them without having to worry about the coronavirus.

People can buy eco-friendly veggies without getting out of their car.

This will protect them from making contact with others.

These packs include vegetables like sweet potatoes, green pumpkins and cucumbers at a 20 to 50 percent discount.

Kang Wi-won, Director of Gyeonggi agroFood Institute said, "We are working with 31 cities and districts in Gyeonggi-do Province on this new distribution channel so we can sell farm goods without risking infection."

There are no commissions at the drive-thru, so farmers get 1-hundred percent of the sales.

The Korean government is implementing programs like this and providing other support to nine cities and provinces to help the farmers and their communities.

Because of the COVID-19 crisis, starting with virus testing, drive-thru products and services have taken off in South Korea and could very well last beyond the outbreak.

Farm produce sold at drive-thru benefits local economy.

드라이브스루에서 판매되는 농산물이 지역 경제에 도움이 되고 있다.

With no school meals being served, these vegetables were going to waste.

학교 급식이 제공되지 않아서, 이 채소들은 폐기될 예정이었다.

So, regional governments have set up drive-thrus in parking lots like this one so people can buy them without having to worry about the coronavirus.

그래서 지자체는 이러한 주차장에 드라이브스루(drive-thrus)를 설치했고 방문객들은 코로나바이러스에 대한 걱정 없이 그 채소들을 살 수 있게 되었다.

☆set up 건립하다, 설립·수립하다

People can buy eco-friendly veggies without getting out of their car.

방문객들은 차에서 내리지 않고도 친환경 채소를 살 수 있다.

This will protect them from making contact with others.

이것은 그들이 다른 사람들과 접촉하는 것을 막아줄 것이다.

☆make contact with ~와 연락 (접촉) 하다

> e.g. She made contact with her mother to confirm she was all right.
> 그녀는 엄마가 괜찮은지 확인하기 위해 엄마에게 연락해 보았다.

These packs include vegetables like sweet potatoes, green pumpkins and cucumbers at a 20 to 50 percent discount.

이 농산물 꾸러미들은 20-50% 할인된 가격의 고구마, 호박, 오이 같은 채소들을 포함한다.

Kang Wi-won, Director of Gyeonggi agroFood Institute said, "we are working with 31 cities and districts in Gyeonggi-do Province on this new distribution channel so we can sell farm goods without risking infection."

강위원 경기농식품유통진흥원장은 "이 신규 유통채널에 대해 경기도 31개 시·군와 함께 일하고 있어서 감염의 위험 없이 농산물을 판매할 수 있다"고 말했다.

There are no commissions at the drive-thru, so farmers get 1-hundred percent of the sales.

드라이브스루에는 수수료가 없기 때문에 농민들은 매출의 100퍼센트를 갖는다.

The Korean government is implementing programs like this and providing other support to nine cities and provinces to help the farmers and their communities.

정부는 이와 같은 프로그램들을 시행하고 있으며 농업인과 그 지역사회를 돕기 위해 9개 시·도에 다른 지원을 하고 있다.

☆implement 시행하다

Because of the COVID-19 crisis, starting with virus testing, drive-thru products and services have taken off in South Korea and could very well last beyond the outbreak.

COVID-19 사태 때문에 바이러스 검사부터 시작해서 드라이브스루 제품과 서비스는 한국에서 급격히 인기를 얻었고, 이것은 코로나 사태를 훨씬 넘어서도 지속될 수 있다.

☆take off 1. 이륙하다 | 2. (특히 서둘러) 떠나다 | 3. 급격히 인기를 얻다

e.g. Since gyms are closed to prevent the spread of the virus, home training has taken off.
바이러스 확산을 방지하기 위해 헬스장들이 문을 닫았기 때문에 홈트레이닝이 급격히 인기를 얻었다.

Writing Exercise

1. 학교 급식이 제공되지 않아서, 이 채소들은 폐기될 예정이었다.

With

2. 그래서 지자체는 이러한 주차장에 드라이브스루(drive-thrus)를 설치했고 방문객들은 코로나바이러스에 대한 걱정 없이 그 채소들을 살 수 있게 되었다.

So, regional

3. 방문객들은 차에서 내리지 않고도 친환경 채소를 살 수 있다.

People

4. 이것은 그들이 다른 사람들과 접촉하는 것을 막아줄 것이다.

    This will

5. 이 농산물 꾸러미들은 20 - 50% 할인된 가격의 고구마, 호박, 오이 같은 채소들을 포함한다.

    These packs

6. 강위원 경기농식품유통진흥원장은 "이 신규 유통채널에 대해 경기도 31개 시군와 함께 일하고 있어서 감염의 위험 없이 농산물을 판매할 수 있다"고 말했다.

    Kang Wi - won,

7. 드라이브스루에는 수수료가 없기 때문에 농민들은 매출의 100퍼센트를 갖는다.

    There are

8. 정부는 이와 같은 프로그램들을 시행하고 있으며 농업인과 그 지역사회를 돕기 위해 9개 시도에 다른 지원을 하고 있다.

    The Korean

9. COVID - 19 사태 때문에 바이러스 검사부터 시작해서 드라이브스루 제품과 서비스는 한국에서 급격히 인기를 얻었고, 이것은 코로나 사태를 훨씬 넘어서도 지속될 수 있다.

    Because of

◎ BRK 457/3
457/3
Today TH

영어 뉴스룸 05

English NewsRoom

BREAKING NEWS

'Untact movement' is bringing changes in an industrial paradigm shift. A designer is introducing his products to potential consumers, but is doing so via a live stream. This is one example of how 'untact movement', minimizing contact between people, is causing the distribution industry to pioneer new sales techniques. An expert says this so-called 'untact movement' will continue to develop, with the COVID-19 outbreak serving as momentum.

접촉하지 않는 사회가 가져온 변화

코로나로 인한 비대면 운동이 산업 패러다임에 변화를 주고 있다는 내용입니다.

NEWS 전체 스크립트

'Untact movement' is bringing changes in an industrial paradigm shift

A designer is introducing his products to potential consumers, but is doing so via a live stream.

This is one example of how 'untact movement', minimizing contact between people, is causing the distribution industry to pioneer new sales techniques.

An expert says this so-called 'untact movement' will continue to develop, with the COVID-19 outbreak serving as momentum.

Kim Tai-gi, Professor of Department of Economics, Dankook University said, "'Untact culture' has been expanding since the COVID-19 outbreak, and it is not going to stop." He added, "People have already realized how nice it is to do things online, such as 'telecommuting' and 'tele-educating', and companies' strategies have changed accordingly."

The distribution industry is not the only sector that is seeing changes from a need to reduce contact. Even movie theaters have been changing how they sell snacks and beverages to customers.

An expert says that revolutionary changes will come as technologies of the fourth industrial revolution are combined with this 'untact movement' but the government needs to prepare for the paradigm shift.

He also advised that the country should have a system that guarantees employment stability.

'Untact movement' is bringing changes in an industrial paradigm shift.
'비대면 운동'이 산업 패러다임 전환에 변화를 가져오고 있다.

☆shift 전환

A designer is introducing his products to potential consumers, but is doing so via a live stream.
한 디자이너가 잠재적 소비자들에게 자신의 제품을 소개하고 있지만, 라이브 스트림을 통해 그렇게 하고 있는 중이다.

☆via 통하여 =going through

This is one example of how 'untact movement', minimizing contact between people, is causing the distribution industry to pioneer new sales techniques.
이것이 사람과 사람 사이의 접촉을 최소화하는 '비대면 운동'이 어떻게 유통업계가 새로운 판매 기술들을 개척하도록 하는지를 보여주는 한 예다.

☆cause A to B A를 B하도록 하다

e.g. The accident caused me to lose some of my memory.
　　그 사고로 난 기억의 일부를 잃었어.

☆pioneer 개척자, 개척하다

e.g. He pioneered in the development of aeroplanes.
　　그는 항공기 개발의 선구자였다.

An expert says this so-called 'untact movement' will continue to develop, with the COVID-19 outbreak serving as momentum.
한 전문가는 COVID-19 전염병 발생이 계기가 되어, 이른바 '비대면 운동'이 계속 발전할 것이라고 말한다.

☆serve as momentum 계기가 되다

e.g. This announcement should serve as momentum for people to continue their work.
　　이 발표는 사람들이 그들의 일을 계속할 수 있는 계기가 되어야 한다.

Kim Tai-gi, Professor of Department of Economics, Dankook University said, "'Untact culture' has been expanding since the COVID-19 outbreak, and it is not going to stop." He added, "People have already realized how nice it is to do things online, such as 'telecommuting' and 'tele-educating', and companies' strategies have changed accordingly."

김태기 단국대 경영학과 교수는 "COVID-19 사태 이후 '비대면 문화'가 확대되고 있어 멈추지 않을 전망"이라고 말했다. 그는 "사람들은 이미 '원격근무'나 '원격교육'과 같은 온라인에서 일을 하는 것이 얼마나 좋은지를 인식했고, 이에 따라 기업의 전략이 달라졌다"고 덧붙였다.

The distribution industry is not the only sector that is seeing changes from a need to reduce contact. Even movie theaters have been changing how they sell snacks and beverages to customers.

접촉을 줄여야 할 필요성을 느껴 변화를 보고 있는 업종은 유통업계뿐만이 아니다. 심지어 영화관들도 손님들에게 과자와 음료를 판매하는 방식을 바꾸고 있다.

An expert says that revolutionary changes will come as technologies of the fourth industrial revolution are combined with this 'untact movement' but the government needs to prepare for the paradigm shift.

한 전문가는 4차 산업혁명의 기술이 이 '비대면 운동'과 결합되면서 혁명적 변화가 올 것이지만 정부는 패러다임 전환에 대비할 필요가 있다고 말한다.

　　☆revolutionary 혁명적인

He also advised that the country should have a system that guarantees employment stability.

그는 또한 국가가 고용 안정성을 보장하는 시스템을 갖춰야 한다고 조언했다.

1. 한 디자이너가 잠재적 소비자들에게 자신의 제품을 소개하고 있지만, 라이브 스트림을 통해 그렇게 하고 있는 중이다.

   A designer

2. 이것이 사람과 사람 사이의 접촉을 최소화하는 비대면 운동이 어떻게 유통업계가 새로운 판매 기술들을 개척하도록 하는지를 보여주는 한 예다.

   This is

3. 한 전문가는 COVID-19 전염병 발생이 계기가 되어, 이른바 비대면 운동이 계속 발전할 것이라고 말한다.

   An expert

4. 김태기 단국대 경영학과 교수는 "COVID-19 사태 이후 '비대면 문화'가 확대되고 있어 멈추지 않을 전망"이라고 말했다. 그는 "사람들은 이미 '원격근무'나 '원격교육'과 같은 온라인에서 일을 하는 것이 얼마나 좋은지를 인식했고, 이에 따라 기업의 전략이 달라졌다"고 덧붙였다.

   Kim Tai-gi,

5. 접촉을 줄여야 할 필요성을 느껴 변화를 보고 있는 업종은 유통업계뿐만이 아니다. 심지어 영화관들도 손님들에게 과자와 음료를 판매하는 방식을 바꾸고 있다.

   The distribution

6. 한 전문가는 4차 산업혁명의 기술이 이 '비대면 운동'과 결합되면서 혁명적 변화가 올 것이지만 정부는 패러다임 전환에 대비할 필요가 있다고 말한다.

   An expert

7. 그는 또한 국가가 고용 안정성을 보장하는 시스템을 갖춰야 한다고 조언했다.

   He also

ⓖ BRK 457/3
457/3
Today TH

영어 뉴스룸 *06*

English NewsRoom

BREAKING NEWS

Korean researchers develop talking signals for plants. When the plant receives water and light, a voice responds. This technology, developed in Korea, can read microbial signals from around a plant's roots. When a plant gets enough water and sun, it carries out photosynthesis and activates microbes. The electric charge from the microbes can then be processed as electronic signals indicating the plant's current state.

말하는 반려 식물이 있다고?

국내 연구진이 식물 뿌리 주변에서 나타나는 신호를 분석해 식물 상태를 음성으로 변환했다는 내용입니다.

Korean researchers develop talking signals for plants

When the plant receives water and light, a voice responds.

This technology, developed in Korea, can read microbial signals from around a plant's roots.

When a plant gets enough water and sun, it carries out photosynthesis and activates microbes.

The electric charge from the microbes can then be processed as electronic signals indicating the plant's current state.

If the plant does not get enough water or sun, the microbes are less activated, resulting in weaker signals.

These signals trigger the voice that comes through the speakers.

Researcher of department of Chemical Engineering, Konkuk University, Lee Eun-bin said, "It was designed to detect the state and activity of the plant within 30 minutes of giving it water."

The electric charge from the microbes around the plant's roots are read and transferred through sensors planted inside the soil.

This way the plant's health can be accurately assessed without damaging it.

Researcher of department of Chemical Engineering of Konkuk University, Yang Yun-jeong said, "I think using this technology can be useful in managing large numbers of plants more easily and increasing plant productivity."

With more people in Korea choosing to grow plants at home for their physical and emotional health, this could also make their hobby more fun.

Korean researchers develop talking signals for plants
국내 연구진이 식물을 위한 말하기 신호를 개발하다

When the plant receives water and light, a voice responds.
식물이 물과 빛을 받으면 음성으로 반응한다.

This technology, developed in Korea, can read microbial signals from around a plant's roots.
국내에서 개발된 이 기술은 식물 뿌리 주변에 있는 미생물의 신호를 읽을 수 있다.

☆microbial 미생물의, 세균의, 세균에 의한
☆signal 신호

When a plant gets enough water and sun, it carries out photosynthesis and activates microbes.
식물이 충분한 물과 태양을 얻을 때, 그것은 광합성을 실행하고 미생물을 활성화시킨다.

☆carry out 실행하다, 수행하다, 완수하다

> e.g. The construction is being carried out by the government.
> 그 공사는 정부에 의해 실행되고 있다.

☆photosynthesis 광합성
☆Microbe 미생물

The electric charge from the microbes can then be processed as electronic signals indicating the plant's current state.
미생물에서 생성된 전하가 식물의 현재 상태를 나타내는 전자 신호로 처리될 수 있다.

☆electric charge 전하
☆process 1. 과정 | 2. 처리하다, 가공하다
   (명사)   (3형식동사)
☆indicate 나타내다, 내비치다

If the plant does not get enough water or sun, the microbes are less activated, resulting in weaker signals.
만약 식물이 충분한 물이나 태양을 얻지 못하면 미생물이 활성화되지 못해, 전기 신호가 약해진다.

☆activated 활성화된

These signals trigger the voice that comes through the speakers.

이 전기 신호들은 스피커를 통해 나오는 음성신호를 촉발시킨다.

☆trigger 1. 방아쇠^(명사) | 2. 촉발시키다^(동사)

Researcher of department of Chemical Engineering, Konkuk University, Lee Eun-bin said, "It was designed to detect the state and activity of the plant within 30 minutes of giving it water."

건국대 생물공학과 이은빈 연구원은 "식물에 물을 주면 30분 내로는 식물의 상태, 식물의 활성도를 알 수 있게끔 설계했다"고 말했다.

☆detect (특히 알아내기 쉽지 않은 것을) 발견하다, 알아내다, 감지하다

The electric charge from the microbes around the plant's roots are read and transferred through sensors planted inside the soil.

식물 뿌리 주변 미생물이 내보내는 전하는 읽혀지고 흙 속에 심은 센서를 통해 전달된다.

☆transferred through ~를 통해 전달되다

This way the plant's health can be accurately assessed without damaging it.

이렇게 하면 식물의 손상없이 식물의 상태를 정확히 평가할 수 있다.

☆accurately 정확히, 정밀하게

☆assess 평가하다

Researcher of department of Chemical Engineering of Konkuk University, Yang Yun-jeong said, "I think using this technology can be useful in managing large numbers of plants more easily and increasing plant productivity."

건국대 생물공학과 양윤정 연구원은 "이 기술을 활용하면 식물을 대량으로 생산하는 데 있어서 식물 관리가 좀 더 쉽고 식물의 생산성을 높이는 데 도움이 될 수 있다고 생각한다"고 말했다.

With more people in Korea choosing to grow plants at home for their physical and emotional health, this could also make their hobby more fun.

한국의 더 많은 사람들이 신체적, 정서적 건강을 위해 집에서 식물을 재배하는 것을 선택함에 따라, 이것은 또한 사람들의 취미를 더 재미있게 만들 수 있다.

☆emotional 정서적인, 감정적인

1. 식물이 물과 빛을 받으면 음성으로 반응한다.

   When _____

   _____

2. 국내에서 개발된 이 기술은 식물 뿌리 주변에 있는 미생물의 신호를 읽을 수 있다.

   This technology, _____

   _____

3. 식물이 충분한 물과 태양을 얻을 때, 그것은 광합성을 실행하고 미생물을 활성화시킨다.

   When _____

   _____

4. 미생물에서 생성된 전하가 식물의 현재 상태를 나타내는 전자 신호로 처리될 수 있다.

   The electric _____

   _____

5. 만약 식물이 충분한 물이나 태양을 얻지 못하면 미생물이 활성화되지 못해, 전기 신호가 약해진다.

   If the plant _____

   _____

6. 이 전기 신호들은 스피커를 통해 나오는 음성신호를 촉발시킨다.

   These _____

   _____

7. 건국대 생물공학과 이은빈 연구원은 "식물에 물을 주면 30분 내로는 식물의 상태, 식물의 활성도를 알 수 있게끔 설계했다"고 말했다.

   Researcher _____

   _____

8. 식물 뿌리 주변 미생물이 내보내는 전하는 읽혀지고 흙 속에 심은 센서를 통해 전달된다.

   The electric _____

   _____

9. 이렇게 하면 식물의 손상없이 식물의 상태를 정확히 평가할 수 있다.

This way

10. 건국대 생물공학과 양윤정 연구원은 "이 기술을 활용하면 식물을 대량으로 생산하는 데 있어서 식물 관리가 좀 더 쉽고 식물의 생산성을 높이는 데 도움이 될 수 있다고 생각한다"고 말했다.

Researcher

11. 한국의 더 많은 사람들이 신체적, 정서적 건강을 위해 집에서 식물을 재배하는 것을 선택함에 따라, 이것은 또한 사람들의 취미를 더 재미있게 만들 수 있다.

With

◎ BRK 457/3
457/3
Today TH

영어 뉴스룸 07

English NewsRoom

BREAKING NEWS

S. Korea's diet foods see sales surge amid pandemic. Konjac is a low-calorie, high-fiber root vegetable grown in Asia. This fried rice product made with rice and rice-shaped konjac just needs to be heated up, and has about half the calories of steamed rice. Such products have become popular as the prolonged COVID-19 outbreak has got more people caring about their weight. According to food company data, sales of konjac rice products increased by...

나는 더 이상 '확찐'자가 아니다

다이어트 식품이 유행병 가운데 매출이 급증했다는 내용입니다.

 전체 스크립트

S. Korea's diet foods see sales surge amid pandemic

Konjac is a low-calorie, high-fiber root vegetable grown in Asia.

This fried rice product made with rice and rice-shaped konjac just needs to be heated up, and has about half the calories of steamed rice.

Such products have become popular as the prolonged COVID-19 outbreak has got more people caring about their weight.

According to food company data, sales of konjac rice products increased by more than 60 percent in March compared to the previous month.

Chung Jung One, Online Planning Team member Park Dae-yeol said, "Sales have increased dramatically as of February." He added, "It seems that customers enjoying home meal replacements have bought them amid the prolonged coronavirus outbreak."

Meanwhile, the popularity of high-calorie delivery foods has been slumping.

Major fried chicken franchises say delivery sales, which were on the rise until February and March started to slow down in May.

In accordance with such trends, the industry is working to launch easy-to-eat diet products.

스크립트 분석

S. Korea's diet foods see sales surge amid pandemic
한국의 다이어트 식품이 팬데믹 가운데서 매출이 급증하다.

☆surge 급등하다

☆amid *(특히 공포심 등이 느껴지는)* 가운데에

Konjac is a low-calorie, high-fiber root vegetable grown in Asia.
곤약은 아시아에서 재배되고 있는 저칼로리 고섬유질 뿌리채소이다.

☆high-fiber 고섬유질의, 식물 섬유의 함유량이 많은

☆root vegetable 뿌리채소

This fried rice product made with rice and rice-shaped konjac just needs to be heated up, and has about half the calories of steamed rice.
쌀과 쌀모양의 곤약으로 만들어진 이 볶음밥 제품은 데우기만 하면 되고, 밥 칼로리의 반 정도 된다.

☆made with ~을 가지고 만든 *(음식 재료에 대해 말할 때 자주 쓰임)*

☆heat up 뜨거워지다, *(경쟁이)* 달아오르다

☆steamed rice 밥

Such products have become popular as the prolonged COVID-19 outbreak has got more people caring about their weight.
장기화된 COVID-19 발병이 더 많은 사람들을 체중에 관심을 가지는 상태가 되게 함으로써 이러한 제품들이 인기를 얻고 있다.

5형식동사
☆get *(준사역 동사 - 시키는 동사)*
- 1. get + 목 + 목적보어 *(to부정사)* : ~을 ~하게 하다
- 2. get + 목 + 목적보어 *(ing)* : ~을 *(~의 상태가)* 되게 하다

☆prolonged 오래 계속되는, 장기적인

☆care about ~에 관심을 가지다

> e.g. I care about fashion because I care about my appearance.
> 난 내 외모에 관심있기 때문에 패션에 신경을 써.
>
> ☆ care about ~에 관심을 가지다

- care for 돌보다 =take care of, =look after

According to food company data, sales of konjac rice products increased by more than 60 percent in March compared to the previous month.

식품회사의 자료에 따르면 3월 곤약쌀 제품의 매출은 전달에 비교하여 60% 이상 증가했다.

Chung Jung One, Online Planning Team member Park Dae-yeol said, "Sales have increased dramatically as of February." He added, "It seems that customers enjoying home meal replacements have bought them amid the prolonged coronavirus outbreak."

청정원 온라인기획 팀 멤버 박대열씨는 "2월 현재 매출이 크게 늘어났다"고 말했다. 그는 "장기화되는 코로나바이러스 발병 가운데 가정간편식을 즐기는 고객들이 구매해 온 것으로 보인다"고 덧붙였다.

☆as of 일자로, 현재

☆home meal replacements (HMR) 가정간편식

Meanwhile, the popularity of high-calorie delivery foods has been slumping.

한편, 고칼로리 배달 음식들의 선호도는 떨어지고 있다.

☆slump 1. (가치/수량/가격 등이) 급락하다, 급락
        2. 폭 쓰러지다

Major fried chicken franchises say delivery sales, which were on the rise until February and March started to slow down in May.

주요 치킨 프랜차이즈 업체들은 2월과 3월까지는 증가세를 보였던 배달 매출이 5월에는 둔화되기 시작했다고 말한다.

☆on the rise (물가 따위가) 오르고 있는, 증가세를 보이는

☆slow down 느긋해지다, 속도를 늦추다

In accordance with such trends, the industry is working to launch easy-to-eat diet products.

이러한 추세에 따라서, 업계는 먹기 쉬운 다이어트 제품들을 출시하기 위해 노력하고 있다.

☆in accordance with ~에 따라서

☆launch 출시하다, 시작하다

☆work 노력하다

Writing Exercise

1. 곤약은 아시아에서 재배되고 있는 저칼로리 고섬유질 뿌리채소이다.

   Konjac

2. 쌀과 쌀모양의 곤약으로 만들어진 이 볶음밥 제품은 데우기만 하면 되고, 밥 칼로리의 반 정도 된다.

   This fried

3. 장기화된 COVID - 19 발병이 더 많은 사람들을 체중에 관심을 가지는 상태가 되게 함으로서 이러한 제품들이 인기를 얻고 있다.

   Such

4. 식품회사의 자료에 따르면 3월 곤약쌀 제품의 매출은 전달에 비교하여 60% 이상 증가했다.

   According to

5. 청정원 온라인기획 팀 멤버 박대열씨는"2월 현재 매출이 크게 늘어났다"고 말했다. 그는 "장기화되는 코로나바이러스 발병 가운데 가정간편식을 즐기는 고객들이 구매해 온 것으로 보인다"고 덧붙였다.

   Chung Jung One,

6. 한편, 고칼로리 배달 음식들의 선호도는 떨어지고 있다.

   Meanwhile,

7. 주요 치킨 프랜차이즈 업체들은 2월과 3월까지는 증가세를 보였던 배달 매출이 5월에는 둔화되기 시작했다고 말한다.

   Major

8. 이러한 추세에 따라서, 업계는 먹기 쉬운 다이어트 제품들을 출시하기 위해 노력하고 있다.

   In accordance

ⓖ BRK 457/3
457/3
Today TH

영어 뉴스룸 08

English NewsRoom

BREAKING NEWS

Indonesia installs "rice ATMs" for people in need amid COVID-19. People are gathering at a military base on the outskirts of Jakarta to receive their daily 1.5 kilogram rations of rice. To help those worst affected by the COVID-19 outbreak, the Indonesian authorities have rolled out these so-called "rice ATMs". The Indonesian government has set up 10 rice dispensers in and around Jakarta, adopting a similar system used in Vietnam.

ATM기에서 돈 대신 쌀이 나온다고?

COVID-19 가운데 도움이 필요한 사람들을 위해 "쌀 ATM"기를 설치하는 나라가 있다고 합니다.

Indonesia installs "rice ATMs" for people in need amid COVID-19

People are gathering at a military base on the outskirts of Jakarta to receive their daily 1.5 kilogram rations of rice.

To help those worst affected by the COVID-19 outbreak, the Indonesian authorities have rolled out these so-called "rice ATMs".

The Indonesian government has set up 10 rice dispensers in and around Jakarta, adopting a similar system used in Vietnam.

Those eligible for the free rice include daily wage earners, people who have lost their jobs and the homeless.

Indonesian Army Official Ibrahim said, "Each day we prepare 1.5 tons of rice for around 1,000 residents." He added, "We will continue doing it everyday, without rest, even on weekends, we will distribute non-stop."

Indonesia announced a 25-billion U.S. dollar stimulus package in March to help shoulder the burden caused by COVID-19, pledging money for food supplies and for discounts on electricity tariffs.

Reuters say that more than 14-thousand Indonesians have contracted the virus since March, with a death toll of almost one-thousand, the highest fatality rate in East Asia outside of China.

The media say that Indonesian President, Joko Widodo, is eager to resume economic activity, but critics have pointed out that it's still too early to return to normal.

스크립트 분석

Indonesia installs 'rice ATMs' for people in need amid COVID-19

인도네시아는 COVID-19 가운데 도움이 필요한 사람들을 위해 '쌀 ATM'을 설치한다

☆ATM (automated teller machine) 현금 자동 입출금기

People are gathering at a military base on the outskirts of Jakarta to receive their daily 1.5 kilogram rations of rice.

사람들이 하루 1.5kg의 쌀 배급을 받기 위해 자카르타 외곽의 군사 기지에 모여들고 있다.

☆outskirts (도시의) 변두리, 교외
☆on the outskirts of ~의 변두리에
☆ration 1. 배급량 | 2. 배급을 주다

To help those worst affected by the COVID-19 outbreak, the Indonesian authorities have rolled out these so-called 'rice ATMs'.

COVID-19 발병으로 인해 최악의 피해를 입은 사람들을 돕기 위해 인도네시아 당국은 소위 "쌀 ATM"을 출시했다.

☆affected by 영향을 받은
☆roll out 출시하다

> e.g. He is planning to roll out various medical devices for the poor.
> 그는 가난한 사람들을 위해 다양한 의료기기를 출시할 계획이다.

☆so-called 소위, 이른바

The Indonesian government has set up 10 rice dispensers in and around Jakarta, adopting a similar system used in Vietnam.

인도네시아 정부는 베트남에서 사용되는 유사한 시스템을 채택하여 자카르타와 그 주변에 10개의 쌀 기계를 설치하였다.

☆set up (기계 등을) 설치하다
☆dispenser (손잡이·단추 등을 눌러 안에 든 것을 바로 뽑아 쓸 수 있는) 기계
☆in and around 안과 주변에
☆adopt 1. 입양하다 | 2. 채택하다

Those eligible for the free rice include daily wage earners, people who have lost their jobs and the homeless.

무상 쌀 지원 대상자는 일용직 근로자, 실직자, 노숙자 등이 포함된다.

☆be eligible for 자격이 있다
☆the homeless 노숙자

Indonesian Army Official Ibrahim said, "Each day we prepare 1.5 tons of rice for around 1,000 residents." He added, "We will continue doing it everyday, without rest, even on weekends, we will distribute non-stop."

인도네시아 군관계자 Ibrahim은 "매일 1000여 명의 주민을 위해 1.5t의 쌀을 준비한다"고 말했다. 그는 "앞으로도 매일, 쉬지 않고, 심지어 주말에도 쉬지 않고 배급할 것"이라고 덧붙였다.

☆distribute 나누어 주다, 분배하다

Indonesia announced a 25-billion U.S. dollar stimulus package in March to help shoulder the burden caused by COVID-19, pledging money for food supplies and for discounts on electricity tariffs.

인도네시아는 지난 3월 COVID-19로 인한 부담을 덜어주기 위한 250억 달러 규모의 경기부양책을 발표하며 식량 지원과 전기요금 할인을 약속했다.

☆stimulus package 경기부양책

☆shoulder the burden 부담을 지다 burden 대신에 cost, responsibility 써도 됨

> e.g. People are being asked to shoulder the burden during this economic crisis.
>   사람들은 이 경제 위기 동안 부담을 져야 한다는 요구를 받고 있다.

☆pledge 약속하다

☆tariff 요금, 관세

Reuters say that more than 14-thousand Indonesians have contracted the virus since March, with a death toll of almost one-thousand, the highest fatality rate in East Asia outside of China.

로이터통신은 지난 3월 이후 1만 4000명 이상의 인도네시아인들이 이 바이러스에 감염됐고, 거의 1000명에 이르는 사망자가 있으며 이는 중국 이외의 동아시아에서 가장 높은 사망률이라고 전한다.

☆contract 1. [ˈkɒntrækt] 계약 | 2. [kənˈtrækt] 계약하다, 감염되다
   명사, 동사 발음 다름 주의!

☆fatality rate 사망률

The media say that Indonesian President, Joko Widodo, is eager to resume economic activity, but critics have pointed out that it's still too early to return to normal.

언론에서는 조코 위도도 인도네시아 대통령이 경제활동 재개를 열망하고 있다고 하지만, 비평가들이 말하길 정상 복귀는 아직 이르다는 지적이 나오고 있다.

☆be eager to 간절히 ~을 하고 싶어하다

☆point out 지적하다, 가리키다

Writing Exercise

1. 사람들이 하루 1.5kg의 쌀 배급을 받기 위해 자카르타 외곽의 군사 기지에 모여들고 있다.

   People _____

   _____

2. COVID - 19 발병으로 인해 최악의 피해를 입은 사람들을 돕기 위해 인도네시아 당국은 소위 "쌀 ATM"을 출시했다.

   To help _____

   _____

3. 인도네시아 정부는 베트남에서 사용되는 유사한 시스템을 채택하여 자카르타와 그 주변에 10개의 쌀 기계를 설치하였다.

   The Indonesian _____

   _____

4. 무상 쌀 지원 대상자는 일용직 근로자, 실직자, 노숙자 등이 포함된다.

   Those _____

   _____

5. 인도네시아 군관계자 Ibrahim은 "매일 1000여 명의 주민을 위해 1.5t의 쌀을 준비한다"고 말했다. 그는 "앞으로도 매일, 쉬지 않고, 심지어 주말에도 쉬지 않고 배급할 것"이라고 덧붙였다.

   Indonesian _____

   _____

6. 인도네시아는 지난 3월 COVID - 19로 인한 부담을 덜어주기 위한 250억 달러 규모의 경기부양책을 발표하며 식량 지원과 전기요금 할인을 약속했다.

   Indonesian _____

   _____

7. 로이터통신은 지난 3월 이후 1만 4000명 이상의 인도네시아인들이 이 바이러스에 감염됐고, 거의 1000명에 이르는 사망자가 있으며 이는 중국 이 외의 동아시아에서 가장 높은 사망률이라고 전한다.

Reuters

8. 언론에서는 조코 위도도 인도네시아 대통령이 경제활동 재개를 열망하고 있다고 하지만, 비평가들이 말하길 정상 복귀는 아직 이르다는 지적이 나오고 있다.

The media

BRK 457/3
457/3
Today TH

영어 뉴스룸 09

English NewsRoom

BREAKING NEWS

Preventive measures enable citizens to enjoy cultural activities amid COVID-19. A group of people, waiting to enter this performance hall, are filling out health questionnaires which ask whether they have any COVID-19 symptoms. Then, they get their temperatures checked before being allowed to go inside. Such measures are to prevent the spread of COVID-19 with the nation practicing the eased social distancing measures known as 'social distancing in...

슬기로운 문화생활을 즐기자

코로나19의 예방조치로 시민들이 다시 문화활동을 즐기기 시작한다는 내용입니다.

NEWS 전체 스크립트

Preventive measures enable citizens to enjoy cultural activities amid COVID-19

A group of people, waiting to enter this performance hall, are filling out health questionnaires which ask whether they have any COVID-19 symptoms.

Then, they get their temperatures checked before being allowed to go inside.

Such measures are to prevent the spread of COVID-19 with the nation practicing the eased social distancing measures known as 'social distancing in daily lives'.

Seoul Arts Center President Yoo In-taek said, "Our performance hall asks visitors to follow general preventive measures." He added, "On top of that, they have to sit one seat apart from others when inside to reduce the risk of infection through contact or droplets in the air."

People feel relieved by such preventive measures being in place.

Museums are no exception. On top of checking visitors' temperatures, museums are only allowing a certain number of visitors in at any one time.

National Museum of Korea, Deptuy Director General Kim Nak-jung said, "The National Museum of Korea is restricting the number of people who can enter to 300 each hour for safety reasons using an online reservation system."

Some foreign tourists say that these measures let them enjoy cultural attractions whilst at the same time being safe.

With people following the preventive measures closely, they can safely enjoy a rich cultural life.

Preventive measures enable citizens to enjoy cultural activities amid COVID-19

예방조치들은 COVID-19가운데 시민들로 하여금 문화활동을 즐길 수 있도록 한다

　　☆preventive 예방을 위한

　　☆enable A to B A로 하여금 B를 가능케 하다

A group of people, waiting to enter this performance hall, are filling out health questionnaires which ask whether they have any COVID-19 symptoms.

이 공연장에 입장하기 위해 대기하고 있는 한 단체의 사람들이 코로나19 증상이 있는지 묻는 건강 설문지를 작성하고 있다.

　　☆fill out 작성하다

　　☆questionnaires 설문지

　　☆symptom 증상

Then, they get their temperatures checked before being allowed to go inside.

그리고 나서, 그들은 실내로 들어가는 것이 허락되기 전에 그들의 체온을 체크 받는다.

　　☆5형식 준사역동사 get
　　get + 목적어A + 목적보어B (to 부정사) A를 B하게 시키다
　　목적어A와 목적보어B가 수동관계라면 목적보어는 to be pp가 됨. 여기서 to be는 생략가능. 따라서 pp만 남음(본문 : get + their temperatures + checked)

Such measures are to prevent the spread of COVID-19 with the nation practicing the eased social distancing measures known as 'social distancing in daily lives'.

이 같은 조치는 '생활 속 거리두기'로 알려진 사회적 거리 두기의 완화 조치를 시행하면서 COVID-19가 확산되는 것을 막기 위한 것이다.

　　☆practice 1. 시행하다 | 2. 실행, 관례

Seoul Arts Center President Yoo In-taek said, "Our performance hall asks visitors to follow general preventive measures." He added, "On top of that, they have to sit one seat apart from others when inside to reduce the risk of infection through contact or droplets in the air."

예술의 전당 유인택 사장은 "우리 공연장은 방문객들에게 일반적인 예방 조치를 따르도록 요구한다"고 말했다. 그는, "뿐만 아니라 접촉이나 공기 중의 물방울(침)을 통한 감염의 위험을 줄이기 위하여 실내에서는 다른 좌석과 한 자리를 떨어져 앉아야만 한다"고 덧붙였다.

　　☆ask A to B A에게 B를 요구하다

☆on top of something 덧붙이자면, 게다가, 분만 아니라, 이외에도

> e.g. He was late for the interview, and on top of that he didn't bring his resume.
> 그는 면접에 늦었고 게다가 이력서도 가져오지 않았어.

☆in the air 공중에, 어떤 기운이 감도는, 어떤 일이 일어날 것 같은 up in the air *(아직)* 미정인

People feel relieved by such preventive measures being in place.
사람들은 그러한 예방책이 마련되어 있어서 안도감을 느낀다.

☆relieved 안도하는, 다행으로 여기는

☆in place ~을 위한 준비가 되어 있는

Museums are no exception. On top of checking visitors' temperatures, museums are only allowing a certain number of visitors in at any one time.
박물관도 예외는 아니다. 방문객들의 체온을 확인하는 것 외에도, 박물관은 한 번에 일정 수의 방문객만 입장할 수 있도록 하고 있다.

☆be no exception 예외가 아니다

☆a certain number of 일정수의

☆at any one time 한 번에 =at a time

National Museum of Korea, Deptuy Director General Kim Nak-jung said, "The National Museum of Korea is restricting the number of people who can enter to 300 each hour for safety reasons using an online reservation system."
국립중앙박물관 김낙중 행정운영단장은 "국립중앙박물관은 온라인 예약 시스템을 이용해 안전상의 이유로 시간당 300명까지 입장할 수 있는 인원을 제한하고 있다"고 말했다.

Some foreign tourists say that these measures let them enjoy cultural attractions whilst at the same time being safe.
일부 외국인 관광객들은 이러한 조치들이 안전하게 하는 동안에 그들이 문화적 명소를 즐길 수 있게 해준다고 말한다.

☆whilst ~하는 동안 =while의 영국식 표현

With people following the preventive measures closely, they can safely enjoy a rich cultural life.
사람들이 예방조치를 꼼꼼히 따름에 따라, 그들은 안전하게 풍부한 문화생활을 즐길 수 있다.

☆closely 꼼꼼히, 자세히

1. 이 공연장에 입장하기 위해 대기하고 있는 한 단체의 사람들이 코로나19 증상이 있는지 묻는 건강 설문지를 작성하고 있다.

   A group
   _____
   _____

2. 그리고 나서, 그들은 실내로 들어가는 것이 허락되기 전에 그들의 체온을 체크 받는다.

   Then,
   _____
   _____

3. 이 같은 조치는 '생활 속 거리두기'로 알려진 사회적 거리 두기의 완화 조치를 시행하면서 COVID - 19가 확산되는 것을 막기 위한 것이다.

   Such
   _____
   _____

4. 예술의 전당 유인택 사장은 "우리 공연장은 방문객들에게 일반적인 예방 조치를 따르도록 요구한다"고 말했다. 그는, "뿐만 아니라 접촉이나 공기 중의 물방울(침)을 통한 감염의 위험을 줄이기 위하여 실내에서는 다른 좌석과 한 자리를 떨어져 앉아야만 한다"고 덧붙였다.

   Seoul
   _____
   _____

5. 사람들은 그러한 예방책이 마련되어 있어서 안도감을 느낀다.

   People
   _____
   _____

6. 박물관도 예외는 아니다. 방문객들의 체온을 확인하는 것 외에도, 박물관은 한 번에 일정 수의 방문객만 입장할 수 있도록 하고 있다.

   Museums
   _____
   _____

7. 국립중앙박물관 김낙중 행정운영단장은 "국립중앙박물관은 온라인 예약 시스템을 이용해 안전상의 이유로 시간당 300명까지 입장할 수 있는 인원을 제한하고 있다"고 말했다.

   National
   _____
   _____

8. 일부 외국인 관광객들은 이러한 조치들이 안전하게 하는 동안에 그들이 문화적 명소를 즐길 수 있게 해준다고 말한다.

Some
_____

_____

9. 사람들이 예방조치를 꼼꼼히 따름에 따라, 그들은 안전하게 풍부한 문화생활을 즐길 수 있다.

With
_____

_____

오디오클립
◀ 바로가기

Have Fun with the English News Room

◉ BRK 457/3
Today TH

◉ BRK 457/3
457/3
Today TH

영어 뉴스룸 10

English NewsRoom

BREAKING NEWS

Two months of telemedicine in S. Korea leads to 130,000 'virtual' prescriptions. Often times, people are just too busy to visit a doctor in person when they feel ill. However, thanks to South Korean government's recent decision to temporarily approve the use of telemedicine, one can speak to a doctor online and even get a prescription. When the doctor is done with the examination, the patient can pick up their prescription at a nearby pharmacy as the doctor...

이제 집에서도 처방전을?

굳이 병원에 가지 않아도 처방전을 발급 받을 수 있게 되었다는 내용입니다.

Two months of telemedicine in S. Korea leads to 130,000 'virtual' prescriptions

Often times, people are just too busy to visit a doctor in person when they feel ill.

However, thanks to South Korean government's recent decision to temporarily approve the use of telemedicine, one can speak to a doctor online and even get a prescription.

When the doctor is done with the examination, the patient can pick up their prescription at a nearby pharmacy as the doctor sends the necessary forms online.

When COVID-19 arrived on South Korea's shores in February, the government decided to green light this system on a trial basis.

Since then, 130,000 prescriptions have written using telemedicine services in the country.

While 26 countries out of 36 OECD countries have telemedicine systems in place, the need for it has been amplified in light of the COVID-19 pandemic.

However, the system is not a fix all for everything.

Korea Physician's Association Park Geun-tae said, "Doctors need to conduct physical examinations when patients have fevers, pneumonia, allergic coughs or asthma."

Despite this, the local medical sector generally agrees telemedicine will only continue to grow and South Korea is looking for ways to make the system even more advanced.

NEWS 스크립트 분석

Two months of telemedicine in S. Korea leads to 130,000 'virtual' prescriptions
두 달 동안 시행된 한국의 원격진료로 인해 13만 건의 '가상' 처방전이 발급되다

　　☆telemedicine 원격진료

　　☆virtual *(컴퓨터를 이용한)* 가상의

　　☆prescription 처방전, 처방

Often times, people are just too busy to visit a doctor in person when they feel ill.
종종, 사람들은 아플 때 너무 바빠서 직접 의사를 방문하지 못한다.

　　☆often times 종종 =on many occasions

　　☆in person 직접

However, thanks to South Korean government's recent decision to temporarily approve the use of telemedicine, one can speak to a doctor online and even get a prescription.
하지만 최근 한국 정부가 원격진료 사용을 잠정 승인한 덕분에 온라인에서 의사와 말할 수 있고 심지어 처방전까지 받을 수 있다.

　　☆thanks to 덕분에

　　☆temporarily 일시적으로, 임시로

　　☆get a prescription 처방을 받다

When the doctor is done with the examination, the patient can pick up their prescription at a nearby pharmacy as the doctor sends the necessary forms online.
의사가 진료를 마치면 의사가 필요한 서식을 온라인으로 보내주므로 환자는 가까운 약국에서 처방전을 받을 수 있다.

　　☆examination 검사 진료

　　☆pharmacy 약국

　　☆as ~함으로

When COVID-19 arrived on South Korea's shores in February, the government decided to green light this system on a trial basis.
2월에 COVID-19가 한국에 도달했을 때, 정부는 시범적으로 이 시스템을 승인하기로 결정했다.

　　☆shore 1. 해안, 해변 | 2. *(해안을 끼고 있는)* 국가

　　☆green-light 1. 승인(명사) | 2. 허가 승인하다(동사)

☆on a trial basis 시험 삼아

e.g. People are using this on a trial basis for 3 weeks.
사람들은 이것을 3주동안 시범적으로 사용하고 있다.

Since then, 130,000 prescriptions have written using telemedicine services in the country.
이후 전국에서 13만 건의 처방전이 원격진료 서비스를 이용해서 쓰여졌다.

While 26 countries out of 36 OECD countries have telemedicine systems in place, the need for it has been amplified in light of the COVID-19 pandemic.
경제협력개발기구(OECD) 36개국 중 26개국이 원격의료 시스템을 갖추고 있지만, COVID-19 대유행이라는 점에서 필요성이 증폭되고 있다.

☆in place ~을 위한 준비가 되어 있는

☆amplify 증폭시키다, (격식) 더 자세히 진술[서술]하다

☆in light of ~을 고려해서 = taking (something) into consideration.

However, the system is not a fix all for everything.
하지만, 이 제도가 모든 것을 해결해주는 것은 아니다.

☆fix (특히 쉽거나 잠정적인) 해결책

Korea Physician's Association Park Geun-tae said, "Doctors need to conduct physical examinations when patients have fevers, pneumonia, allergic coughs or asthma."
대한개원내과협의회 박근태 회장은 "의사들은 열, 폐렴, 알레르기 기침, 천식이 있을 때 신체 검사를 해야 한다"고 말했다.

☆conduct examinations 진찰하다

Despite this, the local medical sector generally agrees telemedicine will only continue to grow and South Korea is looking for ways to make the system even more advanced.
그럼에도 불구하고 국내 의료계는 원격의료가 계속 증가할 것이라는 데 대체로 동의하고 있으며 한국은 이 시스템을 더욱 발전시킬 방법을 찾고 있다.

☆advanced 선진의, 고급[상급]의 =well developed

Writing Exercise

1. 종종, 사람들은 아플 때 너무 바빠서 직접 의사를 방문하지 못한다.

   Often

2. 하지만 최근 한국 정부가 원격진료 사용을 잠정 승인한 덕분에 온라인에서 의사와 말할 수 있고 심지어 처방전까지 받을 수 있다.

   However,

3. 의사가 진료를 마치면 의사가 필요한 서식을 온라인으로 보내주므로 환자는 가까운 약국에서 처방전을 받을 수 있다.

   When

4. 2월에 COVID - 19가 한국에 도달했을 때, 정부는 시범적으로 이 시스템을 승인하기로 결정했다.

   When

5. 이후 전국에서 13만 건의 처방전이 원격진료 서비스를 이용해서 쓰여졌다.

   Since

6. 경제협력개발기구(OECD) 36개국 중 26개국이 원격의료 시스템을 갖추고 있지만, COVID - 19 대유행이라는 점에서 필요성이 증폭되고 있다.

   While

7. 하지만, 이 제도가 모든 것을 해결해주는 것은 아니다.

   However,

8. 대한개원내과협의회 박근태 회장은 "의사들은 열, 폐렴, 알레르기 기침, 천식이 있을 때 신체 검사를 해야 한다"고 말했다.

Korea

9. 그럼에도 불구하고 국내 의료계는 원격의료가 계속 증가할 것이라는 데 대체로 동의하고 있으며 한국은 이 시스템을 더욱 발전시킬 방법을 찾고 있다.

Despite

◉ BRK 457/3
457/3
Today TH

영어 뉴스룸 11

English
NewsRoom

BREAKING NEWS

Elderly S. Koreans feeling lonely as COVID-19 outbreak affects their social lives. Jeong Nam-poong is a retired tool store owner in his late eighties. After his wife passed away some 20 years ago, he has spent countless hours dancing the days away at so-called 'colatecs', daytime discotheques specifically aimed at senior citizens. This colatec reopened as the number of COVID-19 cases went down in South Korea, but was shuttered again after the outbreak...

콜라텍 폐쇄조치로 갈 곳 없는 노인들

코로나19 때문에 내려진 콜라텍 폐쇄 등 조치로 인해 변화된 사회현상에 대한 내용입니다.

Elderly S. Koreans feeling lonely as COVID-19 outbreak affects their social lives

Jeong Nam-poong is a retired tool store owner in his late eighties.

After his wife passed away some 20 years ago, he has spent countless hours dancing the days away at so-called 'colatecs', daytime discotheques specifically aimed at senior citizens.

This colatec reopened as the number of COVID-19 cases went down in South Korea, but was shuttered again after the outbreak in Itaewon clubs.

He needed to talk and dance with people, so Jeong and his friends from the colatec decided to meet at a park in Seoul.

With their face masks on, they let out their energy with some moves, their bodies jigging along with the music.

As elderly people are usually not accustomed to using mobile devices or other types of technology, they have to meet others in person to have a social life.

In South Korea, people over the age of 65 account for almost 16 percent of the population, but the number is rising rapidly.

Statistics Korea says, by 2045, that figure will be 37 percent, the highest in the world.

COVID-19 has naturally made many elderly people nervous, but some are crying out for some face-to-face interaction as loneliness is something that cannot be treated in a hospital.

Elderly S. Koreans feeling lonely as COVID-19 outbreak affects their social lives

COVID-19 발병이 사회생활에 영향을 미치면서 외로움을 느끼는 노인들

☆elderly 연세가 드신 old보다 정중한 표현
☆affect 영향을 미치다 동사

Jeong Nam-poong is a retired tool store owner in his late eighties.

정남풍씨는 80대 후반의 은퇴한 공구점 주인이다.

After his wife passed away some 20 years ago, he has spent countless hours dancing the days away at so-called 'colatecs', daytime discotheques specifically aimed at senior citizens.

약 20년 전 아내가 세상을 떠난 후, 그는 특히 노인들을 겨냥한 주간 디스코텍인 소위 '콜라텍'에서 춤으로 나날들을 보내는 것에 수많은 시간을 소비했다.

☆countless 무수한, 셀 수 없이 많은
☆dance ~ away 춤으로 ~을 보내다

> e.g. dance the days away 춤으로 나날들을 보내다
> dance the night away 춤으로 밤을 지새우다
> dance the youth away 춤으로 젊은 시절을 보내다

· 응용 game ~ away 게임으로 ~을 보내다

> e.g. I'm gaming the days away with friends.
> 난 친구들과 게임으로 나날들을 보내는 중이야.

☆aimed at ~을 목표로 한, ~을 겨냥한

This colatec reopened as the number of COVID-19 cases went down in South Korea, but was shuttered again after the outbreak in Itaewon clubs.

이 콜라텍은 한국에서 COVID-19사례가 감소하면서 다시 문을 열었지만 이태원 클럽에서 발병 후 다시 문을 닫았다.

☆as ~면서 (동시에)
☆shutter 1. 덧문 명사 | 2. 문닫다 동사

He needed to talk and dance with people, so Jeong and his friends from the colatec decided to meet at a park in Seoul.

그는 사람들과 이야기하고 춤추고 싶어서 정씨와 콜라텍 친구들은 서울의 한 공원에서 만나기로 했다.

With their face masks on, they let out their energy with some moves, their bodies jigging along with the music.
마스크를 쓴 채, 그들은 음악에 맞춰 몸으로 춤추며 약간의 동작으로 에너지를 발산했다.

☆along with ~에 따라, ~와 함께

☆jig 춤추다

As elderly people are usually not accustomed to using mobile devices or other types of technology, they have to meet others in person to have a social life.
노인들은 보통 모바일 기기나 다른 종류의 장비를 사용하는 데 익숙하지 않기 때문에, 사회생활을 하기 위해서는 직접 다른 사람들을 만나야 한다.

☆be accustomed to ~ing ~에 익숙한

☆in person 직접

In South Korea, people over the age of 65 account for almost 16 percent of the population, but the number is rising rapidly.
한국에서는 65세 이상 인구가 인구의 거의 16%를 차지하지만, 그 수는 빠르게 증가하고 있다.

Statistics Korea says, by 2045, that figure will be 37 percent, the highest in the world.
통계청은 2045년까지 이 수치가 37%로 세계에서 가장 높을 것이라고 말한다.

COVID-19 has naturally made many elderly people nervous, but some are crying out for some face-to-face interaction as loneliness is something that cannot be treated in a hospital.
COVID-19는 자연스레 많은 노년층을 불안하게 만들었지만, 외로움은 병원에서 치료할 수 없는 것이기 때문에 어떤 이들은 얼굴을 맞대는 상호작용을 절실히 필요로 하고 있다.

☆naturally 물론, 당연히, 자연스럽게

☆cry out for something ~을 절실히 필요로 하다

> e.g. The company is crying out for a strong leader.
> 그 기업은 강한 리더를 절실히 필요로 하고 있다.

☆face-to-face 마주보며 대면하는

☆interaction 상호작용

☆loneliness 외로움

1. 정남풍씨는 80대 후반의 은퇴한 공구점 주인이다.

   Jeong Nam - poong

2. 약 20년 전 아내가 세상을 떠난 후, 그는 특히 노인들을 겨냥한 주간 디스코텍인 소위 '콜라텍'에서 춤으로 나날들을 보내는 것에 수많은 시간을 소비했다.

   After

3. 이 콜라텍은 한국에서 COVID - 19사례가 감소하면서 다시 문을 열었지만 이태원 클럽에서 발병 후 다시 문을 닫았다.

   This

4. 그는 사람들과 이야기하고 춤추고 싶어서 정씨와 콜라텍 친구들은 서울의 한 공원에서 만나기로 했다.

   He

5. 마스크를 쓴 채, 그들은 음악에 맞춰 몸으로 춤추며 약간의 동작으로 에너지를 발산했다.

   With

6. 노인들은 보통 모바일 기기나 다른 종류의 장비를 사용하는 데 익숙하지 않기 때문에, 사회생활을 하기 위해서는 직접 다른 사람들을 만나야 한다.

   As elderly

7. 한국에서는 65세 이상 인구가 인구의 거의 16%를 차지하지만, 그 수는 빠르게 증가하고 있다.

   In South

8. 통계청은 2045년까지 이 수치가 37%로 세계에서 가장 높을 것이라고 말한다.

Statistics

_____

_____

9. COVID-19는 자연스레 많은 노년층을 불안하게 만들었지만, 외로움은 병원에서 치료할 수 없는 것이기 때문에 어떤 이들은 얼굴을 맞대는 상호작용을 절실히 필요로 하고 있다.

COVID-19

_____

_____

◉ BRK 457/3
457/3
Today TH

영어 뉴스룸 12

English NewsRoom

BREAKING NEWS

National Police Agency using packaging tape to try and find missing children. It's common to see clear packaging tape at local post offices across South Korea. But starting May 25th, customers will see blue packaging tape with photo descriptions of missing children in South Korea. The 'Hope Tape' project, implemented by the National Police Agency, is a new way to try and find missing kids. It includes the names and faces of missing children...

택배 포장 테이프에 실종아동 몽타주를?

택배 포장 테이프로 실종아동을 찾는다는 내용입니다.

National Police Agency using packaging tape to try and find missing children

It's common to see clear packaging tape at local post offices across South Korea.

But starting May 25th, customers will see blue packaging tape with photo descriptions of missing children in South Korea.

The 'Hope Tape' project, implemented by the National Police Agency, is a new way to try and find missing kids.

It includes the names and faces of missing children, but most importantly, it has digitally-aged photos of them on the tape.

The National Police Agency says these new type of photos might give them a better chance of helping the children get back to their families.

Chief of Children and Juvenile affairs Division of the Korean National Police Agency, LIM Hee-jin said, "There was one case when we found a missing person because someone saw a person with similar facial features to the digitally-aged photos we made."

The 'Hope Tape' also has QR Codes printed on it so the children's parents can add their kids' fingerprints to the authorities' tracking system.

According to statistics from the National Police Agency, more than 42-thousand kids in South Korea were reported missing in 2019, and more than 6-hundred of them are still unaccounted for.

Officials say the 'Hope Tape' will be located across post offices and logistics centers nationwide, and will be used to seal hundreds of thousands of packages to spread the information as far as possible.

NEWS 스크립트 분석

National Police Agency using packaging tape to try and find missing children
포장 테이프를 이용해 실종아동을 찾으려는 경찰청

It's common to see clear packaging tape at local post offices across South Korea.
한국 전역의 우체국에서 깨끗한 포장테이프를 보는 것은 흔한 일이다.

But starting May 25th, customers will see blue packaging tape with photo descriptions of missing children in South Korea.
하지만 5월 25일부터 고객들은 한국에서 실종된 어린이들의 사진 설명이 들어 있는 파란색 포장 테이프를 보게 될 것이다.

The 'Hope Tape' project, implemented by the National Police Agency, is a new way to try and find missing kids.
경찰청이 시행하는 '호프 테이프(희망테이프)' 사업은 실종된 아이들을 찾기 위한 새로운 시도다.

　☆implement 시행하다

It includes the names and faces of missing children, but most importantly, it has digitally-aged photos of them on the tape.
포장 테이프에는 실종 아동의 이름과 얼굴을 담고 있지만 가장 중요한 것은 테이프에 아이들의 디지털 연령대 사진(나이 변환 몽타주)이 담겨 있다는 점이다.

　☆digitally-aged photos 나이 변환 몽타주

The National Police Agency says these new type of photos might give them a better chance of helping the children get back to their families.
경찰청은 이러한 새로운 형태의 사진들이 경찰청에게 아이들이 가족의 품으로 돌아가도록 도울 수 있는 더 나은 기회를 줄 수 있다고 말한다.

　☆give A B A에게 B를 주다

> e.g. She gives me advice and takes care of me.
> 　　그녀는 나에게 조언을 해주고 나를 돌봐 줘.

Chief of Children and Juvenile affairs Division of the Korean National Police Agency, LIM Hee-jin said, "There was one case when we found a missing person because someone saw a person with similar facial features to the digitally-aged photos we made."

경찰청 아동청소년과 임희진 계장은 "누군가가 우리가 만든 나이변환 몽타주 얼굴사진과 비슷한 사람을 보고 실종자를 찾은 사례가 있었다"고 말했다.

The 'Hope Tape' also has QR Codes printed on it so the children's parents can add their kids' fingerprints to the authorities' tracking system.

'호프 테이프'에도 QR코드가 인쇄돼 있어 어린이 부모가 자녀의 지문을 당국의 추적 시스템에 추가할 수 있다.

☆add A to B A를 B에 추가하다

According to statistics from the National Police Agency, more than 42-thousand kids in South Korea were reported missing in 2019, and more than 6-hundred of them are still unaccounted for.

경찰청의 통계에 따르면, 2019년에 한국에서 4만 2천 명 이상의 아이들이 실종되었다고 보고되었고, 이 중 6백 명 이상이 여전히 행방불명 상태다.

☆unaccounted for 행방불명의

> e.g. More than 10,000 people are still unaccounted for from the war.
> 1만 명 이상의 사람들이 전쟁으로 인해 여전히 행방불명 상태다.

Officials say the 'Hope Tape' will be located across post offices and logistics centers nationwide, and will be used to seal hundreds of thousands of packages to spread the information as far as possible.

관계자들은 '호프테이프'가 전국 우체국과 물류센터에 걸쳐 비치될 것이며, 가능한 한 멀리 정보를 퍼뜨리기 위해 수십만 개의 소포를 봉인하는 데 사용될 것이라고 말한다.

☆seal 봉인하다
☆as far as possible 가능한 한 멀리

Writing Exercise

1. 한국 전역의 우체국에서 깨끗한 포장테이프를 보는 것은 흔한 일이다.

It's

2. 하지만 5월 25일부터 고객들은 한국에서 실종된 어린이들의 사진 설명이 들어 있는 파란색 포장 테이프를 보게 될 것이다.

But

3. 경찰청이 시행하는 '호프 테이프/희망테이프' 사업은 실종된 아이들을 찾기 위한 새로운 시도다.

The 'Hope Tape'

4. 포장 테이프에는 실종 아동의 이름과 얼굴을 담고 있지만 가장 중요한 것은 테이프에 아이들의 디지털 연령대 사진(**나이 변환 몽타주**)이 담겨 있다는 점이다.

It includes

5. 경찰청은 이러한 새로운 형태의 사진들이 경찰청에게 아이들이 가족의 품으로 돌아가도록 도울 수 있는 더 나은 기회를 줄 수 있다고 말한다.

The National

6. 경찰청 아동청소년과 임희진 계장은 "누군가가 우리가 만든 나이변환 몽타주 얼굴사진과 비슷한 사람을 보고 실종자를 찾은 사례가 있었다"고 말했다.

Chief of

7. '호프 테이프'에도 QR코드가 인쇄되어 있어 어린이 부모가 자녀의 지문을 당국의 추적 시스템에 추가할 수 있다.

The 'Hope Tape'

8. 경찰청의 통계에 따르면, 2019년에 한국에서 4만 2천 명 이상의 아이들이 실종되었다고 보고되었고, 이 중 6백 명 이상이 여전히 행방불명 상태다.

According _____

_____

9. 관계자들은 '호프테이프'가 전국 우체국과 물류센터에 걸쳐 비치될 것이며, 가능한 한 멀리 정보를 퍼뜨리기 위해 수십만 개의 소포를 봉인하는 데 사용될 것이라고 말한다.

Officials _____

_____

ⓖBRK 457/3
457/3
Today TH

영어 뉴스룸 13 English NewsRoom

BREAKING NEWS

How Korean dramas are gaining new global fans through Netflix. Korean dramas on Netflix are getting more and more attention from viewers around the world. 'Kingdom' deals with political upheaval in the Joseon dynasty amid a zombie apocalypse. Its first season was named as one of the '30 Best International TV Shows of the Decade' by the New York Times which called it a "most radical departure from Korean-drama norms."

외국인도 드라마 '킹덤'을 보며 떨고 있다

우리 드라마가 세계에 주목 받고 있는 이유에 대한 내용입니다.

 전체 스크립트

How Korean dramas are gaining new global fans through Netflix

Korean dramas on Netflix are getting more and more attention from viewers around the world.

'Kingdom' deals with political upheaval in the Joseon dynasty amid a zombie apocalypse.

Its first season was named as one of the '30 Best International TV Shows of the Decade' by the New York Times which called it a "most radical departure from Korean-drama norms."

Season two has also received positive reviews from fans.

A culture critic says Korean dramas are getting such attention because they are tackling familiar subjects from a fresh perspective.

'Extracurricular' is another "can't miss" Korean show.

This teen crime drama tells the story of a high school student who has been abandoned by his parents and leads a double life.

Critics say fans of Bong Joon-ho's 'Parasite' will enjoy 'extracurricular', which the Los Angeles Times called the "cream of the crop" of the Korean dramas produced by Netflix.

For those unfamiliar with Korean dramas, a culture critic recommends 'Crash Landing on You', a love story set across the divided Korean peninsula.

 스크립트 분석

How Korean dramas are gaining new global fans through Netflix
한국 드라마가 넷플릭스를 통해 새로운 글로벌 팬들을 어떻게 얻고 있는가

Korean dramas on Netflix are getting more and more attention from viewers around the world.
넷플릭스의 한국 드라마가 전 세계 시청자들의 관심을 점점 더 받고 있다.

'Kingdom' deals with political upheaval in the Joseon dynasty amid a zombie apocalypse.
'킹덤'은 좀비 종말론 속에서 조선 왕조의 정치적 격변을 다룬다.

　　☆deals with ~을 다루다

　　☆political upheaval 정치 파동, 격변

　　☆dynasty 왕조, 역대통치자 | 영 ['dɪn.ə.sti], 미 ['daɪ.nə.sti]
　　　영국, 미국 발음 다름 주의!

　　☆apocalypse 종말, 대재앙

Its first season was named as one of the '30 Best International TV Shows of the Decade' by the New York Times which called it a "most radical departure from Korean-drama norms."
첫 시즌은 뉴욕 타임스로부터 '10년간 최고의 국제 TV 쇼 30개' 중 하나로 선정되었는데, 뉴욕 타임스는 그것(킹덤)을 "표준적인 한국 드라마로부터의 가장 급진적인 이탈"이라고 평했다.

　　☆be named 선정되다, 임명되다

　　☆call A B A를 B라고 부르다

　　☆radical 근본적인, 철저한 급진적인, 과격한

　　☆departure 출발, (정도·일상 등으로부터) 벗어남[일탈]

　　☆norm 표준, 규범, 기준

Season two has also received positive reviews from fans.
시즌 2도 팬들의 호평을 받았다.

A culture critic says Korean dramas are getting such attention because they are tackling familiar subjects from a fresh perspective.
한 문화평론가는 한국 드라마가 친숙한 주제를 신선한 시각에서 다루기 때문에 이런 관심을 받고 있다고 말한다.

　　☆tackle 다루다

'Extracurricular' is another "can't miss" Korean show.

인간수업은 또한 놓칠 수 없는 한국 쇼다.

☆extracurricular 과외의 *(형용사)*

This teen crime drama tells the story of a high school student who has been abandoned by his parents and leads a double life.

이 10대 범죄 드라마는 부모로부터 버림받고 이중생활을 하는 고등학생의 이야기를 다룬다.

☆be abandoned 버림받다

Critics say fans of Bong Joon-ho's 'Parasite' will enjoy 'extracurricular', which the Los Angeles Times called the "cream of the crop" of the Korean dramas produced by Netflix.

비평가들은 봉준호 감독의 '기생충' 팬들이 로스엔젤레스타임스가 평했던 넷플릭스가 제작하는 "최고의" 한국 드라마인 '인간수업' 드라마를 즐길 거라고 말한다.

☆Los Angeles 영 [ˌlɒs ˈæn.dʒə.liːz], 미 [ˌlɑːs ˈæn.dʒə.ləs]
  영국, 미국 발음 다름 주의!

☆the cream of the crop : the very best of a particular group of people or things 제일 좋은 것, 알짜 *(인 사람)*

> e.g. People told them he is the cream of the crop in his school.
> 사람들이 그들에게 그가 학교에서 최고라고 말했다.

For those unfamiliar with Korean dramas, a culture critic recommends 'Crash Landing on You', a love story set across the divided Korean peninsula.

한국 드라마에 익숙하지 않은 사람들을 위해, 한 문화평론가는 분단된 한반도로 갈라놓은 러브 스토리인 '사랑의 불시착'을 추천한다.

☆unfamiliar with ~에 익숙하지 못한

1. '킹덤'은 좀비 종말론 속에서 조선 왕조의 정치적 격변을 다룬다.

   'Kingdom'

2. 첫 시즌은 뉴욕 타임스로부터 '10년간 최고의 국제 TV 쇼 30개' 중 하나로 선정되었는데, 뉴욕 타임스는 그것(킹덤)을 "표준적인 한국 드라마로부터의 가장 급진적인 이탈"이라고 평했다.

   Its

3. 시즌2도 팬들의 호평을 받았다.

   Season

4. 한 문화평론가는 한국 드라마가 친숙한 주제를 신선한 시각에서 다루기 때문에 이런 관심을 받고 있다고 말한다.

   A culture

5. 인간수업은 또한 놓칠 수 없는 한국 쇼다.

   'Extracurricular'

6. 이 10대 범죄 드라마는 부모로부터 버림받고 이중생활을 하는 고등학생의 이야기를 다룬다.

   This teen

7. 비평가들은 봉준호 감독의 '기생충' 팬들이 로스엔젤레스타임스가 평했던 넷플릭스가 제작하는 "최고의" 한국 드라마인 '인간수업' 드라마를 즐길 거라고 말한다.

   Critics

8. 한국 드라마에 익숙하지 않은 사람들을 위해, 한 문화평론가는 분단된 한반도로 갈라놓은 러브 스토리인 '사랑의 불시착'을 추천한다.

   For those

영어 뉴스룸 14

English
NewsRoom

BREAKING NEWS

From 3D big 'wave' to future of 'Fourth Screen' in everyday life. Ocean waves crashing loudly in the heart of one of the world's busiest cities. Powerful waves curling and swirling within a see-through water tank. This anamorphic illusion - situated in downtown Seoul - is dazzling visitors. This huge 80-by-20 meter wave trapped inside what appears to be an aquarium is a public art installation displayed on South Korea's largest digital billboard.

전자간판으로 만든 파도의 퀄리티는?

'제 4의 스크린'이라 불리우는 전자간판 산업에 관한 내용입니다.

 전체 스크립트

From 3D big 'wave' to future of 'Fourth Screen' in everyday life

Ocean waves crashing loudly in the heart of one of the world's busiest cities.

Powerful waves curling and swirling within a see-through water tank.

This anamorphic illusion - situated in downtown Seoul - is dazzling visitors.

This huge 80-by-20 meter wave trapped inside what appears to be an aquarium is a public art installation displayed on South Korea's largest digital billboard.

It's also one of many digital information displays that have been deeply immersed in our daily lives.

Dubbed Digital Signage, it's a form of digital installation that beams multimedia content for informational or advertising purposes, and are gradually being seen in major cities around the world.

Samsung Electronics has been dominating the market for over a decade, controlling 27percent of the global market share in 2019, followed by its local rival LG Electronics with 12 percent.

Senior Analyst of Hana Financial Investment KIM Hyun-soo says, "There isn't strong market demand as much of the focus remains on smartphones and display panels. That's the reason why we haven't seen much development within the sector."

Still, while it may not seem essential right now,... it's important that South Korean firms maintain their strong lead in global market before the industry sees an explosion in demand as we head further into the fourth industrial revolution.

From 3D big 'wave' to future of 'Fourth Screen' in everyday life
큰 '파도' 입체 영상에서 일상생활 속 '제4의 스크린'의 미래로
　　☆from A to B A에서 B로

Ocean waves crashing loudly in the heart of one of the world's busiest cities.
세계에서 가장 바쁜 도시들 중 한 곳의 중심부에서 요란하게 부서지는 바다의 물결.
　　☆in the heart of ~의 가운데에

Powerful waves curling and swirling within a see-through water tank.
속이 다 비치는 물탱크 안에서 휘몰아치고 소용돌이치는 강력한 파도.
　　☆curl 돌돌 감기다
　　☆swirl 소용돌이치다
　　☆see-through 속이 다 비치는

This anamorphic illusion - situated in downtown Seoul - is dazzling visitors.
서울 시내에 자리 잡은 이 무정형 환상은 방문객들을 현혹 시키고 있다.
　　☆anamorphic 일그러져 보이는
　　☆illusion 환상
　　☆dazzle 눈부시게 하다, 현혹 시키다

This huge 80-by-20 meter wave trapped inside what appears to be an aquarium is a public art installation displayed on South Korea's largest digital billboard.
수족관으로 보이는 곳 안에 갇힌 이 거대한 가로 80m, 세로 20m 크기의 파도는 한국 최대의 디지털 광고판에 전시된 공공미술 설치물이다.
　　☆80-by-20 meter 가로 80m, 세로 20m
　　☆trap 가두다
　　☆trapped inside 안에 갇힌

It's also one of many digital information displays that have been deeply immersed in our daily lives.

이것은 또한 우리의 일상에 깊이 빠져든 수많은 디지털 정보 디스플레이 중 하나이기도 하다.

☆be immersed in ~에 푹 빠지다, 몰두하다

e.g. She was deeply immersed in classical music.
그녀는 클래식 음악에 깊이 빠져 있었다.

Dubbed Digital Signage, it's a form of digital installation that beams multimedia content for informational or advertising purposes, and are gradually being seen in major cities around the world.

디지털 사이니지(전자간판)라 불리는 이것은 정보 제공이나 광고 목적으로 멀티미디어 콘텐츠를 빔으로 전송하는 디지털 설치의 한 형태로, 이것들은 세계 주요 도시에서 점차 모습을 드러내고 있다.

☆dubbed ~라 불리는, 이름 붙여진

Samsung Electronics has been dominating the market for over a decade, controlling 27 percent of the global market share in 2019, followed by its local rival LG Electronics with 12 percent.

삼성전자는 10년 넘게 시장을 지배해 왔으며 2019년 세계 시장 점유율 27%를 점유하고 있고, 뒤이어 국내 경쟁사인 LG전자가 12%를 점유하고 있다.

☆followed by 뒤이어, 잇달아

Senior Analyst of Hana Financial Investment KIM Hyun-soo says, "There isn't strong market demand as much of the focus remains on smartphones and display panels. That's the reason why we haven't seen much development within the sector."

하나금융투자의 김현수 애널리스트는 "스마트폰과 디스플레이 패널에 수요가 많이 집중 되어 있기 때문에 강력한 시장 수요는 없다. 그것이 그동안 그 분야에서 별다른 발전이 보이지 않았던 이유"라고 말한다.

Still, while it may not seem essential right now,... it's important that South Korean firms maintain their strong lead in global market before the industry sees an explosion in demand as we head further into the fourth industrial revolution.

아직까지는, 지금은 꼭 필요한 것 같진 않지만,... 우리가 4차 산업혁명으로 더 나아가면서 수요가 폭발적으로 증가하기 전에 한국 기업들이 세계 시장에서 강한 우위를 유지하는 것이 중요하다.

☆explosion 1. 폭발, 폭파 | 2. 폭발적인 증가

☆in demand 수요가 많은

e.g. The toy has been in great demand by people of all ages.
그 장난감은 모든 연령대의 사람들에게 큰 인기를 끌었다.

1. 세계에서 가장 바쁜 도시들 중 한 곳의 중심부에서 요란하게 부서지는 바다의 물결.

Ocean

2. 속이 다 비치는 물탱크 안에서 휘몰아치고 소용돌이치는 강력한 파도.

Powerful

3. 서울 시내에 자리 잡은 이 무정형 환상은 방문객들을 현혹 시키고 있다.

This

4. 수족관으로 보이는 곳 안에 갇힌 이 거대한 가로 80m, 세로 20m 크기의 파도는 한국 최대의 디지털 광고판에 전시된 공공미술 설치물이다.

This

5. 이것은 또한 우리의 일상에 깊이 빠져든 수많은 디지털 정보 디스플레이 중 하나이기도 하다.

It's

6. 디지털 사이니지(전자간판)라 불리는 이것은 정보 제공이나 광고 목적으로 멀티미디어 콘텐츠를 빔으로 전송하는 디지털 설치의 한 형태로, 이것들은 세계 주요 도시에서 점차 모습을 드러내고 있다.

Dubbed

7. 삼성전자는 10년 넘게 시장을 지배해 왔으며 2019년 세계 시장 점유율 27%를 점유하고 있고, 뒤이어 국내 경쟁사인 LG전자가 12%를 점유하고 있다.

Samsung

8. 하나금융투자의 김현수 애널리스트는 "스마트폰과 디스플레이 패널에 수요가 많이 집중 되어 있기 때문에 강력한 시장 수요는 없다. 그것이 그동안 그 분야에서 별다른 발전이 보이지 않았던 이유"라고 말한다.

Senior
_____
_____

9. 아직까지는, 지금은 꼭 필요한 것 같진 않지만,... 우리가 4차 산업혁명으로 더 나아가면서 수요가 폭발적으로 증가하기 전에 한국 기업들이 세계 시장에서 강한 우위를 유지하는 것이 중요하다.

Still,
_____
_____

영어 뉴스룸 15

English
NewsRoom

**BREAKING
NEWS**

Europe highlights COVID-19 tracing system. Media in Europe are highlighting South Korea's 'track and trace' system. The BBC has reported on how the country has been tracking down those who've come in contact with infected people and its use of a tracing app for smartphones. There's been some criticism in Europe because of privacy concerns, but a number of countries are introducing similar systems.

이제 유럽이 한국을 따라한다

유럽이 한국의 COVID-19 추적 시스템에 관심을 가지고 따라하고 있다는 내용입니다.

 NEWS 전체 스크립트

Europe highlights COVID-19 tracing system

Media in Europe are highlighting South Korea's 'track and trace' system.

The BBC has reported on how the country has been tracking down those who've come in contact with infected people and its use of a tracing app for smartphones.

There's been some criticism in Europe because of privacy concerns, but a number of countries are introducing similar systems.

The NHS in the UK is developing its own contact-tracing app, and so is France with an app called 'StopCovid'.

The English Premier League is getting ready to resume, so it's using GPS tracking and video analysis to ensure that clubs stick to the safety guidelines.

South Korea's transport ministry is injecting around 7 million U.S. dollars to upgrade its tracing system.

That system, unveiled in March, has helped a great deal in stopping the spread of the virus, taking only about 10 minutes to track down where infected people have been.

The ministry plans to use money from the government's new extra budget to automate the system.

Europe highlights COVID-19 tracing system
유럽이 COVID-19 추적 시스템을 강조하다

Media in Europe are highlighting South Korea's 'track and trace' system.
유럽의 언론들이 한국의 '트랙 앤드 트레이스' 제도를 부각시키고 있다.

　　☆highlight 강조하다, 부각시키다

　　☆track 추적하다

　　☆trace *(추적하여)* 밝혀내다

The BBC has reported on how the country has been tracking down those who've come in contact with infected people and its use of a tracing app for smartphones.
BBC는 감염자와 접촉한 사람들을 어떻게 추적해 왔는지와 스마트폰용 추적 앱의 사용에 대해 보도했다.

　　☆report on ~에 대해 보고하다

　　☆track down ~을 찾아내다

　　☆come in contact with ~와 접촉하다, 만나다

> e.g. Be careful not to come into contact with dead animals.
> 죽은 동물과 접촉하지 않도록 주의하세요.

There's been some criticism in Europe because of privacy concerns, but a number of countries are introducing similar systems.
유럽에서는 사생활 염려에 대한 우려 때문에 비난이 있었지만, 많은 나라들이 유사한 제도를 도입하고 있다.

　　☆privacy 사생활 | 미 ['prɪv.ə.si], 영 ['praɪ.və.si]
　　　영국, 미국 발음 다름 주의!

　　☆privacy concerns 사생활 염려

The NHS in the UK is developing its own contact-tracing app, and so is France with an app called 'StopCovid'.
영국의 NHS(National Health Service)는 자체적인 콘택트레이싱 앱(접촉자 추적앱)을 개발하고 있으며, 프랑스도 'StopCovid'라는 앱을 개발하고 있다.

The English Premier League is getting ready to resume, so it's using GPS tracking and video analysis to ensure that clubs stick to the safety guidelines.

영국 프리미어리그가 재개 준비를 하고 있어서 구단들이 안전지침을 준수하도록 보장하기 위해 GPS 추적과 영상 분석을 활용하고 있다.

☆analysis 분석

☆ensure 확실히 하다, 어떤 특별한 결과를 보장하다

☆stick to 굳게 지키다, 방침을 고수하다

> e.g. **You need to stick to your plans.**
> 넌 너의 계획을 고수할 필요가 있어.

South Korea's transport ministry is injecting around 7 million U.S. dollars to upgrade its tracing system.

한국의 (국토)교통부는 추적 시스템을 업그레이드하기 위해 약 700만 달러를 투입하고 있다.

☆inject *(단체·사업 등이 기능을 발휘하도록 자금을)* 투입하다

That system, unveiled in March, has helped a great deal in stopping the spread of the virus, taking only about 10 minutes to track down where infected people have been.

지난 3월 공개된 이 시스템은 감염자들이 어디에 있었는지 추적하는데 10분밖에 걸리지 않아 바이러스의 확산을 막는 데 큰 도움을 주었다.

☆a great deal 많이, 훨씬 더

The ministry plans to use money from the government's new extra budget to automate the system.

교통부는 정부의 새로운 추경 예산에서 나온 돈을 이 제도를 자동화하는데 사용할 계획이다.

☆automate *(일을)* 자동화하다

Writing Exercise

1. 유럽의 언론들이 한국의 '트랙 앤드 트레이스' 제도를 부각시키고 있다.

   Media

2. BBC는 감염자와 접촉한 사람들을 어떻게 추적해 왔는지와 스마트폰용 추적 앱의 사용에 대해 보도했다.

   The BBC

3. 유럽에서는 사생활 염려에 대한 우려 때문에 비난이 있었지만, 많은 나라들이 유사한 제도를 도입하고 있다.

   There's

4. 영국의 NHS(National Health Service)는 자체적인 콘택트트레이싱 앱(접촉자 추적앱)을 개발하고 있으며, 프랑스도 'StopCovid'라는 앱을 개발하고 있다.

   The NHS

5. 영국 프리미어리그가 재개 준비를 하고 있고 구단들이 안전지침을 지키도록 확실히 하기 위해 GPS 추적과 영상 분석을 활용하고 있다.

   The English

6. 한국의 (국토)교통부는 추적 시스템을 업그레이드하기 위해 약 700만 달러를 투입하고 있다.

   South

7. 지난 3월 공개된 이 시스템은 감염자들이 어디에 있었는지 추적하는데 10분 밖에 걸리지 않아 바이러스의 확산을 막는 데 큰 도움을 주었다.

   That system,

8. 교통부는 정부의 새로운 추경 예산에서 나온 돈을 이 제도를 자동화하는데 사용할 계획이다.

   The ministry

BRK 457/3
457/3
Today TH

영어 뉴스룸 16

English NewsRoom

BREAKING NEWS

Are swimming pools and beaches safe during COVID-19 pandemic?. This is one of the most popular summer destinations in South Korea. Busan's Haeundae beach is normally packed with beach goers, but with the COVID-19 pandemic, the area isn't as crowded as it'd normally be. Generally, many were following the government's guidelines on two-meter social distancing, while most were seen wearing face masks,

수영장에서도 코로나19가 전염될 확률은?

코로나19 대유행 동안 해변과 수영장을 방문하는 것은 안전한가에 대한 내용입니다.

NEWS 전체 스크립트

Are swimming pools and beaches safe during COVID-19 pandemic?

This is one of the most popular summer destinations in South Korea.

Busan's Haeundae beach is normally packed with beach goers, but with the COVID-19 pandemic, the area isn't as crowded as it'd normally be.

Generally, many were following the government's guidelines on two-meter social distancing, while most were seen wearing face masks, except during meal times and when they were in the water.

However, the big question remains.

Is it really safe to visit beaches and swimming pools during the COVID-19 pandemic?

According to experts, if an infected person enters the sea or a pool, the virus can spread via saliva.

However, when mixed with water, the density is significantly lowered, and the risk is greatly reduced.

In particular, swimming pools contain chlorine have a very low chance of spreading the virus.

However, infections are most likely to occur outside the water, and in crowded environments.

Another fear is that mosquitoes, which are rampant in South Korea during summer, could spread the COVID-19 virus, as they can be a carrier of viral diseases.

Fortunately, health experts say there's a near-zero chance that the virus which would have to pass through the mosquito's digestive system could survive in the body, and transmit it through its saliva.

 **스크립트 분석**

Are swimming pools and beaches safe during COVID-19 pandemic?
COVID-19 대유행 동안 수영장과 해변은 안전한가?

This is one of the most popular summer destinations in South Korea.
이곳은 한국에서 가장 인기 있는 여름 여행지 중 하나이다.

　　☆destination 목적지

Busan's Haeundae beach is normally packed with beach goers, but with the COVID-19 pandemic, the area isn't as crowded as it'd normally be.
부산의 해운대 해수욕장은 보통 해변을 찾는 사람들로 붐비지만, COVID-19 대유행으로 이 지역은 평상시만큼 붐비지 않는다.

　　☆be packed with ~로 가득 차다, 붐비다

　　☆beach goers 해변을 찾는 사람들 movie goers 영화 자주 보러 가는 사람들, 영화 팬들

Generally, many were following the government's guidelines on two-meter social distancing, while most were seen wearing face masks, except during meal times and when they were in the water.
일반적으로 2m의 사회적 거리를 두자는 정부의 지침을 따르는 사람이 많았고, 식사시간과 물 속에 있을 때를 제외하고는 대부분 마스크를 착용하고 있는 모습이었다.

However, the big question remains.
그러나 중요한 의문점은 남아 있다.

　　☆question remains 의문점이 남다.

　　　e.g. The question remains whether there will be a party for retirees.
　　　은퇴자들을 위한 파티가 열릴지 의문이다.

Is it really safe to visit beaches and swimming pools during the COVID-19 pandemic?
COVID-19 대유행 동안 해변과 수영장을 방문하는 것이 정말 안전한가?

According to experts, if an infected person enters the sea or a pool, the virus can spread via saliva.
전문가들에 따르면 감염자가 바다나 수영장에 들어가면 침으로 바이러스가 퍼질 수 있다고 한다.

　　☆via 통하여

　　☆saliva 침, 타액

However, when mixed with water, the density is significantly lowered, and the risk is greatly reduced.
그러나 물과 섞이면 밀도가 현저히 낮아져 위험이 크게 줄어든다.

☆density 밀도, 농도

☆significantly 상당히, 크게

In particular, swimming pools contain chlorine have a very low chance of spreading the virus.
특히 염소가 함유된 수영장은 바이러스가 퍼질 확률이 매우 낮다.

☆in particular 특히, 특별히

☆chlorine 염소

☆have a very low chance of 가능성이 낮다

However, infections are most likely to occur outside the water, and in crowded environments.
그러나 감염은 물 밖에서, 그리고 혼잡한 환경에서 발생할 가능성이 가장 높다.

☆occur 발생하다

Another fear is that mosquitoes, which are rampant in South Korea during summer, could spread the COVID-19 virus, as they can be a carrier of viral diseases.
여름철 국내에서 기승을 부리는 모기가 또 다른 걱정거리다. 이 모기는 바이러스성 질환의 매개체가 될 수 있어 COVID-19 바이러스를 확산시킬 수 있다는 우려도 있다.

☆rampant in 걷잡을 수 없는, 만연하는

☆carrier 보균자, 매개체

☆viral 바이러스성의

Fortunately, health experts say there's a near-zero chance that the virus which would have to pass through the mosquito's digestive system could survive in the body, and transmit it through its saliva.
다행히도, 건강 전문가들은 모기의 소화기관을 통과해야만 하는 바이러스가 몸 안에서 살아남아 침으로 전염될 가능성이 거의 없다고 말한다.

☆near-zero chance 희박한 가능성

☆pass through ~에 꿰뚫다[관통하다]

☆digestive 소화의

☆transmit 전염시키다

Writing Exercise

1. 이곳은 한국에서 가장 인기 있는 여름 여행지 중 하나이다.

   This

2. 부산의 해운대 해수욕장은 보통 해변을 찾는 사람들로 붐비지만, COVID - 19 대유행으로 이 지역은 평상시만큼 붐비지 않는다.

   Busan's

3. 일반적으로 2m의 사회적 거리를 두자는 정부의 지침을 따르는 사람이 많았고, 식사시간과 물 속에 있을 때를 제외하고는 대부분 마스크를 착용하고 있는 모습이었다.

   Generally,

4. 그러나 중요한 의문점은 남아 있다.

   However,

5. COVID - 19 대유행 동안 해변과 수영장을 방문하는 것이 정말 안전한가?

   Is it

6. 전문가들에 따르면 감염자가 바다나 수영장에 들어가면 침으로 바이러스가 퍼질 수 있다고 한다.

   According to

7. 그러나 물과 섞이면 밀도가 현저히 낮아져 위험이 크게 줄어든다.

   However,

8. 특히 염소가 함유된 수영장은 바이러스가 퍼질 확률이 매우 낮다.

   In particular, _____

   _____

9. 그러나 감염은 물 밖에서, 그리고 혼잡한 환경에서 발생할 가능성이 가장 높다.

   However, _____

   _____

10. 여름철 국내에서 기승을 부리는 모기가 또 다른 걱정거리다. 이 모기는 바이러스성 질환의 매개체가 될 수 있어 COVID - 19 바이러스를 확산시킬 수 있다는 우려도 있다.

    Another _____

    _____

11. 다행히도, 건강 전문가들은 모기의 소화기관을 통과해야만 하는 바이러스가 몸 안에서 살아남아 침으로 전염될 가능성이 거의 없다고 말한다.

    Fortunately, _____

    _____

⊚ BRK 457/3
457/3
Today TH

영어 뉴스룸 17

English NewsRoom

BREAKING NEWS Students learning Korean language online through King Sejong Institutes. Instead of learning in classrooms as normal, students of the King Sejong Institute in Los Angeles have gathered online to study Korean. During the lesson, students watch the materials set by their teacher and use an online chat function to carry out class discussions. Named after the Joseon Dynasty King Sejong, who invented the Korean alphabet Hangeul, the South...

외국인은 한글을 어떻게 배울까?

세종학당재단의 온라인 화상 수업 시스템 가동에 대한 내용입니다.

Students learning Korean language online through King Sejong Institutes

Instead of learning in classrooms as normal, students of the King Sejong Institute in Los Angeles have gathered online to study Korean.

During the lesson, students watch the materials set by their teacher and use an online chat function to carry out class discussions.

Named after the Joseon Dynasty King Sejong, who invented the Korean alphabet Hangeul, the South Korean state-run institutes offer language and culture education programs.

As of last year, one-hundred-80 King Sejong Institutes in 60 countries have been operating offline.

But, amid the COVID-19 outbreak, roughly 17-thousand students at one-hundred-44 King Sejong Institutes around the world are learning Korean online.

Fueled by a growing popularity for learning the Korean language, 34 more institutes have opened in 30 countries this year.

The King Sejong Institute Foundation plans to have centers open in 76 countries worldwide and develop innovative ways to teach online.

The foundation hopes that by providing online classes, students around the world can continue their passion for learning Korean language and culture despite the coronavirus pandemic.

 **스크립트 분석**

Students learning Korean language online through King Sejong Institutes
세종학당을 통해 온라인으로 한국어를 배우는 학생들

Instead of learning in classrooms as normal, students of the King Sejong Institute in Los Angeles have gathered online to study Korean.
평소처럼 교실에서 배우는 대신 로스앤젤레스 세종학당 학생들이 온라인으로 모여 한국어를 공부하고 있다.

☆as normal 평상시처럼

☆Los Angeles ⑨ [ˌlɒs ˈæn.dʒə.liːz], ⑪ [ˌlɑːs ˈæn.dʒə.ləs]
영국, 미국 발음 다름 주의!

During the lesson, students watch the materials set by their teacher and use an online chat function to carry out class discussions.
수업 중에는 교사가 설정한 자료를 보고 온라인 채팅 기능을 이용해 수업 토론을 진행한다.

☆carry out 진행하다, 수행하다

Named after the Joseon Dynasty King Sejong, who invented the Korean alphabet Hangeul, the South Korean state-run institutes offer language and culture education programs.
한글을 창안한 조선시대 세종대왕의 이름을 딴 이 한국의 국영 기관은 언어와 문화 교육 프로그램들을 제공한다.

☆named after ~의 이름을 따서 명명하다

e.g. The school was named after the founder.
그 학교는 설립자의 이름을 따서 지어졌다.

☆dynasty 왕조, 역대통치자 | ⑨ [ˈdɪn.ə.sti], ⑪ [ˈdaɪ.nə.sti]
영국, 미국 발음 다름 주의!
☆state-run 국영의

As of last year, one-hundred-80 King Sejong Institutes in 60 countries have been operating offline.
지난해 기준 60개국 180개 세종학당이 오프라인으로 운영을 해왔다.

☆as of ~일자로

But, amid the COVID-19 outbreak, roughly 17-thousand students at one-hundred-44 King Sejong Institutes around the world are learning Korean online.

그러나 COVID-19가 발생한 가운데, 전 세계 144개 세종학당에서 약 1만 7천 명의 학생들이 온라인으로 한국어를 배우고 있다.

☆roughly 대략, 거의

Fueled by a growing popularity for learning the Korean language, 34 more institutes have opened in 30 countries this year.

한국어 학습의 인기에 힘입어, 올해 30개국에 34개의 어학당이 더 개설되었다.

☆fueled by ~에 힘입어

e.g. Fueled by anger over racism, some decided not to vote.
인종차별에 대한 분노로, 일부는 투표를 하지 않기로 결정했다.

The King Sejong Institute Foundation plans to have centers open in 76 countries worldwide and develop innovative ways to teach online.

세종학당재단은 전 세계 76개국에 센터를 개설하고 온라인 강의에 혁신적인 방법을 개발할 계획이다.

☆innovative 혁신적인 | 영 ['ɪn.ə.və.tɪv], 미 ['ɪn.ə.veɪ.tɪv]
영국, 미국 발음 다름 주의!

The foundation hopes that by providing online classes, students around the world can continue their passion for learning Korean language and culture despite the coronavirus pandemic.

재단은 온라인 수업을 통해 전 세계 학생들이 코로나바이러스 대유행에도 불구하고 한국어와 한국 문화를 배우는 열정을 이어갈 수 있기를 기대하고 있다.

1. 평소처럼 교실에서 배우는 대신 로스앤젤레스 세종학당 학생들이 온라인으로 모여 한국어를 공부하고 있다.

   Instead

2. 수업 중에는 교사가 설정한 자료를 보고 온라인 채팅 기능을 이용해 수업 토론을 진행한다.

   During

3. 한글을 창안한 조선시대 세종대왕의 이름을 딴 이 한국의 국영 기관은 언어와 문화 교육 프로그램들을 제공한다.

   Named

4. 지난해 기준 60개국 180개 세종학당이 오프라인으로 운영을 해왔다.

   As of

5. 그러나 COVID - 19가 발생한 가운데, 전 세계 144개 세종학당에서 약 1만 7천명의 학생들이 온라인으로 한국어를 배우고 있다.

   But,

6. 한국어 학습의 인기에 힘입어, 올해 30개국에 34개의 어학당이 더 개설되었다.

   Fueled

7. 세종학당재단은 전 세계 76개국에 센터를 개설하고 온라인 강의에 혁신적인 방법을 개발할 계획이다.

   The King

8. 재단은 온라인 수업을 통해 전 세계 학생들이 코로나바이러스 대유행에도 불구하고 한국어와 한국 문화를 배우는 열정을 이어갈 수 있기를 기대하고 있다.

   The foundation

⊚ BRK 457/3
457/3
Today TH

영어 뉴스룸 *18*

English NewsRoom

BREAKING NEWS

S. Korean developers create AI robot to help prevent spread of COVID-19. A self-driving robot equipped with an LED screen and cameras greets visitors and dispenses hand sanitizer at a building in Seoul. It also checks visitors' body temperatures and sets off an alarm if anyone's temperature is over 37.5 degrees Celsius. Using AI technology, it detects gatherings of people and says : "Please follow social distancing measures." It also checks who is wearing...

로봇을 통해 마스크를 썼는지 검사한다?

국내업체가 개발한 AI 로봇을 통해 COVID-19 확산을 방지한다는 내용입니다.

 전체 스크립트

S. Korean developers create AI robot to help prevent spread of COVID-19

A self-driving robot equipped with an LED screen and cameras greets visitors and dispenses hand sanitizer at a building in Seoul.

It also checks visitors' body temperatures and sets off an alarm if anyone's temperature is over 37.5 degrees Celsius.

Using AI technology, it detects gatherings of people and says :

"Please follow social distancing measures."

It also checks who is wearing and who is not wearing a face mask.

"Please wear a face mask."

Armed with ultraviolet lamps and two automatic disinfectant sprays, the robot can disinfect 99 percent of an area of 33 square meters in just ten minutes.

This robot was jointly developed by Korea's largest mobile network operator SK Telecom and industrial automation solution provider Omron Electronics.

It sends data to the control center in real-time over the telecom company's 5G network.

The developers have also added a function to hide faces mirrored in the screen to protect privacy.

Companies in Korea have long been using robotics for tasks like manufacturing and cleaning.

And now, amid coronavirus concerns, the technology has gotten a boost as more companies are looking to reduce human contact.

SK Telecom is set to launch the robot in Korea this year and in global markets next year.

S. Korean developers create AI robot to help prevent spread of COVID-19
국내 개발업체들이 COVID-19 확산 방지를 돕기 위해 AI 로봇을 만들다

A self-driving robot equipped with an LED screen and cameras greets visitors and dispenses hand sanitizer at a building in Seoul.
서울의 한 건물에서 LED 스크린과 카메라를 갖춘 자율주행 로봇이 방문객을 맞이하고 손세정제를 제공한다.

　　☆self-driving 자율 주행의

　　☆equipped with 을 갖춘

　　☆greet 맞다, 환영하다

　　☆dispense 나누어 주다, *(특히 서비스를)* 제공하다, *(약사가 약을)* 조제하다

It also checks visitors' body temperatures and sets off an alarm if anyone's temperature is over 37.5 degrees Celsius.
또한 방문객들의 체온을 확인하고, 37.5도를 넘는 사람이 있으면 경보를 울린다.

　　☆ set something off *(경보 장치를)* 울리다

　　e.g. It can set off a smoke alarm so be careful.
　　　　화재경보기가 울릴 수 있으니 조심하세요.

Using AI technology, it detects gatherings of people and says :
AI 기술을 이용해서 사람의 모임을 감지하여 다음과 같이 말한다.

　　☆detect 감지하다

"Please follow social distancing measures."
"사회적 거리 두기 조치를 따르세요."

It also checks who is wearing and who is not wearing a face mask.
누가 마스크를 쓰고 있는지, 누가 안 쓰고 있는지도 확인한다.

"Please wear a face mask."
"마스크를 쓰세요."

Armed with ultraviolet lamps and two automatic disinfectant sprays, the robot can disinfect 99 percent of an area of 33 square meters in just ten minutes.

자외선 램프와 두 개의 자동 소독 스프레이로 무장한 이 로봇은 불과 10분 만에 33제곱미터 면적의 99%를 소독할 수 있다.

☆armed with ~로 무장한

e.g. He was armed with a gun so people backed off.
그는 총으로 무장하고 있었기 때문에 사람들은 뒤로 물러났다.

☆back off 뒤로 물러나다[뒷걸음질치다]
☆ultraviolet 자외선의
☆disinfectant 소독약, 살균제
☆disinfect 소독하다
☆square meters 평방미터(㎡)

This robot was jointly developed by Korea's largest mobile network operator SK Telecom and industrial automation solution provider Omron Electronics.

국내 최대 이동통신사인 SK텔레콤과 공장 자동화 솔루션 업체 오므론 제어기기가 공동 개발한 로봇이다.

It sends data to the control center in real-time over the telecom company's 5G network.

통신사 5G망을 통해 실시간으로 관제센터에 데이터를 전송한다.

☆real-time 실시간으로

The developers have also added a function to hide faces mirrored in the screen to protect privacy.

개발자들은 사생활 보호를 위해 화면에 비친 얼굴을 숨기는 기능도 추가했다.

☆privacy 사생활 | 영 ['prɪv.ə.si], 미 ['praɪ.və.si]
영국, 미국 발음 다름 주의!

Companies in Korea have long been using robotics for tasks like manufacturing and cleaning.

한국의 기업들은 오랫동안 제조와 청소와 같은 작업에 로봇 기술을 사용해 왔다.

☆robotics 로봇 공학
☆manufacturing 제조업

And now, amid coronavirus concerns, the technology has gotten a boost as more companies are looking to reduce human contact.

그리고 이제, 코로나바이러스 우려 속에서, 점점 더 많은 회사들이 사람간 접촉을 줄이려고 하고 있기 때문에, 이 기술은 힘을 얻었다.

SK Telecom is set to launch the robot in Korea this year and in global markets next year.

SK텔레콤은 올해 국내와 내년 세계 시장에 이 로봇을 출시할 예정이다.

☆be set to ~하도록 예정되어 있다

Writing Exercise

1. 서울의 한 건물에서 LED 스크린과 카메라를 갖춘 자율주행 로봇이 방문객을 맞이하고 손세정제를 제공한다.

A self-driving

2. 또한 방문객들의 체온을 확인하고, 37.5도를 넘는 사람이 있으면 경보를 울린다.

It also

3. AI 기술을 이용해서 사람의 모임을 감지하여 다음과 같이 말한다.

Using

4. "사회적 거리 두기 조치를 따르세요."

"Please

5. 누가 마스크를 쓰고 있는지, 누가 안 쓰고 있는지도 확인한다.

It also

6. "마스크를 쓰세요."

"Please

7. 자외선 램프와 두 개의 자동 소독 스프레이로 무장한 이 로봇은 불과 10분 만에 33제곱미터 면적의 99%를 소독할 수 있다.

Armed

8. 국내 최대 이동통신사인 SK텔레콤과 공장 자동화 솔루션 업체 오므론 제어기기가 공동 개발한 로봇이다.

This robot

9. 통신사 5G망을 통해 실시간으로 관제센터에 데이터를 전송한다.

It sends

10. 개발자들은 사생활 보호를 위해 화면에 비친 얼굴을 숨기는 기능도 추가했다.

The developers

11. 한국의 기업들은 오랫동안 제조와 청소와 같은 작업에 로봇 기술을 사용해 왔다.

Companies

12. 그리고 이제, 코로나바이러스 우려 속에서, 점점 더 많은 회사들이 사람간 접촉을 줄이려고 하고 있기 때문에, 이 기술은 힘을 얻었다.

And now,

13. SK텔레콤은 올해 국내와 내년 세계 시장에 이 로봇을 출시할 예정이다.

SK Telecom

◉ BRK 457/3
457/3
Today TH

영어 뉴스룸 19

English
NewsRoom

BREAKING NEWS

S. Korea installs singing soap dispensers, hand-washing stations to help fight COVID-19. At a bathroom in a museum in Seoul, the soap dispenser plays a song when pressed. The 30-second song encourages children to develop the habit of thorough hand-washing in response to the COVID-19 outbreak. Seoul Resident Kwon Eun-sook says, "Most children struggle to keep track of time. When the song starts to play, children think of hand-washing

노래가 나오는 비누가 있다?

문체부가 COVID-19의 예방을 돕기 위해 여러 곳에 노래나오는 비누와 손세척대들을 설치한다는 내용입니다.

 전체 스크립트

S. Korea installs singing soap dispensers, hand-washing stations to help fight COVID-19

At a bathroom in a museum in Seoul, the soap dispenser plays a song when pressed.

The 30-second song encourages children to develop the habit of thorough hand-washing in response to the COVID-19 outbreak.

Seoul Resident Kwon Eun-sook says, "Most children struggle to keep track of time. When the song starts to play, children think of hand-washing as a fun activity and can better follow the 30-second rule."

Washing hands is the first line of defense against all kinds of pathogens.

Korean health authorities say the sufficient amount of time to properly wash hands is 30 seconds.

Professor of Infectious Diseases at Korea University of Medicine Choi Won-suk says, "Thoroughly washing fingertips and in-between fingers takes at least 30 seconds. If you wash your hands whenever necessary, you will wash your hands more than eight times a day."

However, it's not easy for most people to consciously wash their hands for more than 30 seconds.

The most well-known method is to sing 'Happy Birthday' twice while washing your hands.

Recently, an app was developed to help count those 30 seconds, and hand-washing stations have been installed in parks and on the street.

Wash basins have also been placed inside stores that sell cosmetics and household items.

Under the eased "distancing in daily life" scheme, washing hands is the most simple and easy measure to keep oneself healthy.

NEWS 스크립트 분석

S. Korea installs singing soap dispensers, hand-washing stations to help fight COVID-19
문체부는 COVID-19의 예방을 돕기 위해 노래 비누 디스펜서와 손세척대들을 설치한다

  ☆dispensers 손잡이·단추 등을 눌러 안에 든 것을 바로 뽑아 쓸 수 있는 기계

At a bathroom in a museum in Seoul, the soap dispenser plays a song when pressed.
서울의 한 박물관의 화장실에서, 비누 디스펜서를 누르면 노래가 나온다.

The 30-second song encourages children to develop the habit of thorough hand-washing in response to the COVID-19 outbreak.
이 30초짜리 노래는 아이들이 COVID-19 발병에 대응하여 손씻기를 철저히 하는 습관을 기를 것을 권장한다.

  ☆encourage A to B A가 B하는 것을 권장하다

  ☆thorough 철저한

  ☆in response to ~에 대응하여, 답하여

  > e.g. **We're all writing in response to your letter regarding the service.**
  > 우리 모두는 서비스에 관한 당신의 편지에 대해 답장을 쓰고 있습니다.

Seoul Resident Kwon Eun-sook says, "Most children struggle to keep track of time. When the song starts to play, children think of hand-washing as a fun activity and can better follow the 30-second rule."
서울 시민 권은숙씨는 "대부분의 아이들은 시간을 기록하려고 애쓴다. 노래가 흘러나오기 시작하면 아이들은 손씻기를 즐거운 활동으로 생각하고 30초 룰을 더 잘 따를 수 있다"라고 말한다.

  ☆keep track of 기록하다, 추적하다

Washing hands is the first line of defense against all kinds of pathogens.
손을 씻는 것은 모든 종류의 병원균에 대한 첫 번째 방어선이다.

  ☆defense 방어

  ☆pathogens 병원균

Korean health authorities say the sufficient amount of time to properly wash hands is 30 seconds.
한국 보건 당국은 손을 제대로 씻을 수 있는 충분한 시간은 30초라고 말한다.

Professor of Infectious Diseases at Korea University of Medicine Choi Won-suk says, "Thoroughly washing fingertips and in-between fingers takes at least 30 seconds. If you wash your hands whenever necessary, you will wash your hands more than eight times a day."

최원석 고려대 감염내과 교수는 "손끝과 손가락 사이를 철저히 씻는 것은 최소 30초 이상 걸린다. 필요할 때마다 손을 씻으면 하루에 8번 이상 손을 씻을 것이다"라고 말한다.

☆fingertips 손끝
☆in-between 사이에

However, it's not easy for most people to consciously wash their hands for more than 30 seconds.

하지만 대부분의 사람들에게 30초 이상 의식적으로 손을 씻는 것은 쉽지 않다.

☆consciously 의식적으로, 의식[자각]하여

The most well-known method is to sing 'Happy Birthday' twice while washing your hands.

가장 잘 알려진 방법은 손을 씻으면서 '생일 축하해'를 두 번 부르는 것이다.

Recently, an app was developed to help count those 30 seconds, and hand-washing stations have been installed in parks and on the street.

최근에는, 이 30초를 세는 것을 돕는 앱이 개발되었고, 공원과 거리에 손세척대들이 설치되었다.

Wash basins have also been placed inside stores that sell cosmetics and household items.

화장품과 생활용품 등을 판매하는 매장 내부에도 또한 세면대가 배치되었다.

☆wash basins 세면대
☆place 배치하다, 설치하다

Under the eased "distancing in daily life" scheme, washing hands is the most simple and easy measure to keep oneself healthy.

"생활 속 거리두기"로 완화된 시기 하에서 손을 씻는 것은 몸을 건강하게 유지하기 위한 가장 간단하고 쉬운 방법이다.

Writing Exercise

1. 서울의 한 박물관의 화장실에서, 비누 디스펜서를 누르면 노래가 나온다.

   At a

2. 이 30초짜리 노래는 아이들이 COVID - 19 발병에 대응하여 손씻기를 철저히 하는 습관을 기를 것을 권장한다.

   The 30 - second

3. 서울 시민 권은숙씨는 "대부분의 아이들은 시간을 기록하려고 애쓴다. 노래가 흘러나오기 시작하면 아이들은 손씻기를 즐거운 활동으로 생각하고 30 초 룰을 더 잘 따를 수 있다"라고 말한다.

   Seoul

4. 손을 씻는 것은 모든 종류의 병원균에 대한 첫 번째 방어선이다.

   Washing

5. 한국 보건 당국은 손을 제대로 씻을 수 있는 충분한 시간은 30초라고 말한다.

   Korean

6. 최원석 고려대 감염내과 교수는 "손끝과 손가락 사이를 철저히 씻는 것은 최소 30초 이상 걸린다. 필요할 때마다 손을 씻으면 하루에 8번 이상 손을 씻을 것이다"라고 말한다.

   Professor

7. 하지만 대부분의 사람들에게 30초 이상 의식적으로 손을 씻는 것은 쉽지 않다.

   However,

8. 가장 잘 알려진 방법은 손을 씻으면서 '생일 축하해'를 두 번 부르는 것이다.

The most
_____

_____

9. 최근에는, 이 30초를 세는 것을 돕는 앱이 개발되었고, 공원과 거리에 손세척대들이 설치되었다.

Recently,
_____

_____

10. 화장품과 생활용품 등을 판매하는 매장 내부에도 또한 세면대가 배치되었다.

Wash
_____

_____

11. "생활 속 거리두기"로 완화된 시기 하에서 손을 씻는 것은 몸을 건강하게 유지하기 위한 가장 간단하고 쉬운 방법이다.

Under
_____

_____

ⓒBRK 457/3
457/3
Today TH

영어 뉴스룸 20

English NewsRoom

BREAKING NEWS

Local private cram school holds drive-in college admissions briefing amid COVID-19 outbreak. You might assume this is a drive-in movie theater of sorts, but it's not. Instead, it's more than 3-thousand parents and high school seniors gathered in a parking lot for a briefing. Sat inside cars parked apart from each other, parents and students receive school brochures that include the cram school's analysis on college admissions.

입시설명회도 자동차 극장처럼?

COVID-19 발병 가운데 입시학원이 드라이브인 대학입학설명회를 개최한다는 내용입니다.

NEWS 전체 스크립트

Local private cram school holds drive-in college admissions briefing amid COVID-19 outbreak

You might assume this is a drive-in movie theater of sorts, but it's not.

Instead, it's more than 3-thousand parents and high school seniors gathered in a parking lot for a briefing on college admission.

In order to prevent the spread of COVID-19, one of South Korea's biggest cram schools held a 'Drive-In' college entrance briefing.

Sat inside cars parked apart from each other, parents and students receive school brochures that include the cram school's analysis on college admissions.

Due to the sheer amount of information that had to be explained, the CEO of the cram school said they had no choice but to hold the briefing offline.

Jongro Academy CEO Lim Sung-ho says

"Timing is important for college admissions. Through this briefing, we can share information we couldn't explain online. We also check a person's body temperature if they get out of their vehicles."

South Korea's college entrance examination was originally scheduled for November 19th, but due to the COVID-19 outbreak, it will now be held on December 3rd.

Local private cram school holds drive-in college admissions briefing amid COVID-19 outbreak
COVID-19 발병 가운데 지역 사설학원이 드라이브인 대학입학설명회를 개최한다.

☆cram 1. (좁은 공간 속으로 억지로) 밀어 넣다, (좁은 공간 속으로) 잔뜩 들어가다
       2. 벼락치기 공부를 하다 =swot

☆private cram school 사설학원

You might assume this is a drive-in movie theater of sorts, but it's not.
당신은 이것이 일종의 드라이브인 영화관이라고 생각할지도 모르지만, 그렇지 않다.

☆assume 추정하다 | 영 [əˈsjuːm], 미 [əˈsum]
영국, 미국 발음 다름 주의!

Instead, it's more than 3-thousand parents and high school seniors gathered in a parking lot for a briefing on college admission.
대신, 그것은 3천명이 넘는 학부모와 고3 학생들이 대학 입학 설명회를 위해 주차장에 모여 있는 현장이다.

In order to prevent the spread of COVID-19, one of South Korea's biggest cram schools held a 'Drive-In' college entrance briefing.
COVID-19의 확산을 막기 위해, 한국에서 가장 큰 입시 학원들 중 한곳에서 '드라이브 인' 대학 입학 설명회를 열었다.

Sat inside cars parked apart from each other, parents and students receive school brochures that include the cram school's analysis on college admissions.
서로 떨어져 주차된 차 안에 앉아 학부모와 학생들은 입시학원의 대학입학에 대한 분석 내용이 담긴 학교 안내 책자를 받는다.

☆apart from each other 서로로부터 떨어져서

e.g. Students should wear masks and sit apart from each other in the classroom.
학생들은 마스크를 쓰고 교실에서 서로 떨어져 앉아야 한다.

Due to the sheer amount of information that had to be explained, the CEO of the cram school said they had no choice but to hold the briefing offline.

설명해야 할 정보의 엄청난 양 때문에, 입시 학원의 대표는 오프라인에서 브리핑을 할 수밖에 없었다고 말했다.

☆sheer 엄청난, 순전한 크기, 정도, 양을 강조할 때 앞에 씀

> e.g. sheer weight 엄청난 무게, sheer waste 완전 낭비

☆sheer amount 엄청난 양

> e.g. I saw the sheer amount of time she put into her work.
> 나는 그녀가 그녀의 일에 쏟아붓는 엄청난 시간을 보았다.

☆have no choice but to ~할 수밖에 없다

> e.g. If she's not going to do the laundry, I have no choice but to do it.
> 만약 그녀가 빨래를 안한다면, 내가 할 수밖에 없어.

Jongro Academy CEO Lim Sung-ho says, "Timing is important for college admissions. Through this briefing, we can share information we couldn't explain online. We also check a person's body temperature if they get out of their vehicles."

임성호 종로학원 대표이사는 "타이밍은 대학입학을 위해 중요하다. 이번 브리핑을 통해 우리가 온라인으로 설명할 수 없었던 정보를 공유할 수 있다. 차량에서 내릴 경우 체온도 체크한다"고 말한다.

South Korea's college entrance examination was originally scheduled for November 19th, but due to the COVID-19 outbreak, it will now be held on December 3rd.

한국의 대학입학시험은 당초 11월 19일로 예정되어 있었으나 COVID-19의 발병으로 인해 이제는 12월 3일에 치러지게 되었다.

1. 당신은 이것이 일종의 드라이브인 영화관이라고 생각할지도 모르지만, 그렇지 않다.

You

2. 대신, 그것은 3천명이 넘는 학부모와 고3 학생들이 대학 입학 설명회를 위해 주차장에 모여 있는 현장이다.

Instead,

3. COVID - 19의 확산을 막기 위해, 한국에서 가장 큰 입시 학원들 중 한곳에서 '드라이브 인' 대학 입학 설명회를 열었다.

In order to

4. 서로 떨어져 주차된 차 안에 앉아 학부모와 학생들은 입시학원의 대학입학에 대한 분석 내용이 담긴 학교 안내 책자를 받는다.

Sat

5. 설명해야 할 정보의 엄청난 양 때문에, 입시 학원의 대표는 오프라인에서 브리핑을 할 수밖에 없었다고 말했다.

Due to

6. 임성호 종로학원 대표이사는 "타이밍은 대학입학을 위해 중요하다. 이번 브리핑을 통해 우리가 온라인으로 설명할 수 없었던 정보를 공유할 수 있다. 차량에서 내릴 경우 체온도 체크한다"고 말한다.

Jongro

7. 한국의 대학입학시험은 당초 11월 19일로 예정되어 있었으나 COVID - 19의 발병으로 인해 이제는 12월 3일에 치러지게 되었다.

South

BRK 457/3
457/3
Today TH

영어 뉴스룸 *21*

English NewsRoom

BREAKING NEWS

S. Korea launches digital driver's license on Wednesday. People in South Korea are now able to use a digital version of their driver's license on their smartphones as ID. The service, rolled out on Wednesday, was developed by the National Police Agency in collaboration with the country's three mobile carriers. Unlike an actual license, the digital one only shows the person's photo and QR code. It'll be available through an existing app called PASS.

휴대폰에 운전면허증 담는다?

경찰청의 모바일 운전면허증 도입에 관한 내용입니다.

S. Korea launches digital driver's license on Wednesday

People in South Korea are now able to use a digital version of their driver's license on their smartphones as ID.

The service, rolled out on Wednesday, was developed by the National Police Agency in collaboration with the country's three mobile carriers.

Unlike an actual license, the digital one only shows the person's photo and QR code.

It'll be available through an existing app called PASS.

However, initially it will only be allowed for use at convenience stores operated by CU and GS25.

This will be South Korea's first digital version of an official ID.

S. Korea launches digital driver's license on Wednesday
한국은 수요일에 디지털 운전면허증을 출시한다

　☆launch 출시하다, 착수하다

> e.g. They are going to launch a new app for the kids.
> 　　그들은 아이들을 위한 새로운 앱을 출시할 것이다.

　☆driver's license 운전 면허증 ⑲ driving licence

People in South Korea are now able to use a digital version of their driver's license on their smartphones as ID.
한국 사람들은 이제 스마트폰에서 신분증으로 운전 면허증의 디지털 버전을 사용할 수 있게 되었다.

　☆be able to ~할 수 있다 now와 결합하면 '~할 수 있게 되었다'로 해석
　☆ID 신분증 identification의 약어

The service, rolled out on Wednesday, was developed by the National Police Agency in collaboration with the country's three mobile carriers.
수요일에 출시된 이 서비스는 경찰청이 국내 이동통신 3사와 협력하여 개발되었다.

　☆roll out (신상품을) 출시하다, (새로운 정치 캠페인을) 시작하다 =launch

> e.g. The company rolled out its first self - driving car.
> 　　그 회사는 첫 자율주행차를 출시했다.

　☆in collaboration with 와 협력하여

> e.g. Teachers are working in collaboration with the government to help farmers.
> 　　교사들은 농부들을 돕기 위해 정부와 협력해서 일하고 있다.

Unlike an actual license, the digital one only shows the person's photo and QR code.
실제 면허증과 달리 디지털면허증은 당사자의 사진과 QR코드만 보여준다.

　☆unlike ~와 다른, ~와는 달리

> e.g. Unlike her father, she is very straightforward.
> 　　그녀의 아버지와 달리, 그녀는 매우 솔직하다.

It'll be available through an existing app called PASS.

기존 PASS라는 이름의 앱을 통해 이용할 수 있을 것이다.

☆called ~라는 이름의

☆available 1. 이용할 수 있는 | 2. 시간[여유]이 있는

e.g. It'll be available in some provinces for the first time.
그것은 일부 지방에서 처음으로 이용할 수 있을 것이다.
Are you available to meet me next week?
다음 주에 나 만날 수 있어?

However, initially it will only be allowed for use at convenience stores operated by CU and GS25.

다만 초기에는 CU와 GS25가 운영하는 편의점에서만 사용이 허용될 것이다.

☆initially 처음에

☆operated by ~에 의해 운영되는

This will be South Korea's first digital version of an official ID.

이것은 공식적인 신분증의 한국 최초의 디지털 버전이 될 것이다.

1. 한국 사람들은 이제 스마트폰에서 신분증으로 운전 면허증의 디지털 버전을 사용할 수 있게 되었다.

   People _____

   _____

2. 수요일에 출시된 이 서비스는 경찰청이 국내 이동통신 3사와 협력하여 개발되었다.

   The service, _____

   _____

3. 실제 면허증과 달리 디지털면허증은 당사자의 사진과 QR코드만 보여준다.

   Unlike _____

   _____

4. 기존 PASS라는 이름의 앱을 통해 이용할 수 있을 것이다.

   It'll _____

   _____

5. 다만 초기에는 CU와 GS25가 운영하는 편의점에서만 사용이 허용될 것이다.

   However, _____

   _____

6. 이것은 공식적인 신분증의 한국 최초의 디지털 버전이 될 것이다.

   This will _____

   _____

⊚ BRK 457/3
457/3
Today TH

영어 뉴스룸 22

English NewsRoom

BREAKING NEWS

Blackpink single reaches 100 million YouTube views in record time. The newest music video by K‑pop group Blackpink has become the fastest video ever to top 100 million views on YouTube. According to the group's management agency, YG entertainment, the video for the song "How You Like That" reached the milestone on Sunday Korea time at around 2 : 23 AM. The previous record was set by their fellow K‑pop stars BTS in April 2019...

유튜브를 점령한 블랙핑크의 신곡

블랙핑크 신곡이 유튜브 사상 최단 시간에 1억뷰를 달성했다는 내용입니다.

 전체 스크립트

Blackpink single reaches 100 million YouTube views in record time

The newest music video by K‑pop group Blackpink has become the fastest video ever to top 100 million views on YouTube.

According to the group's management agency, YG entertainment, the video for the song 'How You Like That' reached the milestone on Sunday Korea time at around 2 : 23 AM.

The previous record was set by their fellow K‑pop stars BTS in April 2019 with the song 'Boy With Luv.'

With their new single, Blackpink has also topped the iTunes charts in 60 countries.

They first performed the song live this past Friday on the 'The Tonight Show' with Jimmy Fallon.

Blackpink single reaches 100 million YouTube views in record time
블랙핑크 싱글이 기록적인 시간 안에 유튜브 조회수 1억뷰를 달성하다

☆reach 에 이르다[닿다/도달하다]

☆record 기록 ['rek·ɔ:d] | 기록하다 [rɪ'kɔ:d]
 명사, 동사 발음 다름 주의

☆in record time 기록적인 시간 안에

e.g. It was interesting to know that the building was finished in record time.
 그 건물이 기록적인 시간에 완공되었다는 것을 아는 것은 흥미로웠다.

The newest music video by K-pop group Blackpink has become the fastest video ever to top 100 million views on YouTube.
K-팝 그룹 블랙핑크의 최신 뮤직비디오가 유튜브 조회수 1억뷰를 돌파한 역대 가장 빠른 영상이 되었다.

☆newest 최신의 =latest

☆ever 최상급을 뒤에서 강조하는 부사 by far는 최상급을 주로 앞에서 강조할 때 씀

e.g. She is the best teacher ever.
 그녀는 최고의 선생님이다.
 She is by far the best teacher.
 그녀는 최고의 선생님이다.

According to the group's management agency, YG entertainment, the video for the song 'How You Like That' reached the milestone on Sunday Korea time at around 2 : 23 AM.
그룹 매니지먼트사인 YG엔터테인먼트에 따르면 'How You Like That' 곡의 영상은 한국시간으로 일요일 오전 2시 23분경 대기록을 달성했다.

☆milestone 중요한 단계 =landmark

e.g. Starting a new job is an important milestone in life.
 새로운 일을 시작하는 것은 삶에서 중요한 단계이다.

☆reach the milestone 대기록을 달성하다

> e.g. We reached a milestone in our marketing strategy.
> 우리는 마케팅 전략에서 대기록을 달성했다.
> The company has reached a milestone by making a special kit.
> 그 회사는 특별한 키트를 만들어 대기록을 달성했다.

The previous record was set by their fellow K-pop stars BTS in April 2019 with the song 'Boy With Luv.'
이전 기록은 2019년 4월 동료 K팝 스타 방탄소년단이 'Boy With Luv'(작은 것들을 위한 시)라는 곡으로 세운 것이다.

☆fellow 동료

With their new single, Blackpink has also topped the iTunes charts in 60 countries.
새 싱글로 블랙핑크는 60개국 아이튠즈 차트에서도 1위를 차지했다.

☆top 1. 최고, 정상 | 2. 최고이다, 1위를 하다
　　명사　　　　　동사

> e.g. The album has topped the official charts in the UK.
> 그 앨범은 영국 공식 차트에서 1위를 차지했다.

They first performed the song live this past Friday on the 'The Tonight Show' with Jimmy Fallon.
그들은 지난 금요일 지미 팰런과 함께한 '더 투나잇 쇼'에서 이 노래를 처음으로 라이브로 선보였다.

☆perform 1. 행하다 | 2. 공연하다

> e.g. A computer can perform many tasks at once.
> 컴퓨터는 많은 업무를 한꺼번에 수행할 수 있다.
> His plays are still widely performed in the USA.
> 그의 희곡은 여전히 미국에서 널리 공연되고 있다.

1. K-팝 그룹 블랙핑크의 최신 뮤직비디오가 유튜브 조회수 1억뷰를 돌파한 역대 가장 빠른 영상이 되었다.

   The newest

   _____

2. 그룹 매니지먼트사인 YG엔터테인먼트에 따르면 'How You Like That' 곡의 영상은 한국시간으로 일요일 오전 2시 23분경 대기록을 달성했다.

   According to

   _____

3. 이전 기록은 2019년 4월 동료 K팝 스타 방탄소년단이 'Boy With Luv'(작은 것들을 위한 시)라는 곡으로 세운 것이다.

   The previous

   _____

4. 새 싱글로 블랙핑크는 60개국 아이튠즈 차트에서도 1위를 차지했다.

   With

   _____

5. 그들은 지난 금요일 지미 팰런과 함께한 '더 투나잇 쇼'에서 이 노래를 처음으로 라이브로 선보였다.

   They

   _____

오디오클립
◀ 바로가기

◎ BRK 457/3
457/3
Today TH

영어 뉴스룸 23

English
NewsRoom

BREAKING NEWS

Beaches in S. Korea take extra measures to prevent COVID-19. Local beaches are preparing for a long hot summer, with strict virus prevention guidelines. Visitors to beaches in Gangneung must get their temperature checked and are given wristbands to prove they don't have a fever. They also have to show a QR code on their phone in order to use beach facilities such as showers and restrooms. Gangneung city will disinfect all its beach facilities three times..

해수욕장에서도 코로나19 예방을 위해 특별 조치를 취하고 있다

해수욕장에서도 코로나19 예방을 위해 특별 조치를 취하고 있다는 내용입니다.

Beaches in S. Korea take extra measures to prevent COVID-19

Local beaches are preparing for a long hot summer, with strict virus prevention guidelines.

Visitors to beaches in Gangneung must get their temperature checked and are given wristbands to prove they don't have a fever.

They also have to show a QR code on their phone in order to use beach facilities such as showers and restrooms.

Gangneung city will disinfect all its beach facilities three times a day.

In addition, an online traffic light will track how crowded beaches are.

A green light indicates the beach has the advised number of people.

That's a maximum of one person for every three-point-two square meters

Yellow is between 100 to 200 percent of the recommended number, and red... over 200 percent.

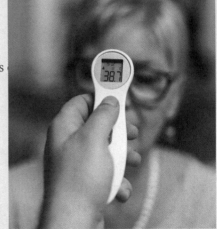

The traffic signal is updated every 30 minutes.

Ten major beaches across the country will use the system from July 1st, and 50 other beaches will adopt the system by mid-July.

Those who plan on visiting beaches in Jeollanam-do Province must reserve their spots online.

Sokcho Beach in Gangwon-do Province will install automatic disinfection systems that sense and spray disinfectant on visitors.

Beaches will be closed at night, and there will be no summer beach festivals.

Beaches in S. Korea take extra measures to prevent COVID-19
한국에 있는 해수욕장들은 코로나19를 예방하기 위해 특별 조치를 취한다

☆take measures 조치를 취하다

> e.g. They took stronger measures to prevent the accident.
> 그들은 사고를 막기 위해 더 강력한 조치를 취했다.

Local beaches are preparing for a long hot summer, with strict virus prevention guidelines.
지역 해수욕장들은 엄격한 바이러스 예방 지침을 지키며 길고 더운 여름을 준비하고 있다.

☆prevention 예방, 방지

Visitors to beaches in Gangneung must get their temperature checked and are given wristbands to prove they don't have a fever.
강릉 해수욕장을 찾는 관광객들은 체온을 재야 하며, 열이 나지 않는다는 것을 증명하기 위해 손목밴드가 주어진다.

☆get something checked ~를 검사 받다 내가 아닌 누군가가 해준 검사

☆wristband [rɪst.bænd] 손목 밴드 장식용으로나 운동 때 땀 흡수를 위해 손목에 차는 띠

☆prove 입증하다

> e.g. Prove that you love me.
> 날 사랑한다는 걸 입증해 봐요.

☆have a fever 열이 있다

> e.g. have a cold 감기에 걸리다
> have a headache 두통이 있다
> have the flu 독감에 걸리다

They also have to show a QR code on their phone in order to use beach facilities such as showers and restrooms.
샤워기, 화장실 등 해변 시설을 이용하려면 휴대전화 QR코드도 보여야 한다.

☆in order to 위하여 목적

> e.g. In order to have a clean environment, we should recycle.
> 깨끗한 환경을 갖기 위해서, 우리는 재활용을 해야 한다.

Gangneung city will disinfect all its beach facilities three times a day.

강릉시는 하루 3회 모든 해수욕장 시설을 소독할 것이다.

☆disinfect 소독하다

In addition, an online traffic light will track how crowded beaches are.

또한, 온라인 교통 신호등은 해변이 얼마나 붐비는지 추적할 것이다.

A green light indicates the beach has the advised number of people.

녹색 신호등은 해변에 권고된 인원수가 있음을 나타낸다.

That's a maximum of one person for every three-point-two square meters of beach.

이는 해변의 3.2제곱미터당 최대 1명꼴이다.

Yellow is between 100 to 200 percent of the recommended number, and red... over 200 percent.

노란색은 권고된 수의 100~200% 사이이고, 빨간색은... 200퍼센트 이상을 말한다.

The traffic signal is updated every 30 minutes.

교통신호는 30분마다 업데이트된다.

Ten major beaches across the country will use the system from July 1st, and 50 other beaches will adopt the system by mid-July.

7월 1일부터는 전국 10개 주요 해수욕장이 이 제도를 이용하고, 그 외 50개 해수욕장은 7월 중순까지 이 제도를 도입할 예정이다.

☆adopt 채택하다, 입양하다

e.g. They will adopt the new technology for customers.
그들은 고객을 위해 새로운 기술을 채택할 것이다.
With much thought, we decided to adopt him.
심사숙고 끝에 우리는 그를 입양하기로 결정했다.

Those who plan on visiting beaches in Jeollanam-do Province must reserve their spots online.

전라남도의 해수욕장 방문을 계획하는 사람들은 온라인으로 장소를 예약해야 한다.

☆reserve 예약하다

☆spot 장소

Sokcho Beach in Gangwon-do Province will install automatic disinfection systems that sense and spray disinfectant on visitors.

강원도 속초해수욕장은 방문객에게 자동으로 감지하고 소독약을 살포하는 자동 소독장치를 설치할 것이다.

☆disinfectant 소독약

Beaches will be closed at night, and there will be no summer beach festivals.

해변은 밤에 문을 닫을 것이고, 여름 해변 축제는 없을 것이다.

Writing Exercise

1. 지역 해수욕장들은 엄격한 바이러스 예방 지침을 지키며 길고 더운 여름을 준비하고 있다.

Local

2. 강릉 해수욕장을 찾는 관광객들은 체온을 재야 하며, 열이 나지 않는다는 것을 증명하기 위해 손목밴드가 주어진다.

Visitors

3. 샤워기, 화장실 등 해변 시설을 이용하려면 휴대전화 QR코드도 보여야 한다.

They

4. 강릉시는 하루 3회 모든 해수욕장 시설을 소독할 것이다.

Gangneung

5. 또한, 온라인 교통 신호등은 해변이 얼마나 붐비는지 추적할 것이다.

In addition,

6. 녹색 신호등은 해변에 권고된 인원수가 있음을 나타낸다.

A green

7. 이는 해변의 3.2제곱미터당 최대 1명꼴이다.

That's

8. 노란색은 권고된 수의 100~200% 사이고, 빨간색은… 200퍼센트 이상을 말한다.

Yellow

9. 교통신호는 30분마다 업데이트된다.

The traffic

10. 7월 1일부터는 전국 10개 주요 해수욕장이 이 제도를 이용하고, 그 외 50개 해수욕장은 7월 중순까지 이 제도를 도입할 예정이다.

Ten major

11. 전라남도의 해수욕장 방문을 계획하는 사람들은 온라인으로 장소를 예약해야 한다.

Those

12. 강원도 속초해수욕장은 방문객에게 자동으로 감지하고 소독약을 살포하는 자동 소독장치를 설치할 것이다.

Sokcho

13. 해변은 밤에 문을 닫을 것이고, 여름 해변 축제는 없을 것이다.

Beaches

BRK 457/3 457/3 Today TH

영어 뉴스룸 24

English NewsRoom

BREAKING NEWS

S. Korean researchers develop robots to remotely collect samples for COVID-19 tests. At COVID-19 screening centers, the medical staff must wear thick protective suits. But despite such efforts, medical teams in Daegu and Gyeongsangbuk-do Province were unable to avoid infections amid a surge in cases in February. Daegu Mayor Kwon Young-jin says, "The surge in cases has led to more infections among medical staff." To protect medical staff, South ...

의료진 감염 예방을 위한 로봇 개발

코로나19 의료진을 위한 원격 샘플 채취 로봇 개발 대한 내용입니다.

 전체 스크립트

S. Korean researchers develop robots to remotely collect samples for COVID-19 tests

At COVID-19 screening centers, the medical staff must wear thick protective suits.

But despite such efforts, medical teams in Daegu and Gyeongsangbuk-do Province were unable to avoid infections amid a surge in cases in February.

Daegu Mayor Kwon Young-jin says, "The surge in cases has led to more infections among medical staff."

To protect medical staff, South Korean researchers have developed a remote sampling technology.

The researcher controls the robot device while watching a monitor from a separate room to check the position of the nostril.

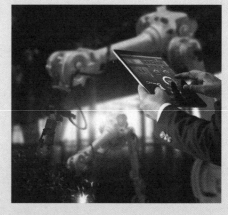

The remote robot then moves as directed and collects the sample.

The sensors on the robot also allow the user to adjust the strength of the swab.

The researchers plan to add artificial intelligence technology to the robot so that it can automatically locate the sample area.

The robot, developed using purely domestic technology, will be deployed to front-line medical facilities immediately after clinical trials.

 스크립트 분석

S. Korean researchers develop robots to remotely collect samples for COVID-19 tests
국내 연구진이 COVID-19 실험을 위해 원격으로 샘플을 채취하는 로봇을 개발하다
　　☆remotely 원격으로
　　☆collect 모으다, 채취하다

At COVID-19 screening centers, the medical staff must wear thick protective suits.
COVID-19 선별진료소에서는 의료진이 두꺼운 방호복을 착용해야 한다.
　　☆protective 보호하는

But despite such efforts, medical teams in Daegu and Gyeongsangbuk-do Province were unable to avoid infections amid a surge in cases in February.
그러나 이러한 노력에도 불구하고 지난 2월 발생건수가 급증하는 가운데 대구경북지역의 의료진은 감염을 피할 수 없었다.
　　☆amid 가운데에

> e.g. The company had to reduce their workforce amid the crisis.
> 　　　그 회사는 위기 가운데 인력을 줄여야 했다.

Daegu Mayor Kwon Young-jin says, "The surge in cases has led to more infections among medical staff."
권영진 대구시장은 "확진 사례의 급증은 의료진들 사이에 더 많은 감염을 초래했다."고 말한다.
　　☆surge 급증, 급증하다

To protect medical staff, South Korean researchers have developed a remote sampling technology.
의료진을 보호하기 위해 국내 연구진이 원격 샘플링 기술을 개발했다.

The researcher controls the robot device while watching a monitor from a separate room to check the position of the nostril.
연구진은 콧구멍의 위치를 확인하기 위해 별도의 방에서 모니터를 보면서 로봇 장치를 조종한다.
　　☆while ~ing ~하면서

The remote robot then moves as directed and collects the sample.
그런 다음 원격 로봇은 지시된 대로 움직이며 샘플을 채취한다.

The sensors on the robot also allow the user to adjust the strength of the swab.
로봇의 센서는 또한 사용자가 스왑(채취 도구)의 강도를 조정할 수 있도록 한다.

☆allow A to B A가 B하는 것을 허락하다

☆adjust 조정하다

> e.g. You can adjust the text size to make reading easier.
> 읽기 쉽도록 텍스트 크기를 조정할 수 있습니다.

☆swab *(세균 샘플 채취 등에 쓰는)* 면봉

The researchers plan to add artificial intelligence technology to the robot so that it can automatically locate the sample area.
연구진은 앞으로 채취 로봇에 인공지능 기술을 추가해 로봇이 샘플 부위를 자동으로 찾을 수 있도록 할 예정이다.

☆add A to B B에 A를 더하다

☆so that+can ~을 할 수 있도록

☆locate 찾다

> e.g. Efforts to locate the suspect were successful.
> 용의자를 찾기 위한 노력은 성공적이었다.

The robot, developed using purely domestic technology, will be deployed to front-line medical facilities immediately after clinical trials.
순수 국내 기술을 이용하여 개발된 이 로봇은 임상시험을 거친 뒤 곧바로 일선 의료 시설에 배치될 것이다.

☆purely 순수히

☆deploy *(군대 무기 등을)* 배치하다

☆front-line 최전선의, 일선의

> e.g. They are the heroes who are on the front line of the battle against the virus.
> 그들은 바이러스와의 싸움의 최전선에 있는 영웅들이다.

☆clinical trials 임상실험

Writing Exercise

1. COVID-19 선별진료소에서는 의료진이 두꺼운 방호복을 착용해야 한다.

At COVID-19 _____

_____

2. 그러나 이러한 노력에도 불구하고 지난 2월 발생건수가 급증하는 가운데 대구경북지역의 의료진은 감염을 피할 수 없었다.

But

3. 권영진 대구시장은 "확진 사례의 급증은 의료진들 사이에 더 많은 감염을 초래했다."고 말한다.

Daegu

4. 의료진을 보호하기 위해 국내 연구진이 원격 샘플링 기술을 개발했다.

To protect

5. 연구진은 콧구멍의 위치를 확인하기 위해 별도의 방에서 모니터를 보면서 로봇 장치를 조종한다.

The researcher

6. 그런 다음 원격 로봇은 지시된 대로 움직이며 샘플을 채취한다.

The remote

7. 로봇의 센서는 또한 사용자가 스왑(채취 도구)의 강도를 조정할 수 있도록 한다.

The sensors

8. 연구진은 앞으로 채취 로봇에 인공지능 기술을 추가해 로봇이 샘플 부위를 자동으로 찾을 수 있도록 할 예정이다.

The researchers

9. 순수 국내 기술을 이용하여 개발된 이 로봇은 임상시험을 거친 뒤 곧바로 일선 의료 시설에 배치될 것이다.

The robot,

ⓒ BRK 457/3
457/3
Today TH

영어 뉴스룸 25

English NewsRoom

BREAKING NEWS

S. Koreans have third most powerful passports in the world. The South Korean passport is the third-most powerful in the world. According to an index by Swiss-based research firm Henley and Partners, South Korea ranks THIRD, down a notch from 2019 tying with Germany. South Korean nationals can travel visa-free to one-hundred-89 destinations. But with South Korea being named as one of the 14 nations allowed to enter EU countries from July,...

전세계에서 통하는 한국 여권의 힘!

한국이 세계에서 세 번째로 강력한 여권을 가지고 있다는 내용입니다.

 전체 스크립트

S. Koreans have third most powerful passports in the world

The South Korean passport is the third-most powerful in the world.

According to an index by Swiss-based research firm Henley and Partners, South Korea ranks THIRD, down a notch from 2019 tying with Germany.

South Korean nationals can travel visa-free to one-hundred-89 destinations.

But with South Korea being named as one of the 14 nations allowed to enter EU countries from July, pundits say its ranking could be considered as second.

Japan continues to top the list with its citizens permitted to travel visa-free to one-hundred-91 countries, followed by Singapore with one-hundred-90.

North Korea meanwhile ranks in one-hundred-and-third place, with its citizens having visa-free waivers to 39 countries.

 **스크립트 분석**

S. Koreans have third most powerful passports in the world
한국인들은 세계에서 세 번째로 강력한 여권을 가지고 있다.

The South Korean passport is the third-most powerful in the world.
한국의 여권은 세계에서 세 번째로 강력하다.

According to an index by Swiss-based research firm Henley and Partners, South Korea ranks THIRD, down a notch from 2019 tying with Germany.
스위스에 본사를 둔 리서치 업체 헨리앤드파트너스의 지수에 따르면, 한국은 독일과 동점인 2019년보다 한 단계 낮은 3위를 차지하고 있다.

☆down a notch 한 단계 낮아진

> e.g. The country's virus risk level moved down a notch from red to orange.
> 그 나라의 바이러스 위험 수준은 적색에서 주황색으로 한 단계 낮아졌다.

☆tie with ~와 동점이 되다, ~로 묶다

> e.g. We tied with a team from Africa in the competition.
> 우리는 그 대회에서 아프리카 팀과 동점이 되었다.

South Korean nationals can travel visa-free to one-hundred-89 destinations.
한국인은 189개 목적지까지는 무비자로 여행할 수 있다.

☆visa-free 무비자 ~free ~가 없는

> e.g. sugar-free 무설탕의, duty-free 면세품, tax-free 면세가 되는

But with South Korea being named as one of the 14 nations allowed to enter EU countries from July, pundits say its ranking could be considered as second.
그러나 한국이 7월부터 EU 국가들에 진입할 수 있는 14개국 중 하나로 선정되면서 전문가들은 한국의 순위가 2위로 고려될 수 있다고 말한다.

☆be named as ~로 선정되다

> e.g. She was named as the student of the year.
> 그녀는 올해의 학생으로 선정되었다.

☆pundit 전문가

Japan continues to top the list with its citizens permitted to travel visa-free to one-hundred-91 countries, followed by Singapore with one-hundred-90.

일본은 191개국으로 자국민들이 비자 없이 여행하는 것으로 계속해서 1위를 차지하고 있고, 그 다음으로는 싱가포르가 190개국으로 그 뒤를 잇고 있다.

☆top the list 1위를 차지하다

e.g. **The country topped the list of 2020 kpop rankings.**
그 나라는 2020년 케이팝 순위에서 1위를 차지했다.

☆followed by 뒤이어, 잇달아

North Korea meanwhile ranks in one-hundred-and-third place, with its citizens having visa-free waivers to 39 countries.

한편 북한은 103위로 39개국에 비자면제를 받고 있다.

☆waiver *(권리 등의)* 포기, 포기 서류

Writing Exercise

1. 한국의 여권은 세계에서 세 번째로 강력하다.

   The South _____

   _____

2. 스위스에 본사를 둔 리서치 업체 헨리앤드파트너스의 지수에 따르면, 한국은 독일과 동점인 2019년보다 한 단계 낮은 3위를 차지하고 있다.

   According to _____

   _____

3. 한국인은 189개 목적지까지는 무비자로 여행할 수 있다.

   South _____

   _____

4. 그러나 한국이 7월부터 EU 국가들에 진입할 수 있는 14개국 중 하나로 선정되면서 전문가들은 한국의 순위가 2위로 고려될 수 있다고 말한다.

   But with _____

   _____

5. 일본은 191개국으로 자국민들이 비자 없이 여행하는 것으로 계속해서 1위를 차지하고 있고, 그 다음으로는 싱가포르가 190개국으로 그 뒤를 잇고 있다.

   Japan _____

   _____

6. 한편 북한은 103위로 39개국에 비자면제를 받고 있다.

   North _____

   _____

ⓖ BRK 457/3
457/3
Today TH

영어 뉴스룸 26 English NewsRoom

BREAKING NEWS

More people turn vegetarian in post-COVID-19 pandemic era. In the post-COVID-19 pandemic era, more people are refraining from eating meat and are turning to a more vegetable-based diet instead. The World Health Organization said that since 1970, around 75 percent of infectious diseases have come from animals. According to the Korea Vegetarian Union, there are around one point five to two-million vegetarians in the country, over three...

강제 채식주의자가 늘고 있다?

포스트코로나 시대가 불러온 '채식 열풍' 대한 내용입니다.

More people turn vegetarian in post-COVID-19 pandemic era

In the post-COVID-19 pandemic era, more people are refraining from eating meat and are turning to a more vegetable-based diet instead.

The World Health Organization said that since 1970, around 75 percent of infectious diseases have come from animals.

According to the Korea Vegetarian Union, there are around one point five to two-million vegetarians in the country, over three percent of the population.

This cooking class teaches Korean temple cuisine.

A monk here demonstrates how to make great meals without using meat.

Monk Yeogu is an instructor who teaches temple cuisine, vegetarian food that is full of vital nutrients.

She believes that greens are good for our immune system and keep us healthy.

Some worry about the nutritional balance of vegetarian diet.

But health experts say that proteins can be consumed by having beans, brown rice and nuts and fermented foods like Kimchi or seaweed for vitamin B_{12}.

NEWS 스크립트 분석

More people turn vegetarian in post-COVID-19 pandemic era
더 많은 사람들이 COVID-19 대유행 이후 시대에 채식주의자가 되다

☆turn 돌리다, 변하다

☆post 후, 다음, 뒤의

> e.g. postscript p.s.편지의 추신,(책 등의) 후기 / postgraduate 대학원생 / post-lunch 점심 후

☆era 시대

In the post-COVID-19 pandemic era, more people are refraining from eating meat and are turning to a more vegetable-based diet instead.
COVID-19 대유행 이후, 더 많은 사람들이 육식을 삼가고 대신 채소 위주의 식단으로 눈을 돌리고 있다.

☆refrain from ~을 삼가다

> e.g. Please refrain from talking in the palace.
> 궁에서는 이야기하는 것은 삼가 주세요.

The World Health Organization said that since 1970, around 75 percent of infectious diseases have come from animals.
세계보건기구는 1970년 이후 전염병의 약 75%가 동물에서 왔다고 말했다.

☆come from ~에서 생겨나다 =originate, ~의 출신이다

> e.g. The virus might have come from a school laboratory.
> 그 바이러스는 학교 실험실에서 생겨났을 수도 있다.

☆laboratory 실험실 영 [ləˈbɒr.ə.tər.i], 미 [ˈlæb.rə.tɔːr.i]
영국, 미국 발음 다름 주의!

According to the Korea Vegetarian Union, there are around one point five to two-million vegetarians in the country, over three percent of the population.
한국채식연합에 따르면, 국내의 채식주의자는 인구의 3퍼센트가 넘는150만명에서 200만명 가량 된다고 한다.

This cooking class teaches Korean temple cuisine.
이 요리 수업은 한국의 사찰 요리를 가르친다.

A monk here demonstrates how to make great meals without using meat.

이곳의 스님은 고기를 사용하지 않고 훌륭한 식사를 만드는 방법을 보여 준다.

☆demonstrate 보여주다, 입증하다

Monk Yeogu is an instructor who teaches temple cuisine, vegetarian food that is full of vital nutrients.

여거 스님은 필수 영양소가 가득한 채식주의자 음식인 사찰음식을 가르치는 강사이다.

She believes that greens are good for our immune system and keep us healthy.

그녀는 푸른채소가 면역체계에 좋고 우리를 건강하게 해준다고 믿는다.

☆greens 푸른채소

☆immune system 면역체계

Some worry about the nutritional balance of vegetarian diet.

어떤 사람들은 채식주의 식단의 영양 균형에 대해 걱정한다.

But health experts say that proteins can be consumed by having beans, brown rice and nuts and fermented foods like Kimchi or seaweed for vitamin B$_{12}$.

그러나 건강 전문가들은 단백질은 콩, 현미, 견과류와 김치나 비타민 B$_{12}$을 위한 해조류같은 발효 식품을 먹음으로써 섭취될 수 있다고 말한다.

☆consume 섭취하다

☆ferment 발효되다

☆seaweed 해조류

☆vitamin 비타민 영 [ˈvɪt.ə.mɪn], 미 [ˈvaɪ.t̬ə mɪn]
영국, 미국 발음 다름 주의!

Writing Exercise

1. COVID - 19 대유행 이후 시대는 더 많은 사람들이 육식을 삼가하고 대신 채소 위주의 식단으로 눈을 돌리고 있다.

In the

2. 세계보건기구는 1970년 이후 전염병의 약 75%가 동물에서 왔다고 말했다.

The World

3. 한국채식연합에 따르면, 국내의 채식주의자는 인구의 3퍼센트가 넘는150만명에서 200만명 가량 된다고 한다.

According to

4. 이 요리 수업은 한국의 사찰 요리를 가르친다.

This

5. 이곳의 스님은 고기를 사용하지 않고 훌륭한 식사를 만드는 방법을 보여 준다.

A monk

6. 여거 스님은 필수 영양소가 가득한 채식주의자 음식인 사찰음식을 가르치는 강사이다.

Monk

7. 그녀는 푸른채소가 면역체계에 좋고 우리를 건강하게 해준다고 믿는다.

She

8. 어떤 사람들은 채식주의 식단의 영양 균형에 대해 걱정한다.

Some

9. 그러나 건강 전문가들은 단백질은 콩, 현미, 견과류와 김치나 비타민 B$_{12}$을 위한 해조류같은 발효 식품을 먹음으로써 섭취될 수 있다고 말한다.

But health

영어 뉴스룸 27　English NewsRoom

BREAKING NEWS
Gov't to recognize restaurants that follow COVID-19 safety guidelines. Traditionally, Koreans eat from the same pot and have a container for spoons and chopsticks. But the government is promoting a policy aimed at making sure these traditions don't lead to the spread of COVID-19. "Safe Restaurant" is a policy recommended to local districts by the Ministry of Agriculture, Food and Rural Affairs. The policy aims to recognize restaurants that make efforts to...

국따로 수저따로 '안심식당'이 생겨나고 있다

'코로나19 예방' 위생수칙 지키는 안심식당에 대한 내용입니다.

 NEWS 전체 스크립트

Gov't to recognize restaurants that follow COVID-19 safety guidelines

Traditionally, Koreans eat from the same pot and have a container for spoons and chopsticks.

But the government is promoting a policy aimed at making sure these traditions don't lead to the spread of COVID-19.

"Safe Restaurant" is a policy recommended to local districts by the Ministry of Agriculture, Food and Rural Affairs.

The policy aims to recognize restaurants that make efforts to protect their customers from the virus.

Local government employees thoroughly check restaurants for three things.

First, are there methods to distribute large dishes in a sanitary way such as providing ladles?

Second, are the spoons and chopsticks distributed in a sanitary fashion?

And, third, are the servers wearing masks?

Restaurants that have passed the city's inspection can display this sticker to show they follow COVID-19 safety standards.

But they have to keep their standards high as they could receive a random spot check.

A restaurant owner who received the sticker says she is motivated to keep her customers safe.

Bucheon city is receiving many requests for the inspection and will give priority to restaurants that have consistently scored high on sanitary and service in the past.

 스크립트 분석

Gov't to recognize restaurants that follow COVID-19 safety guidelines
정부가 COVID-19 안전지침을 따르는 식당을(안심식당으로) 승인할 예정

Traditionally, Koreans eat from the same pot and have a container for spoons and chopsticks.
전통적으로 한국인들은 같은 냄비에서 먹고 숟가락들과 젓가락들을 담은 용기가 주어진다.

But the government is promoting a policy aimed at making sure these traditions don't lead to the spread of COVID-19.
그러나 정부는 이러한 전통이 COVID-19의 확산으로 이어지지 않도록 하는 것을 목표로 한 정책을 추진하고 있다.

　☆promote 추진하다
　☆aimed at ~을 겨냥한, ~을 목표로 한

"Safe Restaurant" is a policy recommended to local districts by the Ministry of Agriculture, Food and Rural Affairs.
"안심식당"은 농림축산식품부가 지역구에 권고한 정책이다.

　☆district 지역, 지구

The policy aims to recognize restaurants that make efforts to protect their customers from the virus.
이 정책은 바이러스로부터 고객을 보호하기 위해 노력하는 식당들을(안심식당으로) 승인하기 위한 것을 목표로 하고 있다.

　☆aim to (do) ~하는 것을 목표로 하다

　e.g. I didn't aim to enter the school but my friend recommended.
　　난 학교에 입학하는 것을 목표로 하지 않았지만 친구가 추천했어.

　☆make an effort 노력하다

　e.g. You should make an effort to overcome this problem.
　　넌 이 문제를 극복하기 위해 노력해야 해.

Local government employees thoroughly check restaurants for three things.
지방 공무원들은 식당의 세 가지를 철저히 점검한다.

　☆thoroughly 철저히

First, are there methods to distribute large dishes in a sanitary way such as providing ladles?

첫째, 국자 제공과 같은 위생적인 방법으로 큰 접시를 분배하는 방법이 있는가?

☆ladle 국자

☆sanitary 위생의, 위생적인

Second, are the spoons and chopsticks distributed in a sanitary fashion?

둘째, 숟가락들과 젓가락들은 위생적인 방법으로 분배되는가?

☆fashion 1. 방법, 방식 | 2. 유행

And, third, are the servers wearing masks?

셋째, 종사자들이 마스크를 쓰고 있는가?

Restaurants that have passed the city's inspection can display this sticker to show they follow COVID-19 safety standards.

시 검사를 통과한 식당에서는 COVID-19 안전기준을 준수함을 보여 주기 위한 이 스티커를 부착할 수 있다.

☆inspection 검사

But they have to keep their standards high as they could receive a random spot check.

하지만 무작위 현장 점검을 받을 수 있기 때문에 기준을 높게 유지해야 해야 한다.

☆spot check (불시에 하는) 검사

A restaurant owner who received the sticker says she is motivated to keep her customers safe.

스티커를 받은 한 식당 주인은 손님들을 안전하게 지키려는 의욕이 생긴다고 말한다.

☆be motivated to ~하도록 동기부여되다, ~할 의욕이 생기다

e.g. I'm motivated to exercise today.
난 오늘 운동할 의욕이 생겨.

Bucheon city is receiving many requests for the inspection and will give priority to restaurants that have consistently scored high on sanitary and service in the past.

부천시는 검사 요청이 많아서 과거 위생 및 서비스 시험에서 지속적으로 높은 점수를 받은 식당에 우선권을 부여할 것이다.

☆give priority to ~에게 우선권을 주다.

Writing Exercise

1. 전통적으로 한국인들은 같은 냄비에서 먹고 숟가락들과 젓가락들을 담은 용기가 주어진다.

   Traditionally,

2. 그러나 정부는 이러한 전통이 COVID - 19의 확산으로 이어지지 않도록 하는 것을 목표로 한 정책을 추진하고 있다.

   But

3. "안심식당"은 농림축산식품부가 지역구에 권고한 정책이다.

   "Safe

4. 이 정책은 바이러스로부터 고객을 보호하기 위해 노력하는 식당들을 (안심식당으로) 승인하기 위한 것을 목표로 하고 있다.

   The policy

5. 지방 공무원들은 식당의 세 가지를 철저히 점검한다.

   Local

6. 첫째, 국자 제공과 같은 위생적인 방법으로 큰 접시를 분배하는 방법이 있는가?

   First,

7. 둘째, 숟가락들과 젓가락들은 위생적인 방법으로 분배되는가?

   Second,

8. 셋째, 종사자들이 마스크를 쓰고 있는가?

   And,

9. 시 검사를 통과한 식당에서는 COVID - 19 안전기준을 준수함을 보여 주기 위한 이 스티커를 부착할 수 있다.

Restaurants
_____

_____

10. 하지만 무작위 현장 점검을 받을 수 있기 때문에 기준을 높게 유지해야 해야 한다.

But
_____

_____

11. 스티커를 받은 한 식당 주인은 손님들을 안전하게 지키려는 의욕이 생긴다고 말한다.

A restaurant
_____

_____

12. 부천시는 검사 요청이 많아서 과거 위생 및 서비스 시험에서 지속적으로 높은 점수를 받은 식당에 우선권을 부여할 것이다.

Bucheon
_____

_____

◎ BRK 457/3
457/3
Today TH

영어 뉴스룸 28

English NewsRoom

BREAKING NEWS

Seoul City government says additional 392 electric buses will be in service by end of year. The city of Seoul is going to put more eco-friendly electric buses on the roads in the months to come to reduce air pollution. Using around 20 million U.S. dollars from the government's budget for the Green New Deal, the city is going to add an extra 166 electric buses to its fleet in the second half of the year. They'll start operating from October.

버스도 이제 전기차로?

서울시의 전기버스 추가 도입에 대한 내용입니다.

 NEWS 전체 스크립트

Seoul City government says additional 392 electric buses will be in service by end of year

The city of Seoul is going to put more eco-friendly electric buses on the roads in the months to come to reduce air pollution.

Using around 20 million U.S. dollars from the government's budget for the Green New Deal, the city is going to add an extra 166 electric buses to its fleet in the second half of the year.

They'll start operating from October.

By the end of the year, there will be almost 400 electric buses operating in Seoul.

They're not only better for the environment, they're much quieter and will save the city 2.3 million U.S. dollars in annual operating costs.

The city also said that, by the end of next year, it's aiming to have a full fleet of eco-friendly buses.

Seoul City government says additional 392 electric buses will be in service by end of year
서울시는 연말까지 392대의 전기버스가 추가로 운행될 것이라고 말한다.

☆additional 추가의

☆be in service 1. 운행 되다 | 2. 군복무 중이다

e.g. The country's new subway will be in service soon.
그 나라의 새 지하철이 곧 운행될 것이다.

The city of Seoul is going to put more eco-friendly electric buses on the roads in the months to come to reduce air pollution.
서울시는 대기 오염을 줄이기 위해 몇 달 안에 더 많은 친환경 전기 버스를 도로에 투입할 것이다.

☆eco-friendly 친환경적인

☆on the roads 도로에, 여행 중인

e.g. I'm on the road right now.
난 지금 도로에 있어.
There's a lion on the road.
도로에 사자가 있다.
She's going to be on the road for a while.
그녀는 잠시 동안 여행을 갈 예정이다.

Using around 20 million U.S. dollars from the government's budget for the Green New Deal, the city is going to add an extra 166 electric buses to its fleet in the second half of the year.
서울시는 그린뉴딜 예산 2000만 달러를 활용해서 하반기 중 166대의 전기버스를 기존 버스들에 추가 도입 예정이다.

☆add A to B A를 B에 추가하다

☆fleet (한 기관이 소유한 전체 비행기버스택시 등의) 무리

☆in the second half of the year 하반기 the first half of the year 상반기

e.g. In the second half of the year, students will be able to use new tables.
하반기에는, 학생들은 새로운 책상을 이용할 수 있게 될 것이다.

They'll start operating from October.
10월부터 운영을 시작할 것이다.

By the end of the year, there will be almost 400 electric buses operating in Seoul.

연말까지 서울에는 거의 400대의 전기버스가 운행될 것이다.

☆by the end of the year 연말까지

They're not only better for the environment, they're much quieter and will save the city 2.3 million U.S. dollars in annual operating costs.

전기버스는 환경에 더 좋을 뿐만 아니라 훨씬 더 조용할 뿐만 아니라 연간 230만 달러의 운영비를 절약할 수 있을 것이다.

☆annual 연간 biennial 2년에 한 번씩의, 격년의

The city also said that, by the end of next year, it's aiming to have a full fleet of eco-friendly buses.

서울시는 또한 내년 말까지 친환경 버스 전량을 보유하는 것을 목표로 한다고 말했다.

☆aim to ~하는 것을 목표로 하다

☆full fleet 전량

1. 서울시는 대기 오염을 줄이기 위해 몇 달 안에 더 많은 친환경 전기 버스를 도로에 투입할 것이다.

   The city

2. 서울시는 그린뉴딜 예산 2000만 달러를 활용해서 하반기 중 166대의 전기버스를 기존 버스들에 추가 도입 예정이다.

   Using

3. 10월부터 운영을 시작할 것이다.

   They'll

4. 연말까지 서울에는 거의 400대의 전기버스가 운행될 것이다.

   By the end

5. 전기버스는 환경에 더 좋을 뿐만 아니라 훨씬 더 조용할 뿐만 아니라 연간 230만 달러의 운영비를 절약할 수 있을 것이다.

   They're

6. 서울시는 또한 내년 말까지 친환경 버스 전량을 보유하는 것을 목표로 한다고 말했다.

   The city

◎ BRK 457/3
457/3
Today TH

영어 뉴스룸 *29*

English NewsRoom

BREAKING NEWS

Incheon to use smart city technology for firefighting, disaster preparation. Fire trucks are dispatched to the scene in a virtual fire drill. While on the move, the firefighters plan how to extinguish the fire by checking the shape and height of the building through high-precision GPS. Information on how many fire trucks are gathering and key facilities around the scene of the fire are also delivered in real-time through the situation room.

이제 화재 진압도 스마트하게!

화재진압과 재난 대비를 위해서 스마트시티 기술을 활용한다는 내용입니다.

 전체 스크립트

Incheon to use smart city technology for firefighting, disaster preparation

Fire trucks are dispatched to the scene in a virtual fire drill.

While on the move, the firefighters plan how to extinguish the fire by checking the shape and height of the building through high-precision GPS.

Information on how many fire trucks are gathering and key facilities around the scene of the fire are also delivered in real-time through the situation room.

The simulation training based on the Geographic Information System platform is designed to use more than 60 types of information from satellites including information on underground facilities and structural safety for smarter firefighting.

It reduces geographical errors that can occur in densely built-up areas and helps those in charge to gain an all-encompassing view of disaster sites.

Incheon, as part of its smart city project, plans to incorporate the GIS system for firefighting and disaster preparation starting next year.

Incheon to use smart city technology for firefighting, disaster preparation
화재진압과 재난 대비를 위해 스마트시티 기술을 활용하는 인천

Fire trucks are dispatched to the scene in a virtual fire drill.
소방차들이 가상 소방훈련 현장에 출동한다.

☆dispatch to ~으로 발송하다, 파견하다

e.g. Officers were dispatched to different departments.
장교들은 각기 다른 부서로 파견되었다.

☆virtual *(컴퓨터를 이용한)* 가상의

e.g. Many leaders are holding a virtual meeting due to the virus.
많은 지도자들이 바이러스 때문에 가상 회의를 열고 있다.

While on the move, the firefighters plan how to extinguish the fire by checking the shape and height of the building through high-precision GPS.
소방대원들은 이동 중에 고정밀 GPS를 통해 건물의 형태와 높이 등을 확인하면서 화재진압 방법을 구상한다.

☆be on the move *(이리저리로)* 옮겨 다니다

e.g. She is always on the move because she doesn't want to stay in one place.
그녀는 한 곳에서 있는 것을 원치 않아서 항상 이러저리 이동한다.

명사
☆precision 정확, 정밀
형용사
☆precise 정확한
부사
☆precisely =with precision 명사를 부사 자리에 쓰기 위해 명사 앞에 전치사를 붙임 정확히, 정확하게

e.g. He's reliable because he chooses his words with precision.
그는 말을 정확하게 선택하기 때문에 믿을 만하다.
More precisely, he doesn't want to invest in your company.
더 정확히 말해서, 그는 너의 회사에 투자하고 싶지 않아..

Information on how many fire trucks are gathering and key facilities around the scene of the fire are also delivered in real-time through the situation room.

얼마나 많은 소방차가 집결하고 있는지, 그리고 화재현장 주변의 주요시설에 대한 정보 등이 상황실을 통해 실시간으로 현장에 전달된다.

☆real-time 실시간

The simulation training based on the Geographic Information System platform is designed to use more than 60 types of information from satellites including information on underground facilities and structural safety for smarter firefighting.

GIS, 지오그래픽 인포메이션 시스템에 기반한 시뮬레이션 교육은 보다 스마트한 화재진압을 위해 인공위성을 통해 지하시설 정보, 구조안전 등 60여 가지 정보를 수신해 활용할 수 있도록 설계되었다.

☆simulation 시뮬레이션, 모의실험

☆based on ~에 기반한

☆underground 지하의

☆structural 구조상의, 구조적인

It reduces geographical errors that can occur in densely built-up areas and helps those in charge to gain an all-encompassing view of disaster sites.

이것(GIS)은 건물밀집지역에서 발생할 수 있는 지리적 오차를 줄이고 현장지휘관들이 재난현장을 한눈에 파악하도록 도와준다.

☆densely 밀집하여

☆all-encompassing 모두를 아우르는

☆in charge ~을 맡은, 담당인

Incheon, as part of its smart city project, plans to incorporate the GIS system for firefighting and disaster preparation starting next year.

스마트도시 구축 사업의 일환으로, 인천시는 내년부터 화재진압과 재난 대비를 위한 GIS시스템을 통합시킬 계획이다.

☆as part of ~의 일환으로

☆incorporate 통합시키다, (법인을) 설립하다

e.g. The new technology can be easily incorporated into existing programs.
새로운 기술은 기존 프로그램에 쉽게 통합될 수 있다.
The company was officially incorporated in 2019.
그 회사는 2019년 공식적으로 법인화가 되었다.

1. 소방차들이 가상 소방훈련 현장에 출동한다.

   Fire

2. 소방대원들은 이동 중에 고정밀 GPS를 통해 건물의 형태와 높이 등을 확인하면서 화재진압 방법을 구상한다.

   While

3. 얼마나 많은 소방차가 집결하고 있는지, 그리고 화재현장 주변의 주요시설에 대한 정보 등이 상황실을 통해 실시간으로 현장에 전달된다.

   Information

4. GIS, 지오그래픽 인포메이션 시스템에 기반한 시뮬레이션 교육은 보다 스마트한 화재진압을 위해 인공위성을 통해 지하시설 정보, 구조안전 등 60여 가지 정보를 수신해 활용할 수 있도록 설계되었다.

   The simulation

5. 이것(GIS)은 건물밀집지역에서 발생할 수 있는 지리적 오차를 줄이고 현장지휘관들이 재난현장을 한눈에 파악하도록 도와준다.

   It reduces

6. 스마트도시 구축 사업의 일환으로, 인천시는 내년부터 화재진압과 재난 대비를 위한 GIS시스템을 통합시킬 계획이다.

   Incheon,

◉BRK 457/3
457/3
Today TH

영어 뉴스룸 *30*

English NewsRoom

BREAKING NEWS

Sprea Editori to print special BTS edition magazine every 2 months for fans of K-pop band. An Italian publisher is printing a regular BTS magazine for K-pop fans around the world. Sprea Editori says it decided to publish the 80-page full-color edition in light of BTS's strong fan base as well as growing interest in the band in Italy. The first edition came out earlier this month. It includes interviews and photos of all seven BTS members.

BTS 전문 잡지를 이탈리아에서도 볼 수 있다?

방탄소년단 전문 잡지가 이탈리아에서도 창간되었다는 내용입니다.

 NEWS 전체 스크립트

Sprea Editori to print special BTS edition magazine every 2 months for fans of K-pop band

An Italian publisher is printing a regular BTS magazine for K-pop fans around the world.

Sprea Editori says it decided to publish the 80-page full-color edition in light of BTS's strong fan base as well as growing interest in the band in Italy.

The first edition came out earlier this month.

It includes interviews and photos of all seven BTS members.

It's one of the few times a K-pop group has been the cover story on a foreign magazine.

The company says it'll publish a new edition featuring BTS every two months.

Sprea Editori to print special BTS edition magazine every 2 months for fans of K-pop band
케이팝 밴드 팬들을 위해 2개월마다 특별한 방탄소년단 에디션 매거진을 발행하는 스프레아 에디토리

☆print 인쇄하다, (책, 신문 등을) 출간·발행하다

e.g. The paperback version of the book is being printed.
그 책의 페이퍼백 버전이 발행되고 있다.

An Italian publisher is printing a regular BTS magazine for K-pop fans around the world.
이탈리아의 한 출판사가 전 세계 케이팝 팬들을 위해 방탄소년단 정규 잡지를 발행하고 있다.

Sprea Editori says it decided to publish the 80-page full-color edition in light of BTS's strong fan base as well as growing interest in the band in Italy.
스프레아 에디토리는 이탈리아에서 밴드에 대한 관심이 높아지는 것은 물론 방탄소년단의 두터운 팬층을 고려해 80여쪽 분량의 전면 컬러판 에디션을 출판하기로 했다고 말한다.

☆B as well as A A뿐만 아니라 B도
동사는 B에 일치시킴에 주의!

e.g. She has a dog as well as three cats.
그녀는 세 마리의 고양이 뿐만 아니라 한 마리의 개도 가지고 있다.

☆in light of ~에 비추어, ~을 고려하여

e.g. In light of recent changes, Facebook privacy settings these days can be a hassle.
최근의 변화에 비추어 볼 때, 요즘 페이스북 개인 정보 설정은 번거로울 수 있다.

☆privacy 개인정보, 사생활 | 영 ['prɪv.ə.si], 미 ['praɪ.və.si]
영국, 미국 발음 다름 주의!

The first edition came out earlier this month.
초판은 이달 초에 나왔다.

☆come out 출간되다

e.g. The previous edition of the book came out in 1999.
그 책의 전판은 1999년에 출간되었다.

It includes interviews and photos of all seven BTS members.
그 잡지에는 방탄소년단 멤버 7명 모두의 인터뷰와 사진이 포함되어 있다.

It's one of the few times a K-pop group has been the cover story on a foreign magazine.
케이팝 그룹이 외국 잡지의 표지 기사가 된 것은 몇 번 안 되는 사례 중 하나이다.

☆one of the few times 몇 안되는 경우 중 하나

e.g. It was one of the few times he smiles during the conversation.
그것은 대화하는 동안 그가 웃는 몇 번 안 되는 순간 중 하나였다.

☆cover story 표지 기사

e.g. The magazine did a cover story on stray cats.
그 잡지는 길고양이에 대한 표지기사를 실었다.

The company says it'll publish a new edition featuring BTS every two months.
이 회사는 두 달에 한 번씩 방탄소년단을 주인공으로 한 신판을 발행할 것이라고 한다.

☆feature 특징, 특징으로 삼다

e.g. The movie features fantastic music and performance.
그 영화는 환상적인 음악과 연기를 특징으로 한다.

1. 이탈리아의 한 출판사가 전 세계 케이팝 팬들을 위해 방탄소년단 정규 잡지를 발행하고 있다.

An Italian
_____
_____

2. 스프레아 에디토리는 이탈리아에서 밴드에 대한 관심이 높아지는 것은 물론 방탄소년단의 두터운 팬층을 고려해 80여쪽 분량의 전면 컬러판 에디션을 출판하기로 했다고 말한다.

Sprea Editori
_____
_____

3. 초판은 이달 초에 나왔다.

The first
_____
_____

4. 그 잡지에는 방탄소년단 멤버 7명 모두의 인터뷰와 사진이 포함되어 있다.

It includes
_____
_____

5. 케이팝 그룹이 외국 잡지의 표지 기사가 된 것은 몇 번 안 되는 사례 중 하나이다.

It's
_____
_____

6. 이 회사는 두 달에 한 번씩 방탄소년단을 주인공으로 한 신판을 발행할 것이라고 한다.

The company
_____
_____

◎ BRK 457/3
457/3
Today TH

영어 뉴스룸 31

English NewsRoom

BREAKING NEWS

Giant panda born for first time in S. Korea. A baby giant panda has been born for the first time in South Korea. The country's largest theme park, Everland said Wednesday that the panda couple in the zoo had a female cub two days ago. The panda couple, Aibao and Lebao had been gifted by Chinese President Xi Jinping in 2016 as a symbol of the two countries' friendship. As pandas have just one childbearing period each year, it is rare to see one giving birth...

한국 출신 아기 판다

한국에서 처음으로 태어난 자이언트 판다에 대한 내용입니다.

 전체 스크립트

Giant panda born for first time in S. Korea

A baby giant panda has been born for the first time in South Korea.

The country's largest theme park, Everland said Wednesday that the panda couple in the zoo had a female cub two days ago.

The panda couple, Aibao and Lebao had been gifted by Chinese President Xi Jinping in 2016 as a symbol of the two countries' friendship.

As pandas have just one childbearing period each year, it is rare to see one giving birth especially without artificial insemination.

Everland said the mother and baby are both healthy but the cub will not be allowed outside until her immune system is strong enough.

The zoo will upload pictures and videos so that fans can see the cub online.

Giant panda born for first time in S. Korea
한국에서 처음으로 태어난 자이언트 판다

A baby giant panda has been born for the first time in South Korea.
아기 자이언트 판다가 한국에서 처음으로 태어났다.

☆for the first time 처음으로

> e.g. For the first time in her life, she stopped worrying about her son.
> 생전 처음으로, 그녀는 아들에 대한 걱정을 멈추었다.

The country's largest theme park, Everland said Wednesday that the panda couple in the zoo had a female cub two days ago.
국내 최대 테마파크인 에버랜드는 동물원에 있는 판다 부부가 이틀 전 새끼 암컷을 낳았다고 수요일에 말했다.

☆theme park 테마파크 놀이공원 =amusement park

☆have =deliver (아기를) 낳다

> e.g. She is about to have a baby.
> 그녀는 곧 아기를 낳을 거야.

☆cub 여우, 곰, 사자 또는 육식성 포유류의 새끼

> e.g. The tiger delivered two healthy male cubs
> 그 호랑이는 두 마리의 건강한 수컷 새끼를 낳았다.

The panda couple, Aibao and Lebao had been gifted by Chinese President Xi Jinping in 2016 as a symbol of the two countries' friendship.
판다 커플 아이바오와 러바오는 2016년 시진핑 중국 국가주석이 한중 친선 도모의 상징으로 보내준 선물이다.

☆as a symbol of ~의 상징으로

> e.g. The ring was given as a symbol of friendship, not of love.
> 그 반지는 사랑의 상징이 아닌 우정의 상징으로 주어졌다.

As pandas have just one childbearing period each year, it is rare to see one giving birth especially without artificial insemination.

판다는 가임기가 1년에 딱 한번 뿐이기 때문에, 특히 인공수정 없이 출산하는 것은 보기 드물다.

☆childbearing 출산

☆childbearing period 가임기

☆childbearing age 가임 연령

e.g. They might have passed childbearing age.
그들은 가임 연령이 지났을지도 모른다.

☆rare 드문

☆it is rare to ~하는 것은 드물다

e.g. It is rare to find someone who is afraid of paper.
종이를 무서워하는 사람을 찾는 것은 드물다.

☆give birth 출산하다

☆artificial 인공의, 인위적인

☆artificial insemination 인공수정

Everland said the mother and baby are both healthy but the cub will not be allowed outside until her immune system is strong enough.

에버랜드는 어미와 새끼 모두 건강하지만 새끼 곰은 면역력이 충분히 강해질 때까지 밖에 나갈 수 없다고 말했다.

☆immune system 면역체계

e.g. The immune system defends our body against invaders, such as viruses.
면역체계는 바이러스와 같은 침입자로부터 우리 몸을 보호한다.

The zoo will upload pictures and videos so that fans can see the cub online.

동물원은 팬들이 새끼 곰을 온라인에서 볼 수 있도록 사진과 동영상을 올릴 예정이다.

☆so that+can ~을 할 수 있도록, ~을 하기 위해서 =in order to

e.g. The father is taking care of his son so that the mother can have a rest.
어머니가 쉴 수 있도록 아버지가 아들을 돌보고 있다.

1. 아기 자이언트 판다가 한국에서 처음으로 태어났다.

   A baby

2. 국내 최대 테마파크인 에버랜드는 동물원에 있는 판다 부부가 이틀 전 새끼 암컷을 낳았다고 수요일에 말했다.

   The country's

3. 판다 커플 아이바오와 러바오는 2016년 시진핑 중국 국가주석이 한중 친선 도모의 상징으로 보내준 선물이다.

   The panda

4. 판다는 가임기가 1년에 딱 한번 뿐이기 때문에, 특히 인공수정 없이 출산하는 것은 보기 드물다.

   As pandas

5. 에버랜드는 어미와 새끼 모두 건강하지만 새끼 곰은 면역력이 충분히 강해질 때까지 밖에 나갈 수 없다고 말했다.

   Everland

6. 동물원은 팬들이 새끼 곰을 온라인에서 볼 수 있도록 사진과 동영상을 올릴 예정이다.

   The zoo

영어 뉴스룸 *32*

English NewsRoom

BREAKING NEWS

New figures show that it would take a South Korean household with an average income in the city to save up all every little penny they make for more than 12 years to afford an average-priced apartment in the capital Seoul. That's according to the National Assembly Research Service which released the 2019 Price to Income Ratio for the city measuring the affordability of homes to come to 12.one-three.As of last December, the average price of an...

월급을 하나도 안쓰고 12년 동안 모아야 집을 살 수 있다?

월급을 안쓰고 모아도 서울에서 아파트를 사려면 평균 12년 걸린다는 내용입니다.

NEWS 전체 스크립트

More than 12 years to buy home in Seoul even if all paychecks were saved : Data

New figures show that it would take a South Korean household with an average income in the city to save up all every little penny they make for more than 12 years to afford an average-priced apartment in the capital Seoul.

That's according to the National Assembly Research Service which released the 2019 Price to Income Ratio for the city measuring the affordability of homes to come to 12.one-three.

As of last December, the average price of an apartment was just under 700-thousand U.S. dollars.

To cool the overheated housing market, the South Korean government is set to soon reveal plans to build more housing units in Seoul and the surrounding area.

NEWS 스크립트 분석

More than 12 years to buy home in Seoul even if all paychecks were saved : Data
데이터에 따르면 급여를 모두 모아도 서울에서 집 사는데 12년 걸려

☆ paychecks 급여

☆ even if 설령 ~라고 할지라도 = even though 비록 ~함에도 불구하고

> e.g. I have to go to the club even though I don't feel like dancing tonight.
> 난 비록 오늘 밤 춤추고 싶지 않음에도 불구하고 클럽에 가야 해.
> I have to go to the club even if I don't feel like dancing tonight.
> 난 설령 오늘 밤 춤출 기분이 아닐지라도 클럽에 가야 해.

New figures show that it would take a South Korean household with an average income in the city to save up all every little penny they make for more than 12 years to afford an average-priced apartment in the capital Seoul.
새로운 수치는 서울에서 평균 소득을 받는 서울에 사는 가구가 월급을 한 푼도 쓰지 않고 모아도 수도 서울에 평균 가격 아파트를 장만하는데 12년 이상 걸린다는 것을 보여 준다.

☆ figure 수치, 숫자, 모형 장난감

☆ average income 평균 소득 (average yearly income 연평균 소득)

> e.g. I would like to know how to save money with an average income.
> 난 평균 수입으로 돈을 모으는 방법을 알고 싶어.

☆ save up 돈을 모으다

> e.g. I'm saving up for a new laptop and car.
> 난 새 노트북과 차를 사기 위해 저축하고 있어.

☆ household 가정, 가구

☆ every penny 동전 한 푼까지 다 (penny 영국의 최소 단위 동전)

☆ average-priced 평균 가격

That's according to the National Assembly Research Service which released the 2019 Price to Income Ratio for the city measuring the affordability of homes to come to 12.one-three.
그것은 국회입법조사처가 제출한 12.13에 이르는 아파트구입의 적정 비용을 측정하는 서울의 2019년도 PIR(Price to Income Ratio)에 따른 것이다.

☆ Price to Income Ratio (PIR) 가구평균소득 대비 아파트 평균 매매가격 비율

☆ affordability 적당한 가격으로 구입할 수 있는 것, 감당할 수 있는 비용

As of last December, the average price of an apartment was just under 700-thousand U.S. dollars.

지난해 12월 일자로 아파트의 평균 가격은 70만 달러를 조금 밑돌았다.

☆as of 일자로, 현재로

> e.g. It takes effect as of the 23rd of July.
> 7월 23일부터 효력이 발생한다.

To cool the overheated housing market, the South Korean government is set to soon reveal plans to build more housing units in Seoul and the surrounding area.

과열된 주택 시장을 진정시키기 위해 정부는 서울과 그 주변에 더 많은 주택 단지를 건설할 계획을 곧 발표할 예정이다.

☆be set to ~할 예정이다

> e.g. After graduating, she is set to work at her father's company.
> 졸업 후, 그녀는 아버지의 회사에서 일할 예정이다.

☆overheated 지나치게 뜨거운, 관심·흥분이 과열된

☆reveal (비밀 등을) 밝히다, 드러내다

☆housing unit 주택

1. 새로운 수치는 서울에서 평균 소득을 받는 서울에 사는 가구가 월급을 한 푼도 쓰지 않고 모아도 수도 서울에 평균 가격 아파트를 장만하는데12년 이상 걸린다는 것을 보여 준다.

New _____

_____

2. 그것은 국회입법조사처가 제출한 12.13에 이르는 아파트구입의 적정 비용을 측정하는 서울의 2019년도 PIR(Price to Income Ratio)에 따른 것이다.

That's _____

_____

3. 지난해 12월 일자로 아파트의 평균 가격은 70만 달러를 조금 밑돌았다.

As of _____

_____

4. 과열된 주택 시장을 진정시키기 위해 정부는 서울과 그 주변에 더 많은 주택 단지를 건설할 계획을 곧 발표할 예정이다.

To cool _____

_____

⊙ BRK 457/3
457/3
Today TH

영어 뉴스룸 *33* English NewsRoom

BREAKING NEWS

Top S. Korean stars donate thousands to flood relief. Several top South Korean entertainers have made donations to help with relief efforts for those affected by the ongoing flooding and landslides caused by the monsoon rains. According to the Korea Disaster Relief Association, entertainer Yoo Jae-seok donated more than 83-thousand U.S. dollars to the agency's 2020 emergency relief campaign. Actor Park Seo-joon is known to have donated a similar...

폭우 피해를 돕기 위한 스타들의 기부행렬

폭우 피해를 돕기 위한 스타들의 기부행렬에 대한 내용입니다.

 **전체 스크립트**

Top S. Korean stars donate thousands to flood relief

Several top South Korean entertainers have made donations to help with relief efforts for those affected by the ongoing flooding and landslides caused by the monsoon rains.

According to the Korea Disaster Relief Association, entertainer Yoo Jae-seok donated more than 83-thousand U.S. dollars to the agency's 2020 emergency relief campaign.

Actor Park Seo-joon is known to have donated a similar amount.

Also, actress Yoo In-na has pitched in around 41-thousand dollars, and so has actor Song Joong-ki.

Top S. Korean stars donate thousands to flood relief
한국의 톱스타들이 수해 구호에 수천 달러를 기부한다.

☆donate 기부하다

☆flood 홍수

☆relief 구호

☆flood relief 수해 구호 (disaster relief 재난 구조 / debt relief 채무 면제)

Several top South Korean entertainers have made donations to help with relief efforts for those affected by the ongoing flooding and landslides caused by the monsoon rains.
몇몇 한국 최고의 연예인들이 계속되는 장맛비로 인한 홍수와 산사태로 피해를 입은 사람들을 위한 구호 활동을 돕기 위해 기부를 했다.

☆make a donation 기부하다

e.g. He made a donation to the school in memory of his late father.
그는 돌아가신 아버지를 추모하기 위해 학교에 기부를 했다.

☆in memory of ~을 추모해서

☆relief effort 구호 활동

☆be affected by 의 영향을 받는

e.g. The signal is affected by weather conditions.
신호는 기상 조건에 의해 영향을 받습니다.

☆ongoing 계속 진행되는

e.g. Tell me about the ongoing legal case against the paper.
현재 진행 중인 신문사 소송에 대해 말해 주세요.

☆landslide 산사태

☆monsoon 장마

According to the Korea Disaster Relief Association, entertainer Yoo Jae-seok donated more than 83-thousand U.S. dollars to the agency's 2020 emergency relief campaign.
희망브리지 전국재해구호협회에 따르면, 연예인 유재석은 이 기구의 2020 수해 피해 긴급구호 캠페인에 8만 3000달러 이상을 기부했다.

Actor Park Seo-joon is known to have donated a similar amount.

배우 박서준이 비슷한 금액을 기부한 것으로 알려졌다.

☆be known to VS be known for VS be known as

· be known to (+동사원형) ~을 한 것으로 알려져 있다

· be known to (+대상) ~에게 알려져 있다

e.g. It is known to everybody in the world.

그것은 세상 모든 사람들에게 알려져 있다.

· be known for (+근거 또는 이유) ~로 알려져 있다 =be famous for

e.g. He is well known for his discovery.

그는 그의 발견으로 잘 알려져 있다.

· be known as (+자격 또는 신분) ~로서 알려져 있다

e.g. Her father is well known as a teacher who takes care of more than hundreds of students.

그녀의 아버지는 수백명 이상의 학생들을 돌보는 선생님으로 잘 알려져 있다.

Also, actress Yoo In-na has pitched in around 41-thousand dollars, and so has actor Song Joong-ki.

또한, 배우 유인나가 약 4만 1천 달러를 도왔고, 배우 송중기도 마찬가지였다.

☆pitch in (자금 등을) 협력하다

e.g. What do you think, if we all pitch in together?

우리 모두 함께 힘을 합치는 거 어떻게 생각해?

1. 몇몇 한국 최고의 연예인들이 계속되는 장맛비로 인한 홍수와 산사태로 피해를 입은 사람들을 위한 구호 활동을 돕기 위해 기부를 했다.

Several

2. 희망브리지 전국재해구호협회에 따르면, 연예인 유재석은 이 기구의 2020 수해 피해 긴급구호 캠페인에 8만 3000달러 이상을 기부했다.

According to

3. 배우 박서준이 비슷한 금액을 기부한 것으로 알려졌다.

Actor

4. 또한, 배우 유인나가 약 4만 1천 달러를 도왔고, 배우 송중기도 마찬가지였다.

Also,

BRK 457/3
457/3
Today TH

영어 뉴스룸 *34*

English NewsRoom

BREAKING NEWS	S. Korean stadiums to operate at up to 30% capacity. More sports fans in South Korea will be able to go to ballparks starting next week. Stadiums have been operating at 10 percent capacity, but the sports ministry says that'll go up to 30 percent starting with KBO games next Tuesday and K League matches on Friday. However, the Korean Baseball Organization says even with the new policy it's only going to open at 25 percent capacity until it's clear...

이제 프로야구를 경기장에서 관람할 수 있다

프로스포츠 관중 입장을 30%로 확대한다는 내용입니다.

S. Korean stadiums to operate at up to 30% capacity

More sports fans in South Korea will be able to go to ballparks starting next week.

Stadiums have been operating at 10 percent capacity, but the sports ministry says that'll go up to 30 percent starting with KBO games next Tuesday and K League matches on Friday.

However, the Korean Baseball Organization says even with the new policy, it's only going to open at 25 percent capacity until it's clear that fans are complying fully with social distancing measures.

S. Korean stadiums to operate at up to 30% capacity

관중 수용인원의 최대 30%까지 운영할 예정인 한국 프로경기장

☆stadium 경기장 (복수형 : stadiums or stadia)

☆up to 최대 (특정한 수·정도 등) ~까지

e.g. We can afford up to 50 guests.

우리는 최대 50명까지 손님을 수용할 수 있다.

· be up to 1. ~에게 달려있다 (e.g. It's up to you.)
          2. 할 수 있다 (e.g. Are you up to playing the game?)

☆operate at 30% capacity 전체 수용능력의 30%를 가동하다

· operate at (full) capacity 수용능력을 최대로 가동하다

e.g. Our factory is working at full capacity.

우리 공장은 최대로 가동 중이다.

More sports fans in South Korea will be able to go to ballparks starting next week.

한국의 더 많은 스포츠 팬들이 다음 주부터 야구장에 갈 수 있을 것이다.

☆Ballpark 1. 야구장 | 2. 대략적인 액수[양]

e.g. As a ballpark figure, it'll be about 7 hundred dollars.

대략적으로, 그것은 700달러 정도 될 겁니다.

· in the ballpark 예상 범위 내에서, 어림잡아

e.g. Four thousand? That could be in the ballpark.

4천 정도 되나? 어림잡아 말하는 거야.

Stadiums have been operating at 10 percent capacity, but the sports ministry says that'll go up to 30 percent starting with KBO games next Tuesday and K League matches on Friday.

경기장은 10% 규모의 관중 입장으로 운영되어 왔지만, 문화체육관광부는 다음주 화요일 KBO 경기와 금요일 K리그 경기를 시작으로 최대 30% 수준으로 확대된다고 말한다.

However, the Korean Baseball Organization says even with the new policy, it's only going to open at 25 percent capacity until it's clear that fans are complying fully with social distancing measures.

하지만, 한국야구위원회는 새로운 방침에도 불구하고, 팬들이 사회적 거리 제한 조치를 완전히 준수하고 있다는 것이 확실해질 때까지, 관중 수용 인원의 최대 25%까지만 개방될 것이라고 말한다.

☆comply with 순응하다, 지키다, 준수하다

e.g. You have to comply with the new regulations.
당신은 새로운 규칙들을 준수해야 합니다.
Please comply fully with the management system.
관리 시스템을 잘 준수하십시오.

☆social distancing 사회적 거리두기

e.g. The capital remains under some social distancing rules for 3 more weeks.
그 수도는 사회적 거리 제한 규정을 3주 더 유지한다.

Writing Exercise

1. 한국의 더 많은 스포츠 팬들이 다음 주부터 야구장에 갈 수 있을 것이다.

More

2. 경기장은 10% 규모의 관중 입장으로 운영되어 왔지만, 문화체육관광부는 다음주 화요일 KBO 경기와 금요일 K리그 경기를 시작으로 최대 30% 수준으로 확대된다고 말한다.

Stadiums

3. 하지만, 한국야구위원회는 새로운 방침에도 불구하고, 팬들이 사회적 거리 제한 조치를 완전히 준수하고 있다는 것이 확실해질 때까지, 관중 수용 인원의 최대 25%까지만 개방될 것이라고 말한다.

However,

ⓒ BRK 457/3
457/3
Today TH

영어 뉴스룸 35

English NewsRoom

BREAKING NEWS

Foreign COVID-19 patients to cover treatment expenses. Starting Monday, foreign COVID-19 patients found to have violated quarantine rules after arriving in South Korea will be required to foot their treatment bill. In addition, from August 24th, foreign patients coming into the country will be required to cover some or all of their treatment expenses although the costs will vary depending on how much their home countries charge Korean nationals for...

외국인 코로나 확진자도 이제는 치료비 낸다

해외유입 외국인 코로나 확진자에게 치료비를 부과한다는 내용입니다.

Foreign COVID-19 patients to cover treatment expenses

Starting Monday, foreign COVID-19 patients found to have violated quarantine rules after arriving in South Korea will be required to foot their treatment bill.

In addition, from August 24th, foreign patients coming into the country will be required to cover some or all of their treatment expenses although the costs will vary depending on how much their home countries charge Korean nationals for coronavirus treatment.

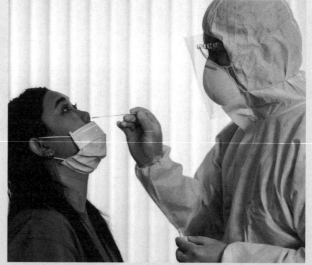

Upon announcement today, the KCDC explained the new measures were due to a recent uptick in imported cases.

Until now, South Korea had offered free coronavirus treatment to foreigners.

However, for foreigners who are infected in South Korea, treatment will still be free of charge.

 스크립트 분석

Foreign COVID-19 patients to cover treatment expenses
치료비를 부담 해야하는 외국인 COVID-19 환자들

　☆cover *(금액을)* 부담하다

> e.g. They have to cover expenses depending on their income.
> 그들은 수입에 따라 비용을 부담해야 한다.

Starting Monday, foreign COVID-19 patients found to have violated quarantine rules after arriving in South Korea will be required to foot their treatment bill.
월요일부터 한국에 도착한 후 검역 규정을 위반한 것으로 밝혀진 외국인 COVID-19 환자들은 그들의 치료비를 부담해야 할 것이다.

　☆quarantine 격리, 격리하다
　☆quarantine rules 검역 규정
　☆be required to ~하도록 요구받다

> e.g. The hospitals are required to provide free masks to visitors.
> 병원들은 방문객들에게 무료 마스크를 제공해야 한다.

　☆foot the bill 비용을 부담하다

> e.g. Her boyfriend footed the bill for her birthday.
> 그녀의 남자친구는 그녀의 생일 비용을 부담했어.

In addition, from August 24th, foreign patients coming into the country will be required to cover some or all of their treatment expenses although the costs will vary depending on how much their home countries charge Korean nationals for coronavirus treatment.
또한 8월 24일부터 국내에 들어오는 외국인 환자들은 치료비의 일부 또는 전부를 부담해야 한다. 하지만 치료비는 해당 국가가 우리 국민에 대해서 얼마나 코로나 바이러스 치료비를 청구하는 지에 따라 달라질 것이다.

　☆expense 비용
　☆although ~에도 불구하고, 그러나, 하지만
　☆vary *(상황에 따라)* 달라지다[다르다]

> e.g. The quantity of learning will vary from student to student.
> 학습량은 학생마다 다를 것이다.

☆charge 청구하다, 충전하다

e.g. I don't know how much they will charge for private tour.
난 그들이 개인 관광에 얼마를 청구할지 모르겠어.
Do not use your phone while it's charging.
충전 중에는 폰을 사용하지 마세요.

Upon announcement today, the KCDC explained the new measures were due to a recent uptick in imported cases.
오늘 발표되자마자, 질병관리본부는 새 조치들은 최근 해외유입 외국인 환자 건수의 증가로 인한 것이었다고 설명했다.

☆upon 하자마자

☆KCDC (Korea Centers for Disease Control and Prevention) 질병관리본부

☆be due to (+ 명사) ~에 기인하다

☆uptick 약간의 증가

Until now, South Korea had offered free coronavirus treatment to foreigners.
지금까지 한국은 외국인들에게 무료 코로나바이러스 치료를 제공해 왔다.

However, for foreigners who are infected in South Korea, treatment will still be free of charge.
그러나 국내에서 감염되는 외국인에게는 여전히 치료비가 무료일 것이다.

☆free of charge 무료의

e.g. The bus service is free of charge for local people.
버스 서비스는 지역 주민들에게는 무료이다.

Writing Exercise

1. 월요일부터 한국에 도착한 후 검역 규정을 위반한 것으로 밝혀진 외국인 COVID - 19 환자들은 그들의 치료비를 부담해야 할 것이다.

   Starting
   _____
   _____

2. 또한 8월 24일부터 국내에 들어오는 외국인 환자들은 치료비의 일부 또는 전부를 부담해야 한다. 하지만 치료비는 해당 국가가 우리 국민에 대해서 얼마나 코로나 바이러스 치료비를 청구하는 지에 따라 달라질 것이다.

   In addition,
   _____
   _____

3. 오늘 발표되자마자, 질병관리본부는 새 조치들은 최근 해외유입 외국인 환자 건수의 증가로 인한 것이었다고 설명했다.

   Upon
   _____
   _____

4. 지금까지 한국은 외국인들에게 무료 코로나바이러스 치료를 제공해 왔다.

   Until now,
   _____
   _____

5. 그러나 국내에서 감염되는 외국인에게는 여전히 치료비가 무료일 것이다.

   However,
   _____
   _____

ⓒ BRK 457/3
457/3
Today TH

영어 뉴스룸 *36* English NewsRoom

BREAKING NEWS

Blackpink becomes world's no. 4 artist by YouTube subscribers. The K-pop girl group, Blackpink, has become the fourth biggest artist in the world in terms of YouTube subscribers. Their record label YG Entertainment said Monday that Blackpink has surpassed 44 million subscribers on their official YouTube channel. Since the group released their latest hit, 'How You Like That' on June 24th, their channel has been growing by a hundred-thousand...

블랙핑크 유튜브 구독자수 세계4위 등극

블랙핑크가 유튜브 구독자수 세계 4위에 등극했다는 내용입니다.

 NEWS 전체 스크립트

Blackpink becomes world's no. 4 artist by YouTube subscribers

The K-pop girl group, Blackpink, has become the fourth biggest artist in the world in terms of YouTube subscribers.

Their record label YG Entertainment said Monday that Blackpink has surpassed 44 million subscribers on their official YouTube channel.

Since the group released their latest hit, 'How You Like That' on June 24th, their channel has been growing by a hundred-thousand subscribers a day, surpassing Eminem and Ariana Grande.

Blackpink still trails Ed Sheeran, Dj Marshmello and Justin Bieber, who continue to be the pop star with the most subscribers in the world.

NEWS 스크립트 분석

Blackpink becomes world's no. 4 artist by YouTube subscribers

블랙핑크, 유튜브 구독자 세계 4위 아티스트 되다

The K-pop girl group, Blackpink, has become the fourth biggest artist in the world in terms of YouTube subscribers.

K-pop 걸그룹 블랙핑크가 유튜브 구독자 기준으로 세계 4위의 아티스트가 됐다.

☆in terms of ~면에서

> e.g. In terms of the quality we offer, we've got the best one.
> 우리가 제공하는 품질에 있어서는, 우리는 최고의 것을 가졌습니다.

Their record label YG Entertainment said Monday that Blackpink has surpassed 44 million subscribers on their official YouTube channel.

그들의 음반사인 YG 엔터테인먼트는 블랙핑크가 공식 유튜브 채널에서 4,400만 명의 구독자를 돌파했다고 월요일 밝혔다.

☆record 1. 음반 [rekɔ:d] (명사) | 2. 기록하다 [rikɔ́:rd] (동사)

명사, 동사 발음 다름 주의!

☆record label 음반 회사

☆surpass 능가하다, 뛰어넘다

> e.g. The figures surpassed even the company's expectations.
> 그 수치는 심지어 회사의 기대치를 능가했다.
> Her father has really surpassed himself with this new painting.
> 그녀의 아버지는 이 새로운 그림으로 정말 자신을 능가했다.

Since the group released their latest hit, 'How You Like That' on June 24th, their channel has been growing by a hundred-thousand subscribers a day, surpassing Eminem and Ariana Grande.

이 그룹은 지난 6월 24일 'How You Like That'을 발매한 이후 에미넴과 아리아나 그란데를 제치고 하루에 10만 명의 구독자가 늘고 있다.

☆release 발매하다, 풀어주다, 석방하다

☆channel has been growing 채널이 성장하다, 구독자수가 늘다

> e.g. Her channel has been growing very quickly over these last few weeks.
> 지난 몇 주 동안 그녀의 채널은 매우 빠르게 성장하고 있다.

☆latest 최신의

e.g. Let me tell you the latest news.
   최근 소식을 알려드리겠습니다.

☆at the latest *(아무리)* 늦어도

e.g. Please fill in the form and submit it at the latest by the 23rd of July.
   양식을 작성하여 늦어도 7월 23일까지 제출해 주십시오.

Blackpink still trails Ed Sheeran, Dj Marshmello and Justin Bieber, who continue to be the pop star with the most subscribers in the world.

세계에서 가장 많은 구독자를 계속 보유하고 있는 팝스타 에드 시런, DJ 마쉬멜로, 저스틴 비버의 뒤를 블랙핑크는 여전히 뒤쫓고 있다.

   명사   동사
☆trail 1. 자국, 자취 | 2. 뒤쫓다, 추적하다

Writing Exercise

1. K-pop 걸그룹 블랙핑크가 유튜브 구독자 기준으로 세계 4위의 아티스트가 됐다.

   The K-pop _____

   _____

2. 그들의 음반사인 YG 엔터테인먼트는 블랙핑크가 공식 유튜브 채널에서 4,400만 명의 구독자를 돌파했다고 월요일 밝혔다.

   Their _____

   _____

3. 이 그룹은 지난 6월 24일 'How You Like That'을 발매한 이후 에미넴과 아리아나 그란데를 제치고 하루에 10만 명의 구독자가 늘고 있다.

   Since _____

   _____

4. 세계에서 가장 많은 구독자를 계속 보유하고 있는 팝스타 에드 시런, DJ 마쉬멜로, 저스틴 비버의 뒤를 블랙핑크는 여전히 뒤쫓고 있다.

   Blackpink _____

   _____

ⓖ BRK 457/3
457/3
Today TH

영어 뉴스룸 37

English NewsRoom

BREAKING NEWS

Seoul 50 Plus Foundation donates 1,500 transparent masks to help students with hearing difficulties. Masks have become a daily necessity, but for those with hearing difficulties, it can be hard to understand people when they talk with a mask on. The Seoul 50 Plus Foundation, an organization run by the city, has made 15-hundred 'transparent masks' that allow others to see your mouth. They were made by a hundred volunteers at home using kits provided...

청각장애인을 위한 마스크가 있다?

서울시가 청각장애학생들의 소통을 위해 입모양이 보이는 '투명 마스크'를 제작하여 일선 교육현장에 기부하였다는 내용입니다.

 NEWS 전체 스크립트

Seoul 50 Plus Foundation donates 1,500 transparent masks to help students with hearing difficulties

Masks have become a daily necessity, but for those with hearing difficulties, it can be hard to understand people when they talk with a mask on.

The Seoul 50 Plus Foundation, an organization run by the city, has made 15-hundred 'transparent masks' that allow others to see your mouth.

They were made by a hundred volunteers at home using kits provided by the foundation.

The foundation will donate 150 of the masks to the Seoul National School for the Deaf and the rest to 44 universities sponsoring students with hearing disabilities.

Seoul 50 Plus Foundation donates 1,500 transparent masks to help students with hearing difficulties

서울시50플러스재단은 청각장애 학생들을 돕기 위해 투명마스크 1,500개를 기증한다

☆transparent 1. *(사물이)* 투명한 | 2. 명백한, 분명한 =obvious

> e.g. Our country is popular for its beautiful transparent blue water.
>
> 우리나라는 아름답고 투명한 푸른 바다로 유명하다.
>
> Doctors should make the instructions more transparent.
>
> 의사들은 지시사항을 좀 더 명확하게 만들어야 한다.

Masks have become a daily necessity, but for those with hearing difficulties, it can be hard to understand people when they talk with a mask on.

마스크는 생활필수품이 됐지만 청각 장애가 있는 사람들에게는 마스크를 쓴 채 대화할 때 사람을 이해하기 어려울 수 있다.

☆necessity 필요*(성)*, 필수품, 불가피한 일

☆daily necessity 생활필수품

> e.g. Mobiles have become our daily necessity of life.
>
> 핸드폰은 우리의 삶에서 생활필수품이 되었다.

☆people with hearing difficulties (= people with hearing loss = people with hearing impairment)

청각장애가 있는 사람들 (the deaf는 무례한 표현이므로 자제)

☆people with visual difficulties (= visually impaired people = people with vision impairment)

시각장애가 있는 사람들 (the blind는 무례한 표현이므로 자제)

☆impairment *(신체적·정신적)* 장애

The Seoul 50 Plus Foundation, an organization run by the city, has made 15-hundred 'transparent masks' that allow others to see your mouth.

시에 의해 운영되는 단체인 서울시50플러스재단은 다른 사람들이 여러분의 입을 보는 것을 허락하는 1,500개의 '투명마스크'를 만들었다.

☆be run by ~에 의해 운영되다 (an organization 뒤에 which is가 생략됨)

☆allow A to B A가 B하는 것을 허락하다

They were made by a hundred volunteers at home using kits provided by the foundation.

그 마스크들은 재단으로부터 제공된 키트를 이용해 집에서 100여 명의 자원봉사자들에 의해 만들어졌다.

☆be provided by ~에 의해 제공되다 (kits뒤에 which are가 생략됨)

The foundation will donate 150 of the masks to the Seoul National School for the Deaf and the rest to 44 universities sponsoring students with hearing disabilities.

재단은 이 마스크 중 150개를 서울국립농학교에 기부하고 나머지는 청각장애 학생들을 후원하는 44개 대학에 기부할 예정이다.

☆the rest 나머지

e.g. You should carry these two heavy luggage, and I'll bring the rest.
너는 이 무거운 짐 두 개를 날라야 하고, 나머지는 내가 가져갈게. 참고로 luggage는 셀 수 없는 명사. 따라서 절대 s를 붙이면 안됨

Writing Exercise

1. 마스크는 생활필수품이 됐지만 청각 장애가 있는 사람들에게는 마스크를 쓴 채 대화할 때 사람을 이해하기 어려울 수 있다.

Masks

2. 시에 의해 운영되는 단체인 서울시50플러스재단은 다른 사람들이 여러분의 입을 보는 것을 허락하는 1,500개의 '투명 마스크'를 만들었다.

The Seoul

3. 그 마스크들은 재단으로부터 제공된 키트를 이용해 집에서 100여명의 자원봉사자들에 의해 만들어졌다.

They

4. 재단은 이 마스크 중 150개를 서울국립농학교에 기부하고 나머지는 청각장애 학생들을 후원하는 44개 대학에 기부할 예정이다.

The foundation

Have Fun with the English News Room

BRK 457/3
Today TH

BRK 457/3
457/3
Today TH

영어 뉴스룸 38

English NewsRoom

BREAKING NEWS

BTS's 'Dynamite' music video shatters record for most views in first 24 hours on YouTube. K-pop sensation BTS has shattered the all-time record for most views on YouTube within 24 hours of a new release with their digital single, 'Dynamite'. Released 12 AM Friday, U.S. eastern standard time, its music video currently has over 120-million views on the online platform and is rapidly approaching 150-million. The boy band's first entirely English song also broke...

BTS 첫 영어신곡 유튜브 최다시청 갱신

BTS의 첫 영어 신곡이 유튜브 최초 공개 후 24시간만에 최다 시청을 기록했다는 내용입니다.

NEWS 전체 스크립트

BTS's 'Dynamite' music video shatters record for most views in first 24 hours on YouTube

K-pop sensation BTS has shattered the all-time record for most views on YouTube within 24 hours of a new release with their digital single, 'Dynamite'.

Released 12 AM Friday, U.S. eastern standard time, its music video currently has over 120-million views on the online platform and is rapidly approaching 150-million.

The boy band's first entirely English song also broke the record for most views in a YouTube premiere.

On top of that, 'Dynamite' has reached number one on regional iTunes charts in more than a hundred countries and territories worldwide.

BTS will be performing 'Dynamite' live for the first time at the 2020 MTV Video Music Awards in New York City, August 30th.

NEWS 스크립트 분석

BTS's 'Dynamite' music video shatters record for most views in first 24 hours on YouTube

방탄소년단의 '다이너마이트' 뮤직비디오가 유튜브에서 첫 (공개이후) 24시간 동안 가장 많이 본 영상 기록을 깨다

☆shatter a record 기록을 깨다 (직역하면 '기록을 산산조각 내다'라는 뜻으로, '큰 차이로 기록을 깨다'는 뜻이다.)

☆shatter 산산이 부서지다, 산산조각 내다

☆record 기록 ['rek.ɔːd], 기록하다 [rɪˈkoːd]
        명사   동사
   명사, 동사 발음 다름 주의!

> e.g. She decided to shatter a record she set last year.
>   그녀는 작년에 세운 기록을 깨기로 결심했다.

K-pop sensation BTS has shattered the all-time record for most views on YouTube within 24 hours of a new release with their digital single, 'Dynamite'.

케이팝 돌풍을 일으키고 있는 방탄소년단이 디지털 싱글 '다이나미트'가 새로 발매된 지 24시간 만에 유튜브 최다 조회수로 사상 최고 기록을 깼다.

☆all-time 시대를 초월한, 사상 (최고[최저]의)

> e.g. The team reached an all-time record score this Summer.
>   그 팀은 이번 여름 사상 최고 기록을 세웠다.

Released 12 AM Friday, U.S. eastern standard time, its music video currently has over 120-million views on the online platform and is rapidly approaching 150-million.

미 동부 표준시간으로 금요일 오전 12시에 발매된 이 뮤직 비디오는 현재 온라인 플랫폼에서 1억 2천만 회 이상의 조회수를 기록하고 있으며 빠르게 1억 5천만 회에 다가가고 있다.

The boy band's first entirely English song also broke the record for most views in a YouTube premiere.

이 보이 밴드의 첫 번째 전체 영어가사로 만든 곡은 또한 유튜브 첫 상영에서 최다 조회 수 기록을 깼다.

☆entirely 완전히

☆break the record 기록을 깨다

> e.g. I had tried so hard to break the record, but eventually failed.
>   나는 기록을 깨기 위해 열심히 노력했지만 결국 실패했어.

☆premiere *(영화의)* 개봉, 첫 상영 | 🔊 ['prem.i.ər]. 🇺🇸 [prɪˈmɪr]
영국, 미국 발음 다름 주의!

> e.g. **The movie I wanted to watch will have its premiere next month.**
> 내가 보고 싶었던 영화는 다음 달에 개봉해.

On top of that, 'Dynamite' has reached number one on regional iTunes charts in more than a hundred countries and territories worldwide.

뿐만 아니라 '다이나마이트'는 전 세계 100여 개 이상의 국가와 지역에서 지역 아이튠즈 차트 1위에 올랐다.

> ☆**on top of that** ~뿐 아니라[~외에] =furthermore, in addition to

---

BTS will be performing 'Dynamite' live for the first time at the 2020 MTV Video Music Awards in New York City, August 30th.

방탄소년단이 오는 8월 30일 미국 뉴욕에서 열리는 2020 MTV 비디오 뮤직 어워드에서 처음으로 '다이나마이트' 라이브 무대를 선보일 것이다.

Writing Exercise

1. 케이팝 돌풍을 일으키고 있는 방탄소년단이 디지털 싱글 '다이나마이트'가 새로 발매된 지 24시간 만에 유튜브 최다 조회수로 사상 최고 기록을 깼다.

   K - pop
   _____

   _____

2. 미 동부 표준시간으로 금요일 오전 12시에 발매된 이 뮤직 비디오는 현재 온라인 플랫폼에서 1억 2천만 회 이상의 조회수를 기록하고 있으며 빠르게 1억 5천만 회에 다가가고 있다.

   Released
   _____

   _____

3. 이 보이 밴드의 첫 번째 전체 영어가사로 만든 곡은 또한 유튜브 첫 상영에서 최다 조회 수 기록을 깼다.

   The boy
   _____

   _____

4. 뿐만 아니라 '다이나마이트'는 전 세계 100여 개 이상의 국가와 지역에서 지역 아이튠즈 차트 1위에 올랐다.

   On top
   _____

   _____

5. 방탄소년단이 오는 8월 30일 미국 뉴욕에서 열리는 2020 MTV 비디오 뮤직 어워드에서 처음으로 '다이나마이트' 라이브 무대를 선보일 것이다.

   BTS will
   _____

   _____

영어 뉴스룸 **39**

**English
NewsRoom**

**BREAKING
NEWS**

Seoul city reviewing whether to raise public transport fares by 20 to 30 U.S. cents. Public transportation in Seoul is likely to get a little more expensive next year. The city government and city council are discussing a hike in the basic bus and subway fares of 200 to 300 won that's around twenty to thirty U.S. cents. They're also looking at raising the surcharge for longer distances from the current ten cents per five kilometers to 20.

지하철 요금 인상을 고려한다고?

서울시가 지하철과 버스 요금 인상을 추진한다는 내용입니다.

 **NEWS 전체 스크립트**

Seoul city reviewing whether to raise public transport fares by 20 to 30 U.S. cents

Public transportation in Seoul is likely to get a little more expensive next year.

The city government and city council are discussing a hike in the basic bus and subway fares of 200 to 300 won that's around twenty to thirty U.S. cents.

They're also looking at raising the surcharge for longer distances from the current ten cents per five kilometers to 20.

The proposal would raise fares in the first quarter of 2021.

The Seoul subway system has been losing money due to policies such as free rides for senior citizens, and the pandemic has only made the system's financial problems worse.

The last hike in fares was in 2015.

 스크립트 분석

Seoul city reviewing whether to raise public transport fares by 20 to 30 U.S. cents
대중교통 요금 20~30센트 인상할지 검토 중인 서울시

☆review 1. 논평 | 2. (특히 필요한 경우 변화를 주기 위해) 검토하다

☆whether ~인지, ~할지

> e.g. He was unsure whether he would be able to confess his feelings.
> 그는 자신의 감정을 고백할 수 있을지 확신하지 못했다.

· whether ~or 와 많이 쓰임

> e.g. Whether he knows it or not, we need to pass the law.
> 그가 그것을 알든 모르든, 우리는 그 법을 통과시켜야 한다.

☆transport 1. 수송, 차량, 이동 (방법) ['træn.spoːt] | 2. 수송하다 [træn'spoːt]
명사, 동사 강세 다름 주의!!

☆fare (교통) 요금

Public transportation in Seoul is likely to get a little more expensive next year.
서울의 대중교통 요금이 내년에 조금 더 비싸질 것 같다.

☆be likely to ~할 것 같다 be more likely to 더욱~할 것 같다

> e.g. He is more likely to be able to accomplish that task than anybody.
> 그는 누구보다도 그 임무를 더욱 완수할 수 있을 것 같다.

The city government and city council are discussing a hike in the basic bus and subway fares of 200 to 300 won that's around twenty to thirty U.S. cents.
시와 시의회는 기본 버스와 지하철 요금을 20-30 센트 정도인 200-300원을 인상하는 방안을 논의하고 있다.

☆hike 1. 도보 여행, (가격의) 대폭 인상 | 2. 도보 여행을 가다, 대폭 인상하다

> e.g. Many pundits are predicting a hike in interest rates.
> 많은 전문가들이 금리 인상을 예측하고 있다.

They're also looking at raising the surcharge for longer distances from the current ten cents per five kilometers to 20.

그들은 또한 현재 5킬로미터당 10센트에서 20센트로 더 먼 거리에 대한 추가요금을 올리는 것을 고려하고 있다.

☆look at ~을 보다, 살피다, 고려하다

> e.g. Officials are looking at building a new pedestrian bridge.
> 공무원들은 새로운 보행자 다리를 건설하는 것을 고려하고 있다.

☆surcharge 추가 요금

The proposal would raise fares in the first quarter of 2021.

그 제안은 2021년 1분기에 요금을 인상할 것이다.

☆the first quarter 1분기 (1년을 3개월씩 4단계로 나눠서 가장 첫 분기-1월~3월)
· 2분기-second quarter, 3분기-third quarter, 4분기-fourth quarter

The Seoul subway system has been losing money due to policies such as free rides for senior citizens, and the pandemic has only made the system's financial problems worse.

서울 지하철은 노인 무임승차 등의 정책으로 인해 손해를 보고 있으며, 코로나19 대유행이 서울 지하철의 재정 문제를 더욱 악화시켰을 뿐이다.

☆free ride 무임승차 (실제 무임승차라는 뜻도 있지만 노력하지 않고 하다라는 뜻의 무임승차의 의미도 있음)

> e.g. I think she got a free ride because she is the President's only daughter.
> 그녀가 대통령의 외동딸이기 때문에 무임승차한 것 같다.

The last hike in fares was in 2015.

마지막 요금 인상은 2015년이었다.

Writing Exercise

1. 서울의 대중교통 요금이 내년에 조금 더 비싸질 것 같다.

   Public _____

   _____

2. 시와 시의회는 기본 버스와 지하철 요금을 20 - 30센트 정도인 200 - 300원을 인상하는 방안을 논의하고 있다.

   The city _____

   _____

3. 그들은 또한 현재 5킬로미터당 10센트에서 20센트로 더 먼 거리에 대한 추가요금을 올리는 것을 고려하고 있다.

   They're _____

   _____

4. 그 제안은 2021년1분기에 요금을 인상할 것이다.

   The proposal _____

   _____

5. 서울 지하철은 노인 무임승차 등의 정책으로 인해 손해를 보고 있으며, 코로나19 대유행이 서울 지하철의 재정 문제를 더욱 악화시켰을 뿐이다.

   The Seoul _____

   _____

6. 마지막 요금 인상은 2015년이었다.

   The last _____

   _____

ⓒ BRK 457/3
457/3
Today TH

영어 뉴스룸 40

**English
NewsRoom**

**BREAKING
NEWS**

Seoul releases detailed guidelines for mandatory mask-wearing. Seoul Metropolitan Government has released detailed guidelines on how its mask-wearing policy will be carried out. Wearing masks in public has been mandatory since last Monday, except for when eating or drinking. The detailed guidelines say people don't need to wear a mask when driving their cars alone or with family members.

이제 마스크를 안 쓰면 과태료를 부과한다고?

서울시가 마련한 마스크 착용 의무화 세부지침에 대한 내용입니다.

 NEWS 전체 스크립트

Seoul releases detailed guidelines for mandatory mask-wearing

Seoul Metropolitan Government has released detailed guidelines on how its mask-wearing policy will be carried out.

Wearing masks in public has been mandatory since last Monday, except for when eating or drinking.

The detailed guidelines say people don't need to wear a mask when driving their cars alone or with family members.

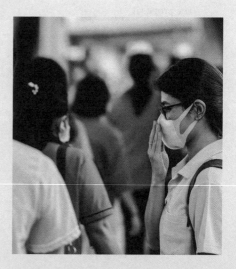

Infants younger than 24 months and people with respiratory diseases are also exempt from the measures, as are people who can't work while wearing a mask, such as musicians and athletes.

Masks must be appropriately sized and cover mouths and noses.

Violators of the policy will be fined from October 13th once the grace period ends.

NEWS 스크립트 분석

Seoul releases detailed guidelines for mandatory mask-wearing
서울시가 마스크 착용 의무화에 대한 세부 지침을 발표하다

☆detailed 상세한

☆mandatory 법에 정해진, 의무적인

☆mandatory military service 의무 군복무

> e.g. The K-pop star has been discharged from mandatory military service last Saturday.
> 그 케이팝 스타는 지난 토요일에 군에서 제대했다.

Seoul Metropolitan Government has released detailed guidelines on how its mask-wearing policy will be carried out.
서울시가 마스크 착용 정책 추진방안에 대한 세부 지침을 내놨다.

☆carry out 수행하다

> e.g. An investigation is being carried out by Sherlock Holmes.
> 셜록 홈즈가 조사를 하고 있다.

Wearing masks in public has been mandatory since last Monday, except for when eating or drinking.
식사나 음주를 할 때를 제외하고는 공공장소에서 마스크를 착용하는 것은 지난 월요일부터 의무적으로 시행되어 왔다.

☆except for ~이 없으면, ~을 제외하고는 | (but for) except for (+구) / except (+절) (주어 동사)

> e.g. I like all fruit except for oriental melons.
> 난 참외 빼고 모든 과일을 좋아해.
> In fact they are very alike, except Sally is slightly taller than Silly.
> 샐리는 실리보다 살짝 크다는 거 빼고는 사실 그들은 닮았다.

The detailed guidelines say people don't need to wear a mask when driving their cars alone or with family members.
이 세부 지침은 사람들이 혼자 또는 가족과 함께 차를 운전할 때 마스크를 착용할 필요가 없다고 말한다.

Infants younger than 24 months and people with respiratory diseases are also exempt from the measures, as are people who can't work while wearing a mask, such as musicians and athletes.

24개월 미만 영유아나 호흡기 질환자도 이번 조치로부터 면제된다. 음악가나 운동선수 등 마스크를 착용한 채 일을 할 수 없는 사람도 마찬가지다.

☆Infant 유아, 아기, 젖먹이

☆exempt from ~을 면제받다

> e.g. He is exempt from paying the tax because of his health.
> 그는 건강 때문에 세금을 면제 받았다.

☆respiratory 호흡의, 호흡 기관의 | 🔊 [rɪˈspɪr.ə.tər.i], 🔊 [ˈres.pə.rə.tɔːr.i]
영국, 미국 발음 다름 주의!

> e.g. If you have respiratory problems, you need to wear a mask when out in public.
> 만약 당신이 호흡기 문제가 있으면, 공공장소에서는 마스크를 써야 합니다.

Masks must be appropriately sized and cover mouths and noses.

마스크는 적절한 크기여야하고 입과 코를 덮어야 한다.

Violators of the policy will be fined from October 13th once the grace period ends.

정책 위반자는 유예기간이 종료되는 10월 13일부터 과태료를 물게 된다.

☆violator 위반자, 방해자

☆fine 1. ^{명사} 벌금, 과태료 | 2. ^{동사} [흔히 수동태로]벌금, 과태료 등을 물리다

☆grace period 유예 기간

> e.g. Because of the grace period, my credit card company will not charge late fees for non - payment.
> 유예 기간 때문에, 내 카드사는 미납료에 대한 연체료를 받지 않을 것이다.

Writing Exercise

1. 서울시가 마스크 착용 정책 추진방안에 대한 세부 지침을 내놨다.

   Seoul

2. 식사나 음주를 할 때를 제외하고는 공공장소에서 마스크를 착용하는 것은 지난 월요일부터 의무적으로 시행되어 왔다.

   Wearing

3. 이 세부 지침은 사람들이 혼자 또는 가족과 함께 차를 운전할 때 마스크를 착용할 필요가 없다고 말한다.

   The detailed

4. 24개월 미만 영유아나 호흡기 질환자도 이번 조치로 부터 면제된다. 음악가나 운동선수 등 마스크를 착용한 채 일을 할 수 없는 사람도 마찬가지다.

   Infants

5. 마스크는 적절한 크기여야하고 입과 코를 덮어야 한다.

   Masks

6. 정책 위반자는 유예기간이 종료되는 10월 13일부터 과태료를 물게 된다.

   Violators

◎ BRK 457/3
457/3
Today TH

영어 뉴스룸 *41*

English NewsRoom

BREAKING NEWS

Chinese fans celebrate BTS member Jungkook's birthday with KTX advertisement, fireworks. Celebrating the 24th birthday of BTS member, Jungkook, Chinese fans wrapped the outside of a nearly 4-hundred-meter-long KTX train with images of the singer. This is the first time in 16 years such a commercial advertisement has covered the exterior of a KTX train. Chinese fans also held an online fireworks event in Busan, which is the city where the singer...

BTS 멤버의 역대급 생일잔치(feat. KTX 전면광고)

KTX 전면광고 등 빌보드 1위 아이돌의 역대급 생일잔치에 대한 내용입니다.

 전체 스크립트

Chinese fans celebrate BTS member Jungkook's birthday with KTX advertisement, fireworks

Celebrating the 24th birthday of BTS member, Jungkook, Chinese fans wrapped the outside of a nearly 4-hundred-meter-long KTX train with images of the singer.

This is the first time in 16 years such a commercial advertisement has covered the exterior of a KTX train.

Chinese fans also held an online fireworks event in Busan, which is the city where the singer grew up.

The birthday event was streamed online for around ten minutes, with fans explaining that it was aimed to provide comfort to the BTS fan base across the world during the pandemic.

NEWS 스크립트 분석

Chinese fans celebrate BTS member Jungkook's birthday with KTX advertisement, fireworks

중국 팬들은 KTX 광고와, 불꽃놀이로 방탄소년단 멤버 정국의 생일을 축하한다

☆advertisement 광고 | 🔵 [ədˈvɜː.tɪs.mənt], 🔴 [æd.vɜˈ.ˈtaɪz.mənt]

영국, 미국 발음 다름 주의!

> e.g. I'm going to shoot an advertisement this Saturday with my dog.
> 이번 주 토요일에 내 강아지와 광고를 찍을 거야.

Celebrating the 24th birthday of BTS member, Jungkook, Chinese fans wrapped the outside of a nearly 4-hundred-meter-long KTX train with images of the singer.

방탄소년단 멤버 정국의 24번째 생일을 기념하여, 중국 팬들은 400m에 가까운 길이의 KTX 열차 바깥쪽을 가수의 사진들로 감쌌다.

☆celebrate 기념하다, 축하하다

☆wrap 싸다, 포장하다

> e.g. Please wrap the inside of the box instead of the outside.
> 박스의 바깥쪽 말고 안쪽을 포장해 주세요.

☆image 이미지 *(인상)*, 사진

> e.g. Now fans can see the images of their favourite musicians in front of the building.
> 이제 팬들은 건물 앞에서 그들이 가장 좋아하는 뮤지션들의 사진을 볼 수 있다.

This is the first time in 16 years such a commercial advertisement has covered the exterior of a KTX train.

이 같은 광고가 KTX 열차 외관을 뒤덮은 것은 16년 만이다.

☆exterior 외부 [ɪkˈstɪə.ri.ər] ↔ interior 내부 [ɪnˈtɪə.ri.ər]

> e.g. I would like to paint the exterior walls of the house.
> 나는 집의 외벽을 페인트칠하고 싶어.

Chinese fans also held an online fireworks event in Busan, which is the city where the singer grew up.

중국 팬들은 가수가 자란 도시인 부산에서 온라인 불꽃놀이 행사도 열었다.

☆hold an event 행사를 열다

> e.g. The organization was supposed to hold an event in Seoul this Summer but cancelled it due to the virus.
> 그 단체는 올 여름 서울에서 행사를 열기로 되어 있었으나 바이러스 때문에 취소했다.

☆grow up 성장하다 → 관련 단어 grown-up

e.g. When you grow up, you might have to work with AIs.
네가 크면 인공지능과 함께 일해야 할지도 몰라.

☆grow-up 1. 다 큰, 어른이 된 | 2. 어른
　　　　　形容詞　　　　　　　名詞

e.g. He is a grown-up man who should shoulder the responsibility of taking care of the family.
그는 가족을 돌봐야 할 책임을 짊어져야 할 어른이다.

☆shoulder the responsibility 책임지다 =take the responsibility

The birthday event was streamed online for around ten minutes, with fans explaining that it was aimed to provide comfort to the BTS fan base across the world during the pandemic.

코로나19 대유행 가운데 세계 방탄소년단 팬층을 위로하기 위한 것이었다는 팬들의 설명과 함께 생일 행사는 10여 분간 온라인에 스트리밍됐다.

☆comfort 1. 안락, 위로 | 2. 위로하다
　　　　　名詞　　　　　　動詞

e.g. How to provide comfort to your partner who doesn't live with you?
당신과 함께 살지 않는 당신의 파트너에게 어떻게 위로할까요?

Writing Exercise

1. 방탄소년단 멤버 정국의 24번째 생일을 기념하여, 중국 팬들은 400m에 가까운 길이의 KTX 열차 바깥쪽을 가수의 사진들로 감쌌다.

Celebrating

2. 이 같은 광고가 KTX 열차 외관을 뒤덮은 것은 16년 만이다.

This is

3. 중국 팬들은 가수가 자란 도시인 부산에서 온라인 불꽃놀이 행사도 열었다.

Chinese

4. 코로나19 대유행 가운데 세계 방탄소년단 팬층을 위로하기 위한 것이었다는 팬들의 설명과 함께 생일 행사는 10여 분간 온라인에 스트리밍됐다.

The birthday

오디오클립
◀ 바로가기

⊚ BRK 457/3
457/3
Today TH

영어 뉴스룸 42

English
NewsRoom

BREAKING NEWS

Driver saved from collapsing bridge thanks to local hero. A man frantically shouts and waves his hands signaling to a car on the other side of a bridge to back up. And as if he had foreseen what was about to come, the bridge collapses and the river below swallows a large section. CCTV footage captures the scene of a man about to save a driver's life just seconds before Typhoon Maysak demolishes a bridge in the city of Pyeongchang, Gangwon-do...

참사를 막은 시민영웅

폭우에 의한 다리 붕괴 직전 참사를 막은 시민 영웅에 대한 내용입니다.

NEWS  전체 스크립트

Driver saved from collapsing bridge thanks to local hero

A man frantically shouts and waves his hands signaling to a car on the other side of a bridge to back up.

And as if he had foreseen what was about to come, the bridge collapses and the river below swallows a large section.

CCTV footage captures the scene of a man about to save a driver's life just seconds before Typhoon Maysak demolishes a bridge in the city of Pyeongchang, Gangwon-do Province on Tuesday.

The country is no longer under the direct influence of Maysak.

But another storm, Typhoon Haishen, is forecast to touch down on the Korean peninsula in a few days, raising concerns that more damage is on the way.

Driver saved from collapsing bridge thanks to local hero
지역 영웅 덕분에 붕괴되는 다리로부터 운전자가 구조됨

☆collapse 붕괴되다, 무너지다

Just moments before disaster
큰 사고가 나기 직전

A man frantically shouts and waves his hands signaling to a car on the other side of a bridge to back up.
한 남자가 미친듯이 소리지르고 다리 반대편에 있는 차에게 후진하라고 사인을 보내며 손을 흔든다.

☆frantically 미친 듯이, 극도로 흥분하여

e.g. He has been working frantically this couple of weeks to take a few days off.
그는 며칠 쉬기 위해 몇 주 동안 미친 듯이 일을 했다.

☆signal 신호, 신호를 보내다
☆back up (차를) 후진시키다

e.g. Please back up your car as it is blocking the driveway.
차가 진입로를 막고 있으니 후진해 주세요.

And as if he had foreseen what was about to come, the bridge collapses and the river below swallows a large section.
그리고 마치 그가 곧 다가올 일을 예견했었던 것처럼 다리가 무너지고 아래 강물이(다리) 큰 부분을 삼켜 버린다.

☆as if 마치 ~인 것처럼
☆foresee 예견하다

e.g. He can foresee the future and see the past.
그는 미래를 예견하고 과거를 볼 수 있다.

☆swallow 삼키다

CCTV footage captures the scene of a man about to save a driver's life just seconds before Typhoon Maysak demolishes a bridge in the city of Pyeongchang, Gangwon-do Province on Tuesday.

화요일 태풍 메이삭이 강원도 평창의 다리를 무너트리기 불과 몇 초 전 운전자를 막 구하려고 하는 한 남성의 장면이 CCTV화면에 포착된다.

☆footage 화면

☆capture 포착하다

☆scene 장면

☆be about to 막~하려고 하다

☆just seconds before 바로 몇 초 전에

> e.g. These photos were taken just seconds before the disaster.
> 이 사진들은 참사 몇 초 전에 찍힌 것이다.

☆demolish *(건물을)* 철거하다, *(사고로 무엇을)* 무너뜨리다

> e.g. The city demolished the building at a cost of about 100 million won.
> 그 시는 약 1억 원을 들여 건물을 철거했다.

The country is no longer under the direct influence of Maysak.

한국은 더 이상 태풍 메이삭의 직접적인 영향을 받지 않는다.

☆the direct influence 직접적인 영향

☆under the influence of ~의 영향 아래

> e.g. The paintings were made under the influence of Korean traditional art.
> 그 그림들은 한국 전통 미술의 영향을 받아 만들어졌다.

But another storm, Typhoon Haishen, is forecast to touch down on the Korean peninsula in a few days, raising concerns that more damage is on the way.

그러나 피해가 더 늘어날 것이라는 우려가 나오고 있는 또 다른 태풍인 하이선이 며칠 안에 한반도에 상륙할 것으로 예상된다.

☆be forecast to ~할 것으로 예상되다

☆touch down 착륙하다

☆raising concerns 우려가 나오고 있는

☆on the way 진행되어, 도중에

1. 큰 사고가 나기 직전

Just
_____

_____

2. 한 남자가 미친듯이 소리지르고 다리 반대편에 있는 차에게 후진하라고 사인을 보내며 손을 흔든다.

A man
_____

_____

3. 그리고 마치 그가 곧 다가올 일을 예견 했었던 것처럼 다리가 무너지고 아래 강물이 (다리) 큰 부분을 삼켜 버린다.

And as
_____

_____

4. 화요일 태풍 메이삭이 강원도 평창의 다리를 무너트리기 불과 몇 초 전 운전자를 막 구하려고 하는 한 남성의 장면이 CCTV화면에 포착된다.

CCTV
_____

_____

5. 한국은 더 이상 태풍 메이삭의 직접적인 영향을 받지 않는다.

The country
_____

_____

6. 그러나 피해가 더 늘어날 것이라는 우려가 나오고 있는 또 다른 태풍인 하이선이 며칠 안에 한반도에 상륙할 것으로 예상된다.

But another
_____

_____

BRK 457/3
457/3
Today TH

영어 뉴스룸 43

English NewsRoom

BREAKING NEWS

Fewer train tickets were sold for this year's Chuseok holiday. Fewer people in South Korea are expected to visit their hometowns for this year's Chuseok holiday due to the resurgence of COVID-19. According to rail operator Korail on Tuesday, only 263-thousand train tickets were sold on the first day of sales, down 55-percent compared to last Chuseok. After the government urged people to stay at home over the holiday, many might be choosing to skip...

추석 철도 예매율 하락?

추석 철도 첫날 예매율이 작년의 55%에 그쳤다는 내용입니다.

 NEWS 전체 스크립트

Fewer train tickets were sold for this year's Chuseok holiday

Fewer people in South Korea are expected to visit their hometowns for this year's Chuseok holiday due to the resurgence of COVID-19.

According to rail operator Korail on Tuesday, only 263-thousand train tickets were sold on the first day of sales, down 55-percent compared to last Chuseok.

After the government urged people to stay at home over the holiday, many might be choosing to skip public transport and use their own vehicles.

From today, Chuseok train tickets for the Honam, Jeolla, Gangneung, Janghang Lines can be bought online.

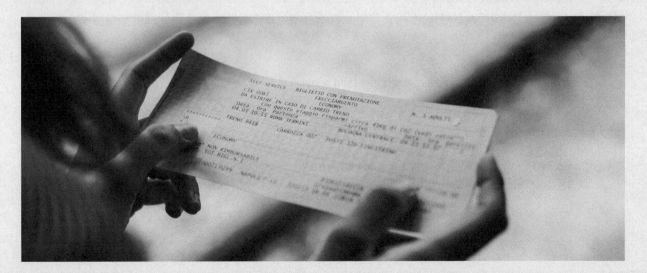

Fewer train tickets were sold for this year's Chuseok holiday

올해 추석에는 더 적은 기차표들이 팔렸다

☆fewer (+복수 명사) 더 적은

> e.g. It was reported that fewer students are going to college.
>
> 대학에 진학하는 학생들이 줄고 있는 것으로 알려졌다.

Fewer people in South Korea are expected to visit their hometowns for this year's Chuseok holiday due to the resurgence of COVID-19.

다시금 COVID-19가 기승을 부림으로 인해 올해 추석연휴는 더 적은 사람들이 고향에 방문할 것으로 예상된다.

☆be expected to 예상되다

> e.g. The talks between two leaders are expected to last two days.
>
> 두 정상간의 회담은 이틀간 계속될 것으로 예상된다.

☆resurgence 부활, 다시 유행, 기승을 부림

> e.g. There has been a resurgence of interest in child caring.
>
> 육아에 대한 관심이 다시 살아났다.

According to rail operator Korail on Tuesday, only 263-thousand train tickets were sold on the first day of sales, down 55-percent compared to last Chuseok.

화요일 철도운영사 코레일에 따르면, 판매 첫날 26만 3000장의 열차표만 팔렸고 지난 추석 대비 55% 감소했다.

☆rail 기차, 철도 _{명사} | 격분하다 _{동사}

> e.g. He railed against the government and expressed anger.
>
> 그는 정부에 대해 격분했고 분노를 표출했다.

☆compare to ~와 비교하다

> e.g. Compared to my small car, his car seemed like a truck.
>
> 내 작은 차에 비하면 그의 차는 마치 트럭처럼 보여.

After the government urged people to stay at home over the holiday, many might be choosing to skip public transport and use their own vehicles.

정부가 사람들에게 명절 동안 집에 머물 것을 촉구한 후, 많은 사람들이 대중교통을 건너뛰고 자가용 차량을 이용하는 것을 선택할 수도 있다.

☆urge A to B A에게 B하도록 권고하다, 촉구하다

e.g. We urge you to reconsider the action that you've taken.
우리는 당신이 취한 행동을 재고해 줄 것을 촉구한다.

☆skip 건너뛰다[생략하다] | 영 줄넘기 하다, 미 '줄넘기 하다'는 jump rope

e.g. He's been skipping classes for three weeks.
그는 3주째 수업을 빠지고 있다.

From today, Chuseok train tickets for the Honam, Jeolla, Gangneung, Janghang Lines can be bought online.

오늘부터 호남 · 전라 · 강릉 · 장항선 추석 열차표를 온라인으로 구입할 수 있다.

Writing Exercise

1. 다시금 COVID - 19가 기승을 부림으로 인해 올해 추석연휴는 더 적은 사람들이 고향에 방문할 것으로 예상된다.

   Fewer

2. 화요일 철도운영사 코레일에 따르면, 판매 첫날 26만3000장의 열차표만 팔렸고 지난 추석 대비 55% 감소했다.

   According to

3. 정부가 사람들에게 명절 동안 집에 머물 것을 촉구한 후, 많은 사람들이 대중교통을 건너뛰고 자가용 차량을 이용하는 것을 선택할 수도 있다.

   After

4. 오늘부터 호남·전라·강릉·장항선 추석 열차표를 온라인으로 구입할 수 있다.

   From

ⓖ BRK 457/3
457/3
Today TH

영어 뉴스룸 44   English NewsRoom

BREAKING NEWS BTS star RM donates US$ 85,000 to local arts scene via MMCA Foundation. On the occasion of his birthday, one of the members of BTS, the rapper RM, has made a big donation to support the contemporary arts. The National Museum of Modern and Contemporary Art said Monday that RM donated 100 million won -- about 85-thousand U.S. dollars -- to help promote a culture of reading about art and to help young people develop their own artistic...

방탄소년단 RM의 미술 업계를 위한 기부

미술을 통해 선한 영향력 전파하는 방탄소년단 RM에 대한 내용입니다.

 NEWS 전체 스크립트

BTS star RM donates US$ 85,000 to local arts scene via MMCA Foundation

On the occasion of his birthday, one of the members of BTS, the rapper RM, has made a big donation to support the contemporary arts.

The National Museum of Modern and Contemporary Art said Monday that RM donated 100 million won--about 85-thousand U.S. dollars--to help promote a culture of reading about art and to help young people develop their own artistic taste.

RM turned 26 over the weekend.

The money will go toward buying 4-thousand art books and distributing them to some 4-hundred public libraries, especially those in rural, mountainous areas where museums and galleries are few and far between.

BTS star RM donates US $85,000 to local arts scene via MMCA Foundation
방탄소년단 스타 RM이 MMCA재단을 통해 지역 예술계에 8만 5000달러를 기부한다(우리나라 돈 1억 원)

　☆scene 현장, 장면, ~계 (music scene 음악계)

> e.g. My father is still involved in the music scene in France.
> 　　저의 아버지는 여전히 프랑스에서 음악계에 종사하십니다.

> ☆via (특정한 사람·시스템 등을) 통하여

> e.g. The flight goes via London and Paris and the journey is more than 20 hours.
> 　　그 비행기는 런던과 파리를 경유하며 그 여정은 20시간 이상 걸린다.

On the occasion of his birthday, one of the members of BTS, the rapper RM, has made a big donation to support the contemporary arts.
그의 생일을 맞아 방탄소년단의 멤버 중 한 명인 래퍼 RM이 현대 예술을 지원하기 위해 거액을 기부했다.

　☆on the occasion of something ~에 즈음하여, (기념일 등) ~을 맞아, 중요한 일 시점에

> e.g. They donated 100,000 won for the poor on the occasion of their wedding anniversary.
> 　　그들은 결혼 기념일을 맞아 가난한 사람들을 위해 10만원을 기부했다.

　☆contemporary 동시대의, 현대의, 당대의 =modern

> e.g. Could you give me more ideas about contemporary fashion?
> 　　현대 패션에 대해 더 많은 아이디어를 주실 수 있나요?

The National Museum of Modern and Contemporary Art said Monday that RM donated 100 million won--about 85-thousand U.S. dollars--to help promote a culture of reading about art and to help young people develop their own artistic taste.
국립현대미술관은 RM이 예술에 대한 독서 문화를 촉진하고 젊은이들이 그들의 예술적 취향을 발전시키는 것을 돕기 위해 1억 원(약 8만 5000달러)을 기부했다고 월요일 밝혔다.

　☆promote 촉진하다, 홍보하다, 승진[진급]시키다

　☆taste 맛, 미각, 기호, 취향

> e.g. How would you describe your taste in music? =what is your music taste?
> 　　네 음악 취향은 어떻게 돼?

RM turned 26 over the weekend.

RM은 주말에 26살이 되었다.

☆turn *(어떤 나이, 시기가)* 되다

> e.g. **She turns 20 in July.** = she becomes 20 years old in July.
> 그녀는 7월에 20살이 된다.

The money will go toward buying 4-thousand art books and distributing them to some 4-hundred public libraries, especially those in rural, mountainous areas where museums and galleries are few and far between.

이 돈은 미술 서적 4천 권을 구입하여 약 4백 권의 공공 도서관, 특히 박물관과 미술관이 거의 없는 시골, 산간 지역에 있는 도서관들에 배포하는 데 쓰일 것이다.

☆go toward something 무언가를 돕기 위해 돈이 사용되다

> e.g. **The donation will go toward rebuilding the children's hospital.**
> 그 기부금은 어린이 병원을 재건하는 데 쓰일 것이다.

☆few and far between 드문드문한, 흔치 않은

> e.g. **Petrol stations are few and far between so we need to take a bus.** 영국에서는 주유소를 petrol station, 미국에서는 gas station
> 주유소가 거의 없어서 우리는 버스를 타야 해.

Writing Exercise

1. 그의 생일을 맞아 방탄소년단의 멤버 중 한 명인 래퍼 RM이 현대 예술을 지원하기 위해 거액을 기부했다.

   On the _____

   _____

2. 국립현대미술관은 RM이 예술에 대한 독서 문화를 촉진하고 젊은이들이 그들의 예술적 취향을 발전시키는 것을 돕기 위해 1억 원(약 8만5000달러)을 기부했다고 월요일 밝혔다.

   The National _____

   _____

3. RM은 주말에 26살이 되었다.

   RM _____

   _____

4. 이 돈은 미술 서적 4천 권을 구입하여 약 4백 권의 공공 도서관, 특히 박물관과 미술관이 거의 없는 시골, 산간 지역에 있는 도서관들에 배포하는 데 쓰일 것이다.

   The money _____

   _____

◎ BRK 457/3
457/3
Today TH

영어 뉴스룸 45

English NewsRoom

BREAKING NEWS

Delivery workers to refuse to sort parcels in protest against overwork. More than four-thousand delivery workers are going to refuse to sort packages ahead of the Chuseok holiday to protest what they say is an unfairly heavy workload. According to a civic group advocating on their behalf, they're going to stop sorting parcels from next Monday if companies don't add more workers to share the burden. The group argues that workers are paid...

택배기사들 분류작업 거부?

택배기사 4천 여명이 21일부터 분류작업을 거부한다는 내용입니다.

 전체 스크립트

Delivery workers to refuse to sort parcels in protest against overwork

More than four-thousand delivery workers are going to refuse to sort packages ahead of the Chuseok holiday to protest what they say is an unfairly heavy workload.

According to a civic group advocating on their behalf, they're going to stop sorting parcels from next Monday if companies don't add more workers to share the burden.

The group argues that workers are paid per delivery but the time-consuming job of sorting goes unpaid.

These are about one tenth of all the delivery workers in the country, so disruptions can be expected because demand is high not only due to Chuseok but also social distancing.

NEWS 스크립트 분석

Delivery workers to refuse to sort parcels in protest against overwork

택배기사들이 과로에 항의해 택배 분류 작업 거부

☆sort 분류하다, 구분하다 →sort out

e.g. She sorted out the cards.
그녀는 카드를 분류했다.

☆parcel 소포, (선물 등의) 꾸러미
☆overwork 과로
☆in protest against something ~에 항의하여

e.g. The party would be launching a hunger strike in protest against the government.
그 정당은 정부에 항의하여 단식 투쟁에 돌입할 것이다.

More than four-thousand delivery workers are going to refuse to sort packages ahead of the Chuseok holiday to protest what they say is an unfairly heavy workload.

4천명 이상의 택배기사들이 자신들이 말하는 불공평한 업무량에 항의하기 위해 추석 연휴를 앞두고 소포를 분류하는 것을 거절할 예정이다.

☆ahead of (공간·시간상으로) ~앞에, (시간적으로) ~보다 빨리 =earlier than planned or expected

e.g. He has always finished ahead of schedule.
그는 예정보다 항상 빨리 끝냈다.

☆what they say 그들이 말하길, 그들이 주장하길

e.g. This is what they say is the first track on the album.
이것은 그들이 말하길 그 앨범의 첫 번째 트랙이다.

☆unfairly 불공평하게

e.g. Former member of the group says he was treated unfairly.
그 그룹의 전 멤버는 그가 부당한 대우를 받았다고 말한다.

☆workload 업무량, 작업량

According to a civic group advocating on their behalf, they're going to stop sorting parcels from next Monday if companies don't add more workers to share the burden.

택배기사들을 지지하는 시민단체에 따르면 기업들이 부담을 분담하기 위한 인력 충원을 하지 않으면 다음 주 월요일부터 소포 분류를 중단한다고 한다.

☆civic group 시민단체

☆advocate *(공개적으로)* 지지하다, 옹호하다

☆on someone's behalf of ~를 대신하여, ~를 대표하여

> e.g. The actor accepted the award on behalf of the program team.
> 그 배우는 프로그램 팀을 대표하여 상을 받았다.

☆add 추가하다, 충원하다

☆share the burden 무거운 짐을 나누어 지다, 부담을 분담하다

> e.g. He wants to share the burden of domestic work.
> 그는 가사 노동을 분담하고 싶어한다.

☆domestic work 가사업무

- - -

The group argues that workers are paid per delivery but the time-consuming job of sorting goes unpaid.

이 단체는 근로자들은 배달 건수에 따라 급여를 받지만 시간이 많이 걸리는 분류작업은 무급이라고 주장한다.

☆paid per delivery 배달 건수에 따라 지급받다

☆paid per hour 시간당으로 지급받다

> e.g. They are paid per hour.
> 그들은 시간당 임금을 받는다.

☆time-consuming *(많은)* 시간이 걸리는, 시간 소모가 큰

> e.g. Writing a book is a very time-consuming job.
> 책을 쓰는 것은 시간이 많이 걸리는 일이다.

- - -

These are about one tenth of all the delivery workers in the country, so disruptions can be expected because demand is high not only due to Chuseok but also social distancing.

(분류작업 거부에 나서는 택배 노동자는) 전국 택배 노동자의 10분의 1 수준이어서 추석뿐 아니라 사회적 거리 두기에 따른 수요도 많아 차질을 예상할 수 있다.

☆disruption 지장, 방해, 붕괴

Writing Exercise

1. 4천명 이상의 택배기사들이 자신들이 말하는 불공평한 업무량에 항의하기 위해 추석 연휴를 앞두고 소포를 분류하는 것을 거절할 예정이다.

   More
   _____
   _____

2. 택배기사들을 지지하는 시민단체에 따르면 기업들이 부담을 분담하기 위한 인력 충원을 하지 않으면 다음 주 월요일부터 소포 분류를 중단한다고 한다.

   According to
   _____
   _____

3. 이 단체는 근로자들은 배달 건수에 따라 급여를 받지만 시간이 많이 걸리는 분류작업은 무급이라고 주장한다.

   The group
   _____
   _____

4. (분류작업 거부에 나서는 택배 노동자는)전국 택배 노동자의 10분의 1 수준이어서 추석뿐 아니라 사회적 거리 두기에 따른 수요도 많아 차질을 예상할 수 있다.

   These
   _____
   _____

ⓒ BRK 457/3
457/3
Today TH

영어 뉴스룸 46

English NewsRoom

BREAKING NEWS

Up to 45% discount on face masks at train stations ahead of Chuseok holiday in Korea. Train stations will start selling face masks at discounted prices - - slashing up to 45 percent - - before the Chuseok holiday in Korea, when many people travel back to their hometowns to spend the thanksgiving period with their families. The finance ministry said Sunday that the masks will go on sale from the last week of September at 282 convenience stores in...

추석맞이 마스크 반값 할인

추석을 맞아 기차역에서 마스크를 최대 45%할인해서 판매한다는 내용입니다.

 전체 스크립트

Up to 45% discount on face masks at train stations ahead of Chuseok holiday in Korea

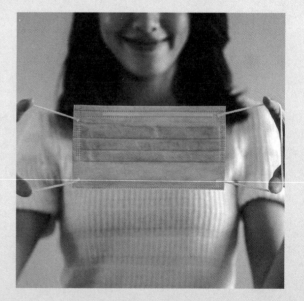

Train stations will start selling face masks at discounted prices - - slashing up to 45 percent - - before the Chuseok holiday in Korea, when many people travel back to their hometowns to spend the thanksgiving period with their families.

The finance ministry said Sunday that the masks will go on sale from the last week of September at 282 convenience stores in train stations nationwide.

Also, to boost small shop owners and businesses amid the COVID-19 pandemic, the government is encouraging the use of Onnuri gift certificates as corporate gifts for employees to mark the Chuseok holiday.

From Monday, prices will be reduced by 10 percent for both online and offline purchases of the gift certificates.

NEWS 스크립트 분석

Up to 45% discount on face masks at train stations ahead of Chuseok holiday in Korea
한국의 추석 연휴 앞두고 기차역에서 마스크 최대 45% 할인

☆up to ~까지 *(특정한 수·정도·위치·시점)*

e.g. Only up to 50 people are allowed to assemble at one place.
50명까지만 한 곳에 모일 수 있다.

· *(예외)* be up to ~에게 달려 있는

e.g. It's up to you.
그것은 너에게 달려있어.

☆discount 1. 할인 ['dɪs.kaʊnt] ^{명사} | 2. 할인하다 [dɪ'skaʊnt] ^{동사}

☆ahead of *(공간·시간상으로)* ~앞에, *(시간적으로)* ~보다 빨리

e.g. She walked on ahead of her mother-in-law.
그녀는 시어머니보다 앞서 걸었다.
Ahead of the meeting, the president said : "I'll resign if you continue to disregard everything I say."
회의에 앞서 회장님은 이렇게 말했다. "당신이 계속 내 말을 무시한다면 사직하겠소."

Train stations will start selling face masks at discounted prices--slashing up to 45 percent--before the Chuseok holiday in Korea, when many people travel back to their hometowns to spend the thanksgiving period with their families.
많은 사람들이 추석연휴기간을 가족들과 보내기 위해 고향으로 돌아가는 추석 연휴를 앞두고 기차역에서는 45퍼센트까지 대폭 할인된 가격으로 마스크 판매를 시작할 것이다.

☆discounted price 할인된 가격

☆slash 대폭 줄이다, 대폭 낮추다

e.g. Prices have been slashed by 30 percent.
가격이 30퍼센트 폭락했다.

The finance ministry said Sunday that the masks will go on sale from the last week of September at 282 convenience stores in train stations nationwide.
기획재정부는 9월 마지막 주부터 전국 282개 기차역의 편의점에서 마스크가 할인되어서 판매될 것이라고 일요일에 말했다.

☆on sale 할인 중인

e.g. Everything in the shop is on sale.
가게의 모든 것이 할인 중이다.

· (비교) for sale 판매 중인

e.g. I'm sorry but these are not for sale.
죄송하지만 이것들은 비매품입니다.

Also, to boost small shop owners and businesses amid the COVID-19 pandemic, the government is encouraging the use of Onnuri gift certificates as corporate gifts for employees to mark the Chuseok holiday.
또한 COVID-19 대유행 속에 소상공인과 사업체들을 활성화하기 위해 추석 명절을 맞아 온누리 상품권을 직원들에게 기업 선물로 사용하도록 독려하고 있다.

☆boost 신장시키다, 북돋우다

e.g. The company is planning to boost the music industry.
그 회사는 음악 산업을 활성화시킬 계획을 하고 있다.

☆gift certificate 상품권 | 😊 gift token, gift voucher
☆mark 기념하다, 축하하다

e.g. The world leaders met to mark the 10th anniversary of the event.
세계 지도자들은 그 행사의 10주년을 기념하기 위해 만났다.

From Monday, prices will be reduced by 10 percent for both online and offline purchases of the gift certificates.
월요일부터 상품권의 온라인과 오프라인 구매 모두 10% 할인된다.

Writing Exercise

1. 많은 사람들이 추석연휴기간을 가족들과 보내기 위해 고향으로 돌아가는 추석 연휴를 앞두고 기차역에서는 45퍼센트까지 대폭 할인된 가격으로 마스크 판매를 시작할 것이다.

Train

2. 기획재정부는 9월 마지막 주부터 전국 282개 기차역의 편의점에서 마스크가 할인되어서 판매될 것이라고 일요일에 말했다.

The finance

3. 또한 COVID - 19 대유행 속에 소상공인과 사업체들을 활성화하기 위해 추석 명절을 맞아 온누리 상품권을 직원들에게 기업 선물로 사용하도록 독려하고 있다.

Also,

4. 월요일부터 상품권의 온라인과 오프라인 구매 모두 10% 할인된다.

From

ⓒ BRK 457/3
457/3
Today TH

영어 뉴스룸 47

English NewsRoom

BREAKING NEWS

N. Korea calls on S. Korea not to violate western sea border in search of official's body. North Korea is warning South Korea not to violate the western sea border in the search for the missing South Korean official who was shot and killed by North Korean soldiers last week. According to a report carried Sunday by the regime's state media, the North Korean navy demanded that South Korea stop what it claimed are search operations that cross the military...

실종 공무원 수색 작업도 못하게 방해하는 북한

북한이 한국의 연평도 실종 공무원 수색 작업을 중단하라고 요구하는 내용입니다.

N. Korea calls on S. Korea not to violate western sea border in search of official's body

North Korea is warning South Korea not to violate the western sea border in the search for the missing South Korean official who was shot and killed by North Korean soldiers last week.

According to a report carried Sunday by the regime's state media, the North Korean navy demanded that South Korea stop what it claimed are search operations that cross the military demarcation line, saying that it cannot overlook intrusions into its waters.

The North said that it plans to carry out its own search and will consider ways to hand over the man's body to South Korea, if found.

Since the man disappeared last week, South Korea has been sending boats to look for him or at this point, for his remains.

NEWS 스크립트 분석

N. Korea calls on S. Korea not to violate western sea border in search of official's body

북한은 한국에 공무원의 시신을 찾아 서해 해상 경계선을 침범하지 말 것을 요구한다

☆call on 요청하다, 촉구하다

> e.g. Teachers called on students to be more tolerant of each other.
> 교사들은 학생들이 서로에 대해 더 관대해질 것을 요구했다.

☆western sea border 서해 해상 경계선

☆in search of ~을 찾아서

> e.g. Police went to several schools in search of him.
> 경찰은 그를 찾기 위해 여러 학교를 돌아다녔다.

☆body 시체

North Korea is warning South Korea not to violate the western sea border in the search for the missing South Korean official who was shot and killed by North Korean soldiers last week.

북한은 지난주 북한군 총탄에 맞아 숨진 실종된 한국 공무원을 찾기 위해 서해 해상 경계선을 침범하지 말라고 한국에게 경고하고 있다.

☆missing 실종된, 없어진

> e.g. The Crime Investigation Department is looking for a missing 7 - year - old boy.
> 범죄 수사국은 실종된 7살 소년을 찾고 있다.

According to a report carried Sunday by the regime's state media, the North Korean navy demanded that South Korea stop what it claimed are search operations that cross the military demarcation line, saying that it cannot overlook intrusions into its waters.

북한 관영 매체(조선중앙통신)에 의해 일요일에 보도된 기사에 따르면, 북한 해군은 자국 영해 침투를 간과할 수 없다고 말하며 / 한국이 주장했던 / 군사분계선을 넘는 수색작전을 중단할 것을 요구했다.

☆report 기사

☆carried by ~에 의해 보도된

☆regime 정권, 제도, 체제 북한을 지칭할 때 많이 쓰임 - the regime's state media 북한 관영 매체

☆demand 요구하다 suggest · propose · insist · demand 등 제안, 요구동사는 that 절에 주어 + (should) + 동사원형이 옴. 여기서 보통 should는 생략됨

> e.g. He demanded that she be silent for a while.
> 그는 그녀에게 잠시 침묵할 것을 요구했다.

☆search operation 수색 작업

e.g. A massive search operation is being conducted along the border.
국경을 따라 대대적인 수색작전이 펼쳐지고 있다.

☆military demarcation line 군사분계선

e.g. There is a military demarcation line between South and North Korea.
남한과 북한 사이에는 군사분계선이 있다.

☆overlook 간과하다, 못 본 체하다

e.g. Don't overlook the signs written on the wall.
벽에 쓰여진 신호들을 간과하지 마세요.

☆intrusion (개인 사생활 등에 대한) 침해, (무단) 침입

e.g. There is too much intrusion into her private life.
그녀의 사생활에 너무 많은 침해가 있다.

The North said that it plans to carry out its own search and will consider ways to hand over the man's body to South Korea, if found.

북한은 자체 수색 작업을 진행할 계획이며 발견될 경우 이 남성의 시신을 한국에 인계하는 방안을 검토할 것이라고 말했다.

☆carry out ~을 수행[이행]하다

e.g. Korean soldiers carried out an attack last night.
한국 군인들이 어젯밤에 공격을 감행했다.

☆hand over 이양하다, 인도하다

e.g. He is going to hand over the important documents.
그는 중요한 서류를 넘겨줄 것이다.

Since the man disappeared last week, South Korea has been sending boats to look for him or at this point, for his remains.

지난 주 그 남자가 사라진 이후, 한국은 그를 찾기 위해, 또는 이 시점에서는 그의 유해를 찾기 위해 배들을 보내고 있는 중이다.

☆remains (죽은 사람·동물의) 유해

e.g. Human remains were found in the forest.
사람의 유해가 숲에서 발견되었다.

Writing Exercise

1. 북한은 지난주 북한군 총탄에 맞아 숨진 실종된 한국 공무원을 찾기 위해 서해 해상 경계선을 침범하지 말라고 한국에게 경고하고 있다.

   North _____

   _____

2. 북한 관영 매체(조선중앙통신)에 의해 일요일에 보도된 기사에 따르면, 북한 해군은 자국 영해 침투를 간과할 수 없다고 말하며 / 한국이 주장했던 /
   군사분계선을 넘는 수색작전을 중단할 것을 요구했다.

   According to _____

   _____

3. 북한은 자체 수색 작업을 진행할 계획이며 발견될 경우 이 남성의 시신을 한국에 인계하는 방안을 검토할 것이라고 말했다.

   The North _____

   _____

4. 지난 주 그 남자가 사라진 이후, 한국은 그를 찾기 위해, 또는 이 시점에서는 그의 유해를 찾기 위해 배들을 보내고 있는 중이다.

   Since _____

   _____

BRK 457/3
457/3
Today TH

영어 뉴스룸 48

English NewsRoom

BREAKING NEWS

More people visiting Korean Cultural Center New York website amid COVID-19 pandemic COVID-19. The spread of the Korean wave, also known as Hallyu, has picked up pace online amid the COVID-19 pandemic. According to the Korean Cultural Center New York, the monthly-average number of web page visitors has increased to 30-thousand this year from 10-thousand during the previous year. From January to August, 500-thousand people visited...

코로나19로 인해 뉴욕문화원 사이트 방문자 증가

코로나19로 인해 뉴욕문화원 사이트 방문자가 3배이상 증가했다는 내용입니다.

 NEWS 전체 스크립트

More people visiting Korean Cultural Center New York website amid COVID-19 pandemic COVID-19

The spread of the Korean wave, also known as Hallyu, has picked up pace online amid the COVID-19 pandemic.

According to the Korean Cultural Center New York, the monthly-average number of web page visitors has increased to 30-thousand this year from 10-thousand during the previous year.

From January to August, 500-thousand people visited the website, which is a four times increase on-year.

The center opened a new section on their web page in April where it features more Korean cultural content related to concerts, exhibitions, Korean food and movies.

Particularly, a special exhibition of Korean movies that aired from April to July has been watched by more than 25-thousand people.

NEWS 스크립트 분석

The spread of the Korean wave, also known as Hallyu, has picked up pace online amid the COVID-19 pandemic.
COVID-19 대유행 속에서 한류라고도 알려진 코리안웨이브의 확산은 온라인상에서 속도를 더 내고 있다.

☆ also known as 또한 ~로 알려진 = aka

e.g. The actor is also known as Mr. Hero.
그 연기자는 미스터 히어로로도 알려져 있다.

☆ pick up the pace 박차를 가해서 속도를 더 내다, 속도를 올리다

e.g. You need to pick up the pace if you're going to finish the project before the deadline.
마감일 전에 그 프로젝트를 끝내려면 속도를 내야 한다.

According to the Korean Cultural Center New York, the monthly-average number of web page visitors has increased to 30-thousand this year from 10-thousand during the previous year.
뉴욕한국문화원에 따르면 웹페이지 방문자 수의 월평균은 지난해 1만 명에서 올해 3만 명으로 늘었다.

☆ monthly-average 월평균

e.g. The monthly average of people who were fired stood at 100.
해고된 사람들의 한 달 평균은 100명을 기록했다.

☆ yearly-average 연 평균

From January to August, 500-thousand people visited the website, which is a four times increase on-year.
1월부터 8월까지 50만 명이 방문했는데 이는 작년 동기 대비 4배 증가한 수치다.

☆ from A to B 어느 한 장소에서 다른 장소로, A부터 B까지
☆ (year) on-year 전년 동기 대비 = year-over-year

The center opened a new section on their web page in April where it features more Korean cultural content related to concerts, exhibitions, Korean food and movies.
센터는 4월, 센터 홈페이지에 콘서트, 전시회, 한국 음식, 영화와 관련된 더 많은 한국 문화 콘텐츠들을 특징으로 하는 새로운 코너를 개설했다.

☆ feature 특징으로 하다

e.g. It features almost everything that you would expect from a smartphone.
그것은 당신이 스마트폰으로부터 기대할 수 있는 거의 모든 것을 특징으로 한다.

☆related to ~와 관련 있는

Particularly, a special exhibition of Korean movies that aired from April to July has been watched by more than 25-thousand people.

특히 4월부터 7월까지 방영된 한국영화 특별전은 2만 5000여 명 이상이 관람했다.

　　　　명사　　동사
☆air 공기 | 방영되다, 방송되다

Writing Exercise

1. 뉴욕한국문화원에 따르면 웹페이지 방문자 수의 월평균은 지난해 1만 명에서 올해 3만 명으로 늘었다.

According to
_____

_____

2. 1월부터 8월까지 50만 명이 방문했는데 이는 작년 동기 대비 4배 증가한 수치다.

From
_____

_____

3. 센터는 4월, 센터 홈페이지에 콘서트, 전시회, 한국 음식, 영화와 관련된 더 많은 한국 문화 콘텐츠들을 특징으로 하는 새로운 코너를 개설했다.

The center
_____

_____

4. 특히 4월부터 7월까지 방영된 한국영화 특별전은 2만5000여 명 이상이 관람했다.

Particularly,
_____

_____

BRK 457/3
457/3
Today TH

영어 뉴스룸 49 English NewsRoom

BREAKING NEWS

Fast food franchises in S. Korea could serve hamburgers without tomatoes due to lack of supply. Major hamburger franchises are on alert as they are experiencing delays in the supply of tomatoes. Fast food companies such as Lotteria, McDonald's and Burger King have announced that their hamburgers may not include tomatoes, as the string of typhoons that hit South Korea this summer hampered supply. Due to this, some companies will sell...

햄버거에 토마토만 쏙 뺐다

올여름 태풍으로 인해 토마토 수급에 비상이 걸린 햄버거 프렌차이즈 업체들에 대한 내용입니다.

Fast food franchises in S. Korea could serve hamburgers without tomatoes due to lack of supply

Major hamburger franchises are on alert as they are experiencing delays in the supply of tomatoes.

Fast food companies such as Lotteria, McDonald's and Burger King have announced that their hamburgers may not include tomatoes, as the string of typhoons that hit South Korea this summer hampered supply.

Due to this, some companies will sell hamburgers at a lowered price, and some others will replace tomatoes with other vegetables or hand out drink coupons instead.

Industry experts expect tomato supplies to become stable by late October.

Fast food franchises in S. Korea could serve hamburgers without tomatoes due to lack of supply

한국의 패스트푸드 체인점들은 공급 부족으로 토마토 없이 햄버거를 제공할 수도 있다

☆tomato 토마토 | 영 [tə'mɑ:.təʊ], 미 [tə'meɪ.toʊ]

영국, 미국 발음 다름 주의!

☆lack of supply 공급 부족 (lack of something 무언가가 부족한 것)

e.g. I have a lack of knowledge about biotechnology.
나는 생명공학에 대한 지식이 부족하다.

Major hamburger franchises are on alert as they are experiencing delays in the supply of tomatoes.

주요 햄버거 프랜차이즈 업체들이 토마토 공급 지연을 겪고 있어 비상상황을 맞고 있다.

☆be on (the) alert 비상상황을 맞다, 경계태세를 갖추다

e.g. Korean soldiers are on alert to ensure the safety of the people.
한국 군인들은 국민의 안전을 위해 경계 태세를 갖추고 있다.

☆delay 1. 지연, 지체 (명사) | 2. 지연하다, 지체하다 (동사)

e.g. This problem needs to be tackled without delay.
이 문제는 지체 없이 해결해야 한다

Fast food companies such as Lotteria, McDonald's and Burger King have announced that their hamburgers may not include tomatoes, as the string of typhoons that hit South Korea this summer hampered supply.

롯데리아, 맥도날드, 버거킹과 같은 패스트푸드 회사들은 올 여름 한국에 타격을 준 일련의 태풍들이(토마토의) 공급을 방해했기 때문에 패스트푸드 햄버거에 토마토를 포함하지 않을 수도 있다고 발표했다.

☆string of 일련의

e.g. A string of incidents have been reported since July.
7월 이후 일련의 사건들이 보고되었다.

☆hit ~에 타격을 주다

e.g. The tax increases will hit business rather than consumers.
세금 인상은 소비자보다는 사업에 타격을 줄 것이다.

☆hamper 방해하다

e.g. Bad weather hampered the rescue efforts.
악천후가 구조 작업을 방해했다.

Due to this, some companies will sell hamburgers at a lowered price, and some others will replace tomatoes with other vegetables or hand out drink coupons instead.

이 때문에 햄버거를 싸게 파는 업체도 있고 토마토 대신 다른 채소로 대체하거나 음료 쿠폰을 나눠주는 업체도 있을 것이다.

☆at a lowered price 할인된 가격

e.g. This is the first time their cars are being sold at a lowered price.
그들의 차가 더 낮은 가격에 팔리는 것은 이번이 처음이다.

☆hand out something 뿌리다, 나눠주다

√hand in 내다, 제출하다 (케쥬얼하게 씀), submit (비지니스에서 많이 씀)

e.g. Please hand out the documents to the visitors.
방문객들에게 서류를 나눠주세요.

Industry experts expect tomato supplies to become stable by late October.

업계 전문가들은 10월 말쯤 토마토 공급이 안정될 것으로 예상한다.

☆stable 안정된, 안정적인

e.g. She got a stable job in a bank and a good flat.
그녀는 은행에서 안정적인 직장을 얻었고 좋은 아파트를 얻었다.

1. 주요 햄버거 프랜차이즈 업체들이 토마토 공급 지연을 겪고 있어 비상상황을 맞고 있다.

   Major
   _____
   _____

2. 롯데리아, 맥도날드, 버거킹과 같은 패스트푸드 회사들은 올 여름 한국에 타격을 준 일련의 태풍들이 **(토마토의)** 공급을 방해했기 때문에 패스트푸드 햄버거에 토마토를 포함하지 않을 수도 있다고 발표했다.

   Fast
   _____
   _____

3. 이 때문에 햄버거를 싸게 파는 업체도 있고 토마토 대신 다른 채소로 대체하거나 음료 쿠폰을 나눠주는 업체도 있을 것이다.

   Due to
   _____
   _____

4. 업계 전문가들은 10월 말쯤 토마토 공급이 안정될 것으로 예상한다.

   Industry
   _____
   _____

BRK 457/3
457/3
Today TH

영어 뉴스룸 50

English NewsRoom

BREAKING NEWS

Kickboard batteries will have to be removed when stored next year. For the popular electric kickboards seen these days on South Korean streets, the government's decided to strengthen safety standards when it comes to their batteries in response to fires that have occurred recently. The Ministry of Trade, Industry and Energy said Wednesday that from next August kickboard owners will have to take the batteries out when they store the device.

킥보드 보관 시 배터리를 분리해야

안전상의 문제로 전동킥보드 배터리 관리기준을 강화한다는 내용입니다.

 NEWS 전체 스크립트

Kickboard batteries will have to be removed when stored next year

For the popular electric kickboards seen these days on South Korean streets, the government's decided to strengthen safety standards when it comes to their batteries in response to fires that have occurred recently.

The Ministry of Trade, Industry and Energy said Wednesday that from next August kickboard owners will have to take the batteries out when they store the device.

This applies also to the companies that run kickboard sharing apps.

There will also be more rigorous testing of their charging limits.

Kickboards, the government says, have been involved in dozens of fires and explosions over the past three years.

Kickboard batteries will have to be removed when stored next year
내년부터 킥보드 배터리는(킥보드를) 보관할 때 분리해야 한다.

☆remove 제거하다, *(배터리를)* 분리하다

For the popular electric kickboards seen these days on South Korean streets, the government's decided to strengthen safety standards when it comes to their batteries in response to fires that have occurred recently.
요즘 한국 거리에서 볼 수 있는 인기 있는 전동 킥보드에 대해, 정부는 최근 발생한 화재에 대응하여 배터리에 관한 안전 기준을 강화하기로 결정했다.

☆strengthen 강화하다 (strengthen safety standards 안전 기준을 강화하다)

> e.g. Let me tell you ways to strengthen family bonds.
> 가족간의 유대감을 강화하는 방법을 알려줄게.

☆when it comes to ~에 관한 한

> e.g. When it comes to studying language, it is important to consider input and output.
> 언어를 공부하는 것에 관한 한 입출력을 고려하는 것이 중요하다.

☆in response to ~에 응하여,~에 답하여

> e.g. The manager is writing in response to the customer's request for additional information.
> 그 관리자는 고객의 추가 정보에 요청에 대한 답변을 쓰고 있다.

The Ministry of Trade, Industry and Energy said Wednesday that from next August kickboard owners will have to take the batteries out when they store the device.
산업통상자원부는 내년 8월부터 킥보드 주인들이 그 장치(킥보드)를 보관할 때 배터리를 제거해야 할 것이라고 수요일 밝혔다.

☆take something out 제거하다, 빼다

> e.g. Take this sentence out from your resume.
> 당신의 이력서에서 이 문장을 빼세요.

This applies also to the companies that run kickboard sharing apps.
이는 킥보드 공유 앱을 운영하는 기업에도 적용된다.

☆apply to 적용되다

e.g. The law applies to all EU countries ; Britain is no exception.
그 법은 모든 EU 국가에 적용된다. 영국도 예외는 아니다.

There will also be more rigorous testing of their charging limits.
또한 충전 한도에 대한 더 엄격한 테스트가 있을 것이다.

☆rigorous 철저한, 엄격한

e.g. The school has rigorous standards.
그 학교는 엄격한 기준을 가지고 있다.

☆charge 1. 충전하다(동사) | 2. 요금(명사)

Kickboards, the government says, have been involved in dozens of fires and explosions over the past three years.
킥보드는 지난 3년 동안 수십 건의 화재와 폭발에 연루되었다고 정부는 말한다.

☆involved in ~에 관련된, ~에 연루된

e.g. I don't want to get involved in a serious relationship.
저는 진지한 관계에는 관여하고 싶지 않아요.

☆dozens of 수십의, 많은

e.g. Dozens of accidents were reported last night due to the typhoon.
어젯밤 태풍으로 수십 건의 사고가 보고되었다.

1. 요즘 한국 거리에서 볼 수 있는 인기 있는 전동 킥보드에 대해, 정부는 최근 발생한 화재에 대응하여 배터리에 관한 안전 기준을 강화하기로 결정했다.

   For the

2. 산업통상자원부는 내년 8월부터 킥보드 주인들이 그 장치(킥보드)를 보관할 때 배터리를 제거해야 할 것이라고 수요일 밝혔다.

   The Ministry

3. 이는 킥보드 공유 앱을 운영하는 기업에도 적용된다.

   This

4. 또한 충전 한도에 대한 더 엄격한 테스트가 있을 것이다.

   There

5. 킥보드는 지난 3년 동안 수십 건의 화재와 폭발에 연루되었다고 정부는 말한다.

   Kickboards,

BRK 457/3
457/3
Today TH

영어 뉴스룸 51

English
NewsRoom

BREAKING NEWS

S. Korea to resume free flu shots next week after safety concerns addressed. The South Korean government is going to start giving out free flu shots again next week, having suspended the program last month because some of the vaccines had not been stored properly. The free flu shots will restart next Tuesday, first for middle and high school students aged 13 to 18. Shots will also be available for pregnant women, children of all ages and seniors...

독감 무료 접종 받으세요

안전문제로 중단된 정부의 무료 독감 예방접종 사업을 재개한다는 내용입니다.

 전체 스크립트

S. Korea to resume free flu shots next week after safety concerns addressed

The South Korean government is going to start giving out free flu shots again next week, having suspended the program last month because some of the vaccines had not been stored properly.

The free flu shots will restart next Tuesday, first for middle and high school students aged 13 to 18.

Shots will also be available for pregnant women, children of all ages and seniors from age 62.

The government has checked the vaccines and found no safety problems, though it has taken back about half a million of them just in case.

The goal this winter is to prevent a major flu outbreak, which could seriously complicate efforts to stop COVID-19.

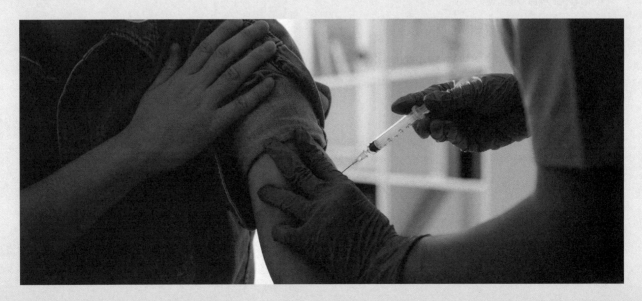

S. Korea to resume free flu shots next week after safety concerns addressed
한국, 안전 문제가 다루어진 후 다음 주 무료 독감접종 재개 예정

☆resume 재개하다

e.g. The suspended flights are going to be resumed.
운항이 중단된 항공편이 재개될 예정이다.

☆address 1. 주소, 연설 (명사) | 2. (문제·상황 등에 대해) 다루다, 연설하다, 호칭을 쓰다, 호칭으로 부르다 (동사)

e.g. This problem has to be addressed in the next meeting.
이 문제는 다음 회의에서 다뤄져야 한다.
She likes to be addressed as "Ms. Anaconda."
그녀는 "아나콘다양"으로 불리는 것을 좋아한다.

The South Korean government is going to start giving out free flu shots again next week, having suspended the program last month because some of the vaccines had not been stored properly.
정부는 일부 백신이 제대로 보관되지 않아 지난달 중단되었던 프로그램(무료 독감 국가예방접종 사업)을 다음 주부터 다시 시작할 예정이다.

☆give out something 사람들에게 각각 나누어 주다

e.g. The president is giving out free tickets to anyone who followed him on twitter.
회장은 트위터에서 그를 팔로우한 모든 사람들에게 무료 티켓을 나눠주고 있다.

☆flu shot 독감 예방접종
☆suspend (공식적으로) 중단하다

e.g. My mobile service has been suspended due to late payments.
내 휴대폰 서비스는 지불 연기로 인해 중단되었다.

☆stored properly 제대로 보관되다

e.g. All the information is stored properly in a file.
모든 정보는 파일에 적절하게 저장됩니다.

The free flu shots will restart next Tuesday, first for middle and high school students aged 13 to 18.
무료 독감 예방접종은 우선13세에서 18세 사이의 중고등학생을 대상으로 다음 주 화요일에 재개될 것이다.

Shots will also be available for pregnant women, children of all ages and seniors from age 62.

임산부, 모든 연령의 어린이, 62세 이상의 노인에 대해서도 무료 예방접종 이용이 가능할 것이다.

☆be available for something or someone ~에 대해 이용가능하다

> e.g. The team has not yet said when it will be available for purchase.
> 그 팀은 아직 그것이 언제 구매가 가능한지 말하지 않았다.

The government has checked the vaccines and found no safety problems, though it has taken back about half a million of them just in case.

정부는 백신을 검사했고 만약을 대비해 50만 개 정도를 회수했지만 안전상의 문제는 발견되지 않았다.

☆though (비록) 접속사 ~이지만 | 부사 하지만

☆take something back 회수하다, (자기가 한말을) 취소하다

> e.g. My mother is going to take it back and ask for a refund instead of me.
> 엄마가 저 대신 회수해서 환불을 요구하실 거예요.
> Take back what you said about my best friend.
> 네가 내 가장 친한 친구에 대해 했던 말 취소해.

☆just in case 만약을 대비해

The goal this winter is to prevent a major flu outbreak, which could seriously complicate efforts to stop COVID-19.

올 겨울 목표는 대규모 독감 발병을 예방하는 것인데, 이것은 COVID-19를 막기 위한 노력을 심각하게 복잡하게 할 수 있다.

1. 정부는 일부 백신이 제대로 보관되지 않아 지난달 중단되었던 프로그램(무료 독감 국가예방접종 사업)을 다음 주부터 다시 시작할 예정이다.

   The South

2. 무료 독감 예방접종은 우선13세에서 18세 사이의 중고등학생을 대상으로 다음 주 화요일에 재개될 것이다.

   The free

3. 임산부, 모든 연령의 어린이, 62세 이상의 노인에 대해서도 무료 예방접종 이용이 가능할 것이다.

   Shots

4. 정부는 백신을 검사했고 만약을 대비해 50만 개 정도를 회수했지만 안전상의 문제는 발견되지 않았다.

   The government

5. 올 겨울 목표는 대규모 독감 발병을 예방하는 것인데, 이것은 COVID - 19를 막기 위한 노력을 심각하게 복잡하게 할 수 있다.

   The goal

영어 뉴스룸 52 English NewsRoom

BREAKING NEWS

Netflix documentary on K-pop megastars Blackpink to be released on Wednesday. A documentary on K-pop megastars Blackpink will be unveiled on Wednesday, offering fans and viewers an intimate look behind-the-scenes as well as down-to-earth stories from their journey to success. Netflix's latest documentary "Blackpink : Light Up the Sky" will be released in 190 countries, becoming the first-ever Netflix documentary on a K-pop band.

블랙핑크가 인생 내막을 공개하다

블랙핑크가 K팝 가수 최초로 넷플릭스 다큐멘터리의 주인공이 되었다는 내용입니다.

 전체 스크립트

Netflix documentary on K-pop megastars Blackpink to be released on Wednesday

A documentary on K-pop megastars Blackpink will be unveiled on Wednesday, offering fans and viewers an intimate look behind-the-scenes as well as down-to-earth stories from their journey to success.

Netflix's latest documentary "Blackpink : Light Up the Sky" will be released in 190 countries, becoming the first-ever Netflix documentary on a K-pop band.

At an online press conference on Tuesday, member Rose noted it's the story of how Blackpink became the Blackpink that they are today.

Directed by Caroline Suh, the documentary is the fourth Netflix production to focus on female artists after Lady Gaga, Beyonce and Taylor Swift.

Netflix documentary on K-pop megastars Blackpink to be released on Wednesday
수요일에 개봉되는 케이팝 슈퍼스타 블랙핑크에 대한 넷플릭스 다큐멘터리

☆documentary 다큐멘터리, 기록물

☆megastar 초대형 스타, 슈퍼스타 *(가수 · 배우 · 연예인)*

☆release 석방하다, 발표하다, 개봉하다

A documentary on K-pop megastars Blackpink will be unveiled on Wednesday, offering fans and viewers an intimate look behind-the-scenes as well as down-to-earth stories from their journey to success.
팬들과 시청자들에게 성공에 이르는 현장 스토리 뿐만 아니라 무대 뒤의 친밀한 모습을 선사하는 K팝 슈퍼스타 블랙핑크를 소재로 한 다큐멘터리가 수요일에 공개될 것이다.

☆unveil 발표하다

e.g. The revised policy was unveiled yesterday at the summit.
개정된 정책은 어제 정상회담에서 공개되었다.

4형식동사
☆offer A B A에게 B를 제공하다

e.g. A waiter offered him the menu.
웨이터가 그에게 메뉴를 제공했다.

☆intimate 친밀한, 개인적인

e.g. The actor likes to mention the intimate details of his life on social media.
그 배우는 SNS에 자신의 삶의 친밀한 내용을 언급하는 것을 좋아한다.

☆behind-the-scenes 무대 뒤의

e.g. Manager's hard work has been going on behind the scenes.
매니저의 고된 일이 무대 뒤에서 진행되어 왔다.

☆down-to-earth 현실적인, 실제적인

e.g. I love meeting her every Saturday because she is down to earth.
난 그녀가 현실적이어서 매주 토요일 마다 그녀를 만나는 것을 좋아해.

☆B as well as A A뿐만 아니라 B역시 =not only A but also B

Netflix's latest documentary "Blackpink : Light Up the Sky" will be released in 190 countries, becoming the first-ever Netflix documentary on a K-pop band.

K팝 밴드 사상 첫 넷플릭스 다큐멘터리가 되는 넷플릭스의 최신 다큐멘터리 "블랙핑크 : 세상을 밝혀라"가 190개국에서 개봉될 것이다.

　　☆latest 최근의, 최신의

　　☆light up *(빛·색으로)* 환하게 만들다, 행복하게 보이다

> e.g. The full moon will light up the sky soon.
> 　　　보름달이 곧 하늘을 밝힐 것이다.

　　☆first-ever 생전 처음의, 사상 최초의

> e.g. It's the first-ever meeting between my mother and mother-in-law.
> 　　　우리 어머니와 시어머니의 첫 만남이에요.

At an online press conference on Tuesday, member Rose noted it's the story of how Blackpink became the Blackpink that they are today.

멤버 로제는 화요일 온라인 기자회견에서 블랙핑크가 어떻게 지금의 블랙핑크가 됐는지에 대한 이야기라고 언급했다.

　　☆note *(중요하거나 흥미로운 것을)* 언급하다

> e.g. At the executive meeting, he noted the importance of having a museum in the company.
> 　　　임원 회의에서 그는 회사 내에 박물관이 있는 것의 중요성을 언급했다.

Directed by Caroline Suh, the documentary is the fourth Netflix production to focus on female artists after Lady Gaga, Beyonce and Taylor Swift.

캐롤라인 서 감독이 연출을 맡은 이 다큐멘터리는 레이디 가가, 비욘세, 테일러 스위프트에 이어 여성 아티스트에 초점을 맞춘 네 번째 넷플릭스 작품이다.

　　☆directed by ~에 의해 감독된

> e.g. The film was directed by people who love music.
> 　　　그 영화는 음악을 사랑하는 사람들에 의해 연출되었다.

1. 팬들과 시청자들에게 성공에 이르는 현장 스토리 뿐만 아니라 무대 뒤의 친밀한 모습을 선사하는 K팝 슈퍼스타 블랙핑크를 소재로 한 다큐멘터리가 수요일에 공개될 것이다.

A documentary _____

_____

2. K팝 밴드 사상 첫 넷플릭스 다큐멘터리가 되는 넷플릭스의 최신 다큐멘터리 "블랙핑크 : 세상을 밝혀라"가 190개국에서 개봉될 것이다.

Netflix's _____

_____

3. 멤버 로제는 화요일 온라인 기자회견에서 블랙핑크가 어떻게 지금의 블랙핑크가 됐는지에 대한 이야기라고 언급했다.

At an _____

_____

4. 캐롤라인 서 감독이 연출을 맡은 이 다큐멘터리는 레이디 가가, 비욘세, 테일러 스위프트에 이어 여성 아티스트에 초점을 맞춘 네 번째 넷플릭스작품이다.

Directed _____

_____

영어 뉴스룸 53

English NewsRoom

BREAKING NEWS

Tteokbokki selected as S. Koreans' favorite comfort food in new survey. Tteokbokki, or spicy Korean rice cakes, has been selected as South Korea's favorite comfort food. According to a survey conducted by the Seoul city government, the dish ranked top after a survey of around ten-thousand residents. It was followed by fried chicken, Kimchi stew, grilled pork belly and ginseng chicken soup. A survey of 50 foreign residents also selected similar foods.

위안을 주는 음식 1위는 떡볶이

나를 위로하는 음식 1위에 선정된 떡볶이에 대한 내용입니다.

Tteokbokki selected as S. Koreans' favorite comfort food in new survey

Tteokbokki, or spicy Korean rice cakes, has been selected as South Korea's favorite comfort food.

According to a survey conducted by the Seoul city government, the dish ranked top after a survey of around ten-thousand residents.

It was followed by fried chicken, Kimchi stew, grilled pork belly and ginseng chicken soup.

A survey of 50 foreign residents also selected similar foods.

The surveys were conducted as part of the 'Taste of Seoul' week set to be held from November 11th to 15th.

Officials say it's aimed at comforting fatigued residents and small business owners amid the COVID-19 outbreak.

Tteokbokki selected as S. Koreans' favorite comfort food in new survey
새 설문조사에서 한국인이 가장 좋아하는 위안을 주는 음식으로 선정된 떡볶이

☆select as ~로 선택하다

e.g. The professor has been selected as a member of the community.
그 교수는 그 공동체의 일원으로 선출되었다.

☆comfort 위로, 위안

e.g. It is true that she has been a great comfort to me.
그녀가 나에게 큰 위로가 된 것은 사실이다.

☆comfort food 위안을 주는 음식, 추억의 음식

Tteokbokki, or spicy Korean rice cakes, has been selected as South Korea's favorite comfort food.
떡볶이 혹은 매운 한국 떡은 한국이 가장 좋아하는 위안 음식으로 선정되었다.

According to a survey conducted by the Seoul city government, the dish ranked top after a survey of around ten-thousand residents.
서울시 조사에 따르면, 이 요리는 약 1만 명의 주민을 대상으로 한 설문 조사 결과 1위를 차지했다.

☆conducted by ~에 의해 실시된

e.g. The poll was conducted by a secret agency.
그 여론조사는 비밀 기관에 의해 실시되었다.

☆dish 요리, 접시
☆ranked top 1위를 차지했다

e.g. The country's software program ranked top in the world.
그 나라의 소프트웨어 프로그램은 세계 1위를 차지했다.

It was followed by fried chicken, Kimchi stew, grilled pork belly and ginseng chicken soup.
그 다음으로는 닭튀김, 김치찌개, 삼겹살(구이), 인삼닭국(삼계탕) 순이었다.

☆followed by 뒤이어, 잇달아

e.g. Bananas are still the most popular fruits, followed by apples.
바나나는 여전히 가장 인기 있는 과일이고, 그 다음이 사과입니다.

☆stew 스튜 고기와 채소를 넣고 국물이 좀 있게 해서 천천히 끓인 요리, soup는 stew에 비해 liquid를 많이 넣어 재료들이 푹 담긴 요리를 말함

A survey of 50 foreign residents also selected similar foods.
외국인 거주자 50명을 대상으로 한 설문조사에서도 비슷한 음식을 선정했다.

The surveys were conducted as part of the 'Taste of Seoul' week set to be held from November 11th to 15th.
이번 조사는 11월 11일부터 15일까지 열릴 예정인 '서울의 맛'('서울 미식주간') 주간의 일환으로 실시되었다.

☆as part of ~의 일환으로

e.g. We welcome 예지 as part of our family.
예지를 우리 가족의 일원으로 환영합니다.

☆be set to ~하기로 예정되어 있다

e.g. The event is set to be held online this year due to the Covid-19 pandemic.
그 행사는 코로나19 대유행으로 인해 올해 온라인으로 개최될 예정이다.

Officials say it's aimed at comforting fatigued residents and small business owners amid the COVID-19 outbreak.
관계자(공무원)들은 이것이 COVID-19 사태 속에서 지친 시민들과 소상공인들을 위로하기 위한 것이라고 말한다.

☆aim at ~을 겨냥한

e.g. The campaign is aimed at encouraging citizens to drive safe.
그 캠페인은 시민들이 안전 운전을 장려하기 위한 것이다.

☆fatigue 심신이 지친, 피로한

e.g. The lack of rest and 2 hours of driving had fatigued him.
휴식 부족과 2시간의 운전은 그를 지치게 했다.

1. 떡볶이 혹은 매운 한국 떡은 한국이 가장 좋아하는 위안 음식으로 선정되었다.

Tteokbokki,

2. 서울시 조사에 따르면, 이 요리는 약 1만 명의 주민을 대상으로 한 설문 조사 결과 1위를 차지했다.

According

3. 그 다음으로는 닭튀김, 김치찌개, 삼겹살 (구이), 인삼닭국(삼계탕) 순이었다.

It was

4. 외국인 거주자 50명을 대상으로 한 설문조사에서도 비슷한 음식을 선정했다.

A survey

5. 이번 조사는 11월 11일부터 15일까지 열릴 예정인 '서울의 맛'('서울 미식주간') 주간의 일환으로 실시되었다.

The surveys

6. 관계자(공무원)들은 이것이 COVID - 19 사태 속에서 지친 시민들과 소상공인들을 위로하기 위한 것이라고 말한다.

Officials

영어 뉴스룸 54 English NewsRoom

BREAKING NEWS

S. Korea to hand out 'consumption coupons' to 10 million citizens. The South Korean government is going to be giving out coupons to more than 10 million people in its latest bid to boost the local economy in the pandemic. The finance ministry said Sunday that the coupons will be distributed starting in late October, offering discounts in eight key sectors including tourism, sports, entertainment, food and hospitality. The coupon package comes ahead...

정부가 1천만명에게 소비쿠폰을 뿌린다

정부가 경제를 살리기 위해 소비쿠폰을 배포한다는 내용입니다.

S. Korea to hand out 'consumption coupons' to 10 million citizens

The South Korean government is going to be giving out coupons to more than 10 million people in its latest bid to boost the local economy in the pandemic.

The finance ministry said Sunday that the coupons will be distributed starting in late October, offering discounts in eight key sectors including tourism, sports, entertainment, food and hospitality.

The coupon package comes ahead of a retail event known as the 'Korea Sale Festa', which begins on November first.

The government says it will hold more events to promote the consumption of cultural and tourism products and of food products.

S. Korea to hand out 'consumption coupons' to 10 million citizens
대한민국, 1000만 시민에게 '소비 쿠폰'을 배포할 예정이다

☆hand out 나눠주다, 배포하다

e.g. He's going to hand out life jackets to everybody who wants to swim.
　　그는 수영 하고 싶은 모든 사람들에게 구명조끼를 나눠줄 것이다.

The South Korean government is going to be giving out coupons to more than 10 million people in its latest bid to boost the local economy in the pandemic.
한국 정부는 세계적인 유행병가운데 지역 경제를 활성화시키기 위한 최근 노력의 일환으로 1,000만 명 이상의 사람들에게 쿠폰을 배포할 예정이다.

☆give out something 나누어주다, 배포하다, (열·빛 등을) 내다

e.g. The company is giving out free meals to the vulnerable.
　　그 회사는 취약계층에게 무료 급식을 나눠주고 있다.

☆in a bid 노력의 일환으로, ~하기 위해

e.g. In a bid to gain more voters, he provided free coupons to people.
　　더 많은 유권자들을 얻기 위한 노력의 일환으로, 그는 사람들에게 무료 쿠폰을 제공했다.

☆boost 신장시키다, 북돋우다

e.g. Lawmakers agreed on ways to boost the economy.
　　국회의원들은 경제 활성화 방안에 합의했다.

The finance ministry said Sunday that the coupons will be distributed starting in late October, offering discounts in eight key sectors including tourism, sports, entertainment, food and hospitality.
기획재정부는 관광, 스포츠, 오락, 음식, 숙박 등 8개 주요 업종에서 할인 혜택을 제공하는 쿠폰이 10월 말부터 배포될 것이라고 일요일 밝혔다.

☆distribute (사람들에게) 나누어 주다, 배부하다

e.g. The books will be distributed free of charge for educational purposes.
　　그 책들은 교육용으로 무료로 배포될 것이다.

The coupon package comes ahead of a retail event known as the 'Korea Sale Festa', which begins on November first.

이 쿠폰 패키지는 11월 1일부터 시작되는 '코리아 세일 페스타'로 알려진 소매 행사 보다 앞서 나온다.

☆ahead of *(시간상으로)* ~보다 빨리, *(시간·공간상으로)* ~앞에

e.g. Ahead of a meeting with his team members, he explained why they have to retire.
그는 팀원들과의 회의를 앞두고 왜 그들이 은퇴해야 하는지 설명했다.

☆retail 소매 (wholesale 도매)

☆known as ~으로 알려진

e.g. Her name is Sally Kwon, but she is known as Kwon Anaconda.
그녀의 이름은 샐리권이지만, 그녀는 권아나콘다로 알려져 있다.

The government says it will hold more events to promote the consumption of cultural and tourism products and of food products.

정부는 문화관광 상품과 식료품의 소비를 촉진하기 위해 더 많은 행사를 개최할 것이라고 말한다.

☆hold an event 행사를 개최하다

e.g. The authorities will hold events to promote sharing culture.
당국은 나눔 문화를 촉진하기 위한 행사를 개최할 것이다.

☆promote 촉진하다

e.g. There are lots of campaigns to promote the consumption of drinking water.
식수 소비를 촉진하기 위한 캠페인이 많이 있다.

Writing Exercise

1. 한국 정부는 세계적인 유행병가운데 지역 경제를 활성화시키기 위한 최근 노력의 일환으로 1,000만 명 이상의 사람들에게 쿠폰을 배포할 예정이다.

The South
_____
_____

2. 기획재정부는 관광, 스포츠, 오락, 음식, 숙박 등 8개 주요 업종에서 할인 혜택을 제공하는 쿠폰이 10월 말부터 배포될 것이라고 일요일 밝혔다.

The finance
_____
_____

3. 이 쿠폰 패키지는 11월 1일부터 시작되는 '코리아 세일 페스타'로 알려진 소매 행사 보다 앞서 나온다.

The coupon
_____

4. 정부는 문화관광 상품과 식료품의 소비를 촉진하기 위해 더 많은 행사를 개최할 것이라고 말한다.

The government
_____

◉ BRK 457/3
457/3
Today TH

영어 뉴스룸 55

English NewsRoom

BREAKING NEWS

Late chairman made Samsung a global tech giant. In his three decades as the chairman of Samsung Group, Lee Kun-hee grew the company into a global tech giant. When he took over as chairman in 1987 after the death of his father, who founded the company, Samsung's market cap was around 900 billion won. Under Lee Kun-hee's management, it rose by almost 350 fold to around 282 billion U.S. dollars.

삼성 이건희 회장 별세

항상 혁신과 변화를 도모한 삼성 이건희 회장의 별세 관한 내용입니다.

 NEWS 전체 스크립트

Late chairman made Samsung a global tech giant

In his three decades as the chairman of Samsung Group, Lee Kun-hee grew the company into a global tech giant.

When he took over as chairman in 1987 after the death of his father, who founded the company, Samsung's market cap was around 900 billion won.

Under Lee Kun-hee's management, it rose by almost 350 fold to around 282 billion U.S. dollars.

Lee Kun-hee's success as a leader is often attributed to his deep-rooted philosophy of change and innovation.

His famous slogan was "change everything, except for your wife and children."

He pushed the company to become the world's biggest memory chip maker in the early 90s, surging ahead of its Japanese and American competitors.

By 2012, Samsung Electronics had become number one in the mobile industry as well.

He died as the richest man in South Korea.

Now his son, Lee Jae-yong, who is the current vice chairman of Samsung Electronics, is widely expected to take over.

Late chairman made Samsung a global tech giant

고인이 된 회장은 삼성을 세계적인 기술 대기업으로 만들었다

☆tech =technology 기술, 기술상의, 전문적인

☆giant 거인, 거대 조직[기업]

☆make A B (5형식 사역동사 : 주어 + 동사 + 목적어 + 목적보어) A를 B하도록 만들다

In his three decades as the chairman of Samsung Group, Lee Kun-hee grew the company into a global tech giant.

삼성그룹 회장으로서 30년 동안, 이건희 회장은 이 회사를 세계적인 기술 대기업으로 성장시켰다.

☆decade 10년

☆grow into ~로 성장하다.

e.g. The young man grew the startup company into one of the leading consulting firms in Korea.
그 젊은이는 그 스타트업 회사를 한국의 일류 컨설팅 회사 중 하나로 성장시켰다.

When he took over as chairman in 1987 after the death of his father, who founded the company, Samsung's market cap was around 900 billion won.

그가 창업한 아버지(이병철 회장)의 사망 이후 1987년 회장직을 승계했을 때 삼성의 시가총액은 9000억 원 안팎이었다.

☆take over ~을 인수하다, 승계하다

e.g. They wanted someone to take over the company for a day.
그들은 누군가가 회사를 하루 동안 인수하기를 원했다.

☆market cap 시가총액

Under Lee Kun-hee's management, it rose by almost 350 fold to around 282 billion U.S. dollars.

이건희 회장의 경영 아래(시가총액은) 약 350배 증가한 2820억 달러 올랐다.

☆fold 1. 접다(동사) | 2. 배(명사)

e.g. Within 20 years, the population increased ten fold.
20년 안에, 인구는 10배 증가했다.

Lee Kun-hee's success as a leader is often attributed to his deep-rooted philosophy of change and innovation.
지도자로서 이건희 회장의 성공은 그의 뿌리 깊은 변화와 혁신의 철학에 기인하는 경우가 많다.

　　☆be attributed to ~에 기인하다
　　☆deep-rooted 뿌리 깊은

His famous slogan was "change everything, except for your wife and children."
그의 유명한 슬로건은 "마누라와 자식 빼놓고 다 바꿔봐"라는 것이었다.

　　☆except for ~을 제외하고는

> e.g. She hadn't eaten a thing except for snacks.
> 　　그녀는 간식을 제외하고는 아무것도 먹지 않았다.

He pushed the company to become the world's biggest memory chip maker in the early 90s, surging ahead of its Japanese and American competitors.
그는 90년대 초반, 일본과 미국 등의 경쟁사들보다 앞서서 급등하는 세계 최대의 메모리 칩 제조사가 되기 위해 회사를 몰아붙였다.

　　☆surge 급등하다, 급증하다

> e.g. Prices of red pepper powder surged last month due to the bad weather.
> 　　악천후로 지난달 고춧가루 가격이 급등했다

By 2012, Samsung Electronics had become number one in the mobile industry as well.
2012년까지 삼성전자는 모바일 업계에서도 1위를 차지했다.

He died as the richest man in South Korea.
그는 대한민국 최고의 부자로 세상을 떠났다.

Now his son, Lee Jae-yong, who is the current vice chairman of Samsung Electronics, is widely expected to take over.
이제 현 삼성전자 부회장인 아들 이재용씨가 승계할 것이라는 전망이 우세하다.

　　☆be widely expected 널리 예상되다, 전망이 우세하다

> e.g. It is widely expected that the bank will ease the policy.
> 　　그 은행이 정책을 완화할 것이라는 전망이 우세하다.

1. 삼성그룹 회장으로서 30년 동안, 이건희 회장은 이 회사를 세계적인 기술 대기업으로 성장시켰다.

In his

2. 그가 창업한 아버지(이병철 회장)의 사망 이후 1987년 회장직을 승계했을 때 삼성의 시가총액은 9000억 원 안팎이었다.

When

3. 이건희 회장의 경영 아래 (시가총액은) 약 350배 증가한 2820억 달러 올랐다.

Under

4. 지도자로서 이건희 회장의 성공은 그의 뿌리 깊은 변화와 혁신의 철학에 기인하는 경우가 많다.

Lee Kun - hee's

5. 그의 유명한 슬로건은 "마누라와 자식 빼놓고 다 바꿔봐"라는 것이었다.

His

6. 그는 90년대 초반, 일본과 미국 등의 경쟁사들보다 앞서서 급등하는 세계 최대의 메모리 칩 제조사가 되기 위해 회사를 몰아붙였다.

He pushed

7. 2012년까지 삼성전자는 모바일 업계에서도 1위를 차지했다.

By 2012,

8. 그는 대한민국 최고의 부자로 세상을 떠났다.

He died _____

_____

9. 이제 현 삼성전자 부회장인 아들 이재용씨가 승계할 것이라는 전망이 우세하다.

Now _____

_____

BRK 457/3
457/3
Today TH

영어 뉴스룸 56

English NewsRoom

BREAKING NEWS

2020 Korea Sale Festa to kick off Nov. in its largest scale ever. 'Korea Sale Festa', South Korea's biggest shopping festival, is to kick off next month and it is going to be the largest one ever. According to the Ministry of Trade and Industry, more than 13-hundred firms will take part during this year's event. This is almost double the number of companies from last year. This year, all 17 major cities and provinces will join the festival with products close to...

역대 최대 규모의 코리아세일페스타

역대 최대 규모로 열리는 '코리아세일페스타'에 관한 내용입니다.

2020 Korea Sale Festa to kick off Nov. in its largest scale ever

'Korea Sale Festa', South Korea's biggest shopping festival, is to kick off next month and it is going to be the largest one ever.

According to the Ministry of Trade and Industry, more than 13-hundred firms will take part during this year's event.

This is almost double the number of companies from last year.

This year, all 17 major cities and provinces will join the festival with products close to people's everyday life, such as cars, clothes, electronics and cosmetics will be on display.

The festival runs until November 15th.

Purchases can be made both on and offline.

NEWS 스크립트 분석

2020 Korea Sale Festa to kick off Nov. in its largest scale ever
11월에 사상 최대 규모로 개막하는 2020 코리아세일페스타

☆kick off *(경기, 이벤트, 미팅 등을)* 시작하다

> e.g. We are going to kick off the month by talking about love.
> 우리는 사랑에 대한 이야기로 한 달을 시작할 것이다.

☆largest scale 대규모로

> e.g. The festival is celebrating its 2nd birthday in largest scale ever.
> 그 축제는 역대 최대 규모로 2번째 생일을 맞이하고 있다.

'Korea Sale Festa', South Korea's biggest shopping festival, is to kick off next month and it is going to be the largest one ever.
국내 최대 쇼핑 축제인 '코리아세일페스타'가 다음 달 개막해 역대 최대 규모로 열릴 예정이다.

According to the Ministry of Trade and Industry, more than 13-hundred firms will take part during this year's event.
산업통상자원부에 따르면 올해 행사 기간 동안 1300개 이상의 기업이 참가한다.

This is almost double the number of companies from last year.
이는 지난해의 두 배 가까운 기업 수다.

This year, all 17 major cities and provinces will join the festival with products close to people's everyday life, such as cars, clothes, electronics and cosmetics will be on display.
올해는 자동차, 의류, 가전, 화장품 등 국민 생활과 직결된 제품이 전시되는 등 17개 주요 시·도가 모두 동참한다.

☆close to 아주 가까이에서, 가까운

> e.g. Think about nature, animals and everything that is close to our life.
> 자연, 동물 그리고 우리의 삶과 가까운 모든 것에 대해 생각해 보세요.

☆everyday life 일상생활

> e.g. In our everyday life, sometimes we judge people by their appearances.
> 우리의 일상 생활에서, 때때로 우리는 사람들을 외모로 판단합니다.

☆on display 전시된, 진열된

e.g. Paintings of animals will be on display in the palace.
동물 그림들이 궁전에 전시될 것이다.

The festival runs until November 15th.
축제는 11월 15일까지 계속된다.

☆run 진행되다, *(얼마 기간동안)* 유효하다

e.g. The event runs from 7am to 9am on Saturday, so please register asap.
행사는 토요일 오전 7시부터 9시까지 진행되니 최대한 빨리 등록해 주세요.

Purchases can be made both on and offline.
온 · 오프라인 구매가 가능하다.

☆Purchases can be made 구입이 가능하다

e.g. Purchases can be made in advance from Wednesday.
수요일부터 미리 구매가 가능합니다.

Writing Exercise

1. 국내 최대 쇼핑 축제인 '코리아세일페스타'가 다음 달 개막해 역대 최대 규모로 열릴 예정이다.

   'Korea
   _____

   _____

2. 산업통상자원부에 따르면 올해 행사 기간 동안 1300개 이상의 기업이 참가한다.

   According to
   _____

   _____

3. 이는 지난해의 두 배 가까운 기업 수다.

   This
   _____

   _____

4. 올해는 자동차, 의류, 가전, 화장품 등 국민 생활과 직결된 제품이 전시되는 등 17개 주요 시·도가 모두 동참한다.

   This year,
   _____

   _____

5. 축제는 11월 15일까지 계속된다.

   The festival
   _____

   _____

6. 온·오프라인 구매가 가능하다.

   Purchases
   _____

   _____

◎ BRK 457/3
457/3
Today TH

영어 뉴스룸 57

English NewsRoom

BREAKING NEWS

S. Korea resumes distribution of discount coupons for travel packages, dining out. The South Korean government will resume its distribution of discount coupons on Friday for travel packages, lodging and dining out to drive domestic spending in areas hit hard by the COVID-19 pandemic. Starting Friday afternoon, the government will provide up to 30 percent discounts for over 11-hundred tour items. The coupon can be downloaded from 2 PM...

여행과 외식을 할인된 가격으로!

정부가 코로나 피해 지역의 내수를 촉진시키기 위해 여행상품과 외식 할인쿠폰을 지급한다는 내용입니다.

S. Korea resumes distribution of discount coupons for travel packages, dining out

The South Korean government will resume its distribution of discount coupons on Friday for travel packages, lodging and dining out to drive domestic spending in areas hit hard by the COVID-19 pandemic.

Starting Friday afternoon, the government will provide up to 30 percent discounts for over 11-hundred tour items.

The coupon can be downloaded from 2PM from the website of travel agency Tidesquare.

The government will also resume its cashback program for dining out at restaurants.

If people eat out at restaurants three times, they will get a refund of around nine dollars on their fourth meal.

Card users can apply for the cashback through their card websites from 4 PM today.

 스크립트 분석

S. Korea resumes distribution of discount coupons for travel packages, dining out
(한국)정부는 여행상품과 외식을 위한 할인쿠폰 지급을 재개한다

☆distribution 분배, 지급

e.g. There are rules to protect customers from the illegal distribution of goods.
불법 상품 유통으로부터 고객을 보호하기 위한 규정들이 있다.

☆dining out 외식 (dine out 외식하다)

e.g. We like to dine out and enjoy outdoor activities.
우리는 외식을 하고 야외 활동을 즐기는 것을 좋아한다.

The South Korean government will resume its distribution of discount coupons on Friday for travel packages, lodging and dining out to drive domestic spending in areas hit hard by the COVID-19 pandemic.
한국 정부는 COVID-19 대유행으로 큰 피해를 입은 지역의 내수를 촉진하기 위해 금요일부터 여행 상품, 숙박, 외식 등에 대한 할인 쿠폰 지급을 재개할 예정이다.

☆lodging 숙소, 숙박

e.g. The price includes lodging and two meals a day.
그 가격에는 숙박과 하루 두 끼가 포함되어 있다.

☆drive 촉진하다

e.g. What drives consumer spending when the economy is unstable?
경제가 불안정할 때 무엇이 소비자 소비를 촉진하는가?

☆domestic spending 국내 소비, 내수 소비

e.g. It was true that domestic spending was still weak because of the typhoon.
태풍 때문에 국내 소비가 여전히 부진한 것은 사실이었다.

☆be hit hard (안좋은 쪽으로) 큰 타격을 받다

e.g. The country was hit hard by the virus last year.
그 나라는 작년에 그 바이러스로 인해 큰 타격을 받았다.

Starting Friday afternoon, the government will provide up to 30 percent discounts for over 11-hundred tour items.
정부는 금요일 오후부터 1100개가 넘는 관광(여행) 상품에 대해 최대 30%의 할인 혜택을 제공할 예정이다.

☆up to 최대

The coupon can be downloaded from 2PM from the website of travel agency Tidesquare.
쿠폰은 여행사 타이드스퀘어 홈페이지에서 오후 2시부터 다운로드 받을 수 있다.

The government will also resume its cashback program for dining out at restaurants.
정부는 또한 식당에서의 외식을 위한 캐시백 프로그램을 재개할 것이다.

If people eat out at restaurants three times, they will get a refund of around nine dollars on their fourth meal.
식당에서 세 번 외식을 하면 네 번째 식사 때 9달러 안팎의 환불을 받는다.

☆eat out 외식하다

e.g. We used to eat out all the time when we were in Korea.
우리는 한국에 있을 때 항상 외식을 하곤 했다.

☆get a refund 환불받다, 변제받다

e.g. How can I get a refund on a used product?
중고 제품을 어떻게 환불 받을 수 있나요?

Card users can apply for the cashback through their card websites from 4 PM today.
카드 이용자들은 오늘 오후 4시부터 카드 홈페이지를 통해 캐시백을 신청할 수 있다.

☆apply for 신청하다, 지원하다

e.g. He is going to apply for a job as a panda nanny.
그는 팬더 유모직에 지원할 예정이다.

Writing Exercise

1. 한국 정부는 COVID - 19 대유행으로 큰 피해를 입은 지역의 내수를 촉진하기 위해 금요일부터 여행 상품, 숙박, 외식 등에 대한 할인 쿠폰 지급을 재개할 예정이다.

   The South

2. 정부는 금요일 오후부터 1100개가 넘는 관광(여행)상품에 대해 최대 30%의 할인 혜택을 제공할 예정이다.

   Starting

3. 쿠폰은 여행사 타이드스퀘어 홈페이지에서 오후 2시부터 내려 받을 수 있다.

   The coupon

4. 정부는 또한 식당에서의 외식을 위한 캐시백 프로그램을 재개할 것이다.

   The government

5. 식당에서 세 번 외식을 하면 네 번째 식사 때 9달러 안팎의 환불을 받는다.

   If people

6. 카드 이용자들은 오늘 오후 4시부터 카드 홈페이지를 통해 캐시백을 신청할 수 있다.

   Card

BRK 457/3
457/3
Today TH

영어 뉴스룸 58

English NewsRoom

BREAKING NEWS

'Baby Shark' becomes YouTube's most-watched video with over 7 bil. Views. With an addictive hook and easy-to-follow dance moves, 'Baby Shark', a megahit children's song made by the South Korean educational brand Pinkfong, has become YouTube's most-played video as of Monday. According to the company, the sing-and-dance video received international attention by reaching more than 7 billion views. The song made its way to the top of YouTube's ...

아기상어, 유튜브 최다 조회수 기록하다

유튜브 역대 조회수 1위를 기록한 아기상어에 관한 내용입니다.

NEWS  전체 스크립트

'Baby Shark' becomes YouTube's most-watched video with over 7 bil. Views

With an addictive hook and easy-to-follow dance moves, 'Baby Shark', a megahit children's song made by the South Korean educational brand Pinkfong, has become YouTube's most-played video as of Monday.

According to the company, the sing-and-dance video received international attention by reaching more than 7 billion views.

The song made its way to the top of YouTube's most-watched chart 4 years after it was first uploaded in 2016.

The number of views for 'Baby Shark' has surpassed those of Luis Fonsi and Daddy Yankee's "Despacito", which had previously held the most watched top spot since 2017.

 스크립트 분석

'Baby Shark' becomes YouTube's most-watched video with over 7 bil. Views
'아기 상어'가 유튜브에서 70억 뷰 이상의 조회수를 기록하며 가장 많이 본 영상이 되다

☆the most-watched video 가장 많이 본 영상
· the most-visited place 가장 많이 간 장소
· the most-listened song 가장 많이 들은 노래
· the most-read book 가장 많이 읽은 책

With an addictive hook and easy-to-follow dance moves, 'Baby Shark', a megahit children's song made by the South Korean educational brand Pinkfong, has become YouTube's most-played video as of Monday.
중독성 있는 구절과 따라 하기 쉬운 춤으로 국내 교육 브랜드 핑크퐁이 만든 메가히트 동요 '아기상어'가 월요일자로 유튜브에서 가장 많이 재생된 영상이 된다.

☆addictive 중독성이 있는

e.g. It is a highly addictive drug for the young.
그것은 젊은이들에게 매우 중독성이 강한 약물이다.

☆hook 귀에 맴도는 노래의 구절
☆easy-to-follow 따라하기 쉬운

e.g. This is an easy-to-follow recipe.
이것은 쉽게 따라 할 수 있는 요리법이다.

☆made by ~에 의해 만들어진

e.g. The toy is made by using computer software.
그 장난감은 컴퓨터 소프트웨어를 사용하여 만들어졌다.

☆as of ~일자로, ~현재로

e.g. As of now, I will no longer drink coffee for my brain.
지금부터, 나는 뇌를 위해 더 이상 커피를 마시지 않을 거야.

According to the company, the sing-and-dance video received international attention by reaching more than 7 billion views.

그 회사에 따르면, 그 노래와 춤 영상은 70억 이상의 조회수를 기록함으로써 국제적인 주목을 받았다고 한다.

☆receive attention 주목받다

> e.g. It received attention thanks to the video uploaded by her.
> 그녀가 올린 영상 덕분에 주목을 받았다.

The song made its way to the top of YouTube's most-watched chart 4 years after it was first uploaded in 2016.

이 곡은 2016년 처음 업로드된 지 4년 만에 유튜브 최다 조회 차트 1위에 올랐다.

☆make one's way 나아가다, 가다, 출세하다

> e.g. After military service, he made his way as a reporter.
> 군복무 후 그는 기자로 출세했다.

The number of views for 'Baby Shark' has surpassed those of Luis Fonsi and Daddy Yankee's 'Despacito', which had previously held the most watched top spot since 2017.

'아기상어' 조회수가 2017년 이후 가장 많은 시청률을 기록했던 루이스 폰시와 대디 양키의 '데스파시토' 조회수를 넘어섰다.

☆surpass 능가하다, 뛰어넘다

> e.g. The number of confirmed virus cases in the country surpassed 2 million.
> 국내 바이러스 확진 건수가 200만 건을 돌파했다.

☆top spot 최고의 자리, 1등

> e.g. The company has remained top spot for safety issues.
> 그 회사는 안전 문제에서 여전히 1위를 유지하고 있다.

Writing Exercise

1. 중독성 있는 구절과 따라 하기 쉬운 춤으로 국내 교육 브랜드 핑크퐁이 만든 메가히트 동요 '아기상어'가 월요일자로 유튜브에서 가장 많이 재생된 영상이 된다.

With _____

_____

2. 그 회사에 따르면, 그 노래와 춤 영상은 70억 이상의 조회수를 기록함으로서 국제적인 주목을 받았다고 한다.

According to _____

_____

3. 이 곡은 2016년 처음 업로드된 지 4년 만에 유튜브 최다 조회 차트 1위에 올랐다.

The song _____

_____

4. '아기상어' 조회수가 2017년 이후 가장 많은 시청률을 기록했던 루이스 폰시와 대디 양키의 '데스파시토' 조회수를 넘어섰다.

The number _____

_____

ⓖ BRK 457/3
457/3
Today TH

영어 뉴스룸 59

English NewsRoom

BREAKING NEWS

Biden heads to church after victory... Trump golfing for second straight day. A day after the U.S. presidential election was finally called by major TV networks, both President Trump and President-elect Joe Biden were seen out and about on Sunday. Biden began his day attending Mass in Delaware with his family, after which Biden visited the cemetery where his parents, first wife, young daughter and son are buried.

바이든은 교회로, 트럼프는 골프장으로

미국 대선을 승리한 바이든은 성당을 찾았고 이에 불복하는 트럼프는 이틀째 골프를 치고 있다는 내용입니다.

 NEWS 전체 스크립트

Biden heads to church after victory... Trump golfing for second straight day

A day after the U.S. presidential election was finally called by major TV networks, both President Trump and President-elect Joe Biden were seen out and about on Sunday.

Biden began his day attending Mass in Delaware with his family, after which Biden visited the cemetery where his parents, first wife, young daughter and son are buried.

President Trump was seen golfing in Virginia, greeted by supporters as well as demonstrators.

CNN reports that Jared Kushner has approached the president to concede, while First Lady Melania Trump also advised her husband to accept the loss.

However, the First Lady later tweeted that the American people deserve fair elections, adding every legal-not illegal-vote should be counted.

NEWS 스크립트 분석

Biden heads to church after victory... Trump golfing for second straight day
바이든은 승리 후 교회로 향해... 트럼프, 이틀째 골프

☆head to ~로 향하다

> e.g. He is heading to the Presidential Office after the victory.
> 그는 우승 후 대통령 집무실로 향하고 있다.

☆straight 연속적인, 끊이지 않는

> e.g. The town has 10 criminal cases for three straight days.
> 그 도시는 3일 연속 10건의 형사 사건이 있었다.

A day after the U.S. presidential election was finally called by major TV networks, both President Trump and President-elect Joe Biden were seen out and about on Sunday.
미국 대선결과가 마침내 주요 TV 방송국에 의해 발표된 지 하루 만인 일요일에 트럼프 대통령과 조 바이든 대통령 당선자 모두 다시 바깥으로 모습을 드러냈다.

☆out and about 다시 나다니는, *(어디를)* 돌아다니는

> e.g. The doctor says after the treatment, she should be out and about in a few days.
> 의사는 치료 후에 그녀가 며칠 안에 돌아다닐 수 있을 것이라고 말했다.

Biden began his day attending Mass in Delaware with his family, after which Biden visited the cemetery where his parents, first wife, young daughter and son are buried.
바이든은 가족과 함께 델라웨어 주에서 미사에 참석하며 하루를 시작했고, 그 후 바이든은 부모와 첫째 아내, 어린 딸과 아들이 묻혀 있는 묘지를 방문했다.

☆begin the day 하루를 시작하다

> e.g. He begins the day with a cup of coffee with his wife.
> 그는 아내와 커피 한 잔으로 하루를 시작한다.

☆Mass 미사
☆after which 그리고 나서, 그 후, 그런 다음에

> e.g. He went to the bank, after which he visited my office.
> 그는 은행에 갔고 그 후에 내 사무실을 방문했다.

☆cemetery 묘지

☆bury *(시신을)* 묻다

> e.g. 10 members of the family are buried in the same graveyard.
> 가족 10명이 같은 묘지에 묻혔다.

☆graveyard *(흔히 교회 근처에 있는)* 묘지

President Trump was seen golfing in Virginia, greeted by supporters as well as demonstrators.

트럼프 대통령은 시위대는 물론 지지자들의 환영을 받으며 버지니아주에서 골프를 치는 모습이 목격되었다.

☆be seen 목격되다, 보여지다

☆greeted by ~로부터 환영 받다

> e.g. She was greeted by her parents and friends.
> 그녀는 부모님과 친구들의 환영을 받았다.

☆demonstrator 시위대

CNN reports that Jared Kushner has approached the president to concede, while First Lady Melania Trump also advised her husband to accept the loss.

영부인 멜라니아 트럼프도 남편에게 패배를 받아들이라고 조언하는 동안 재러드 쿠슈너가*(사위)* 대통령에게 패배를 인정하라고 접촉했다고 CNN은 보도한다.

☆concede *(패배를)* 인정하다

However, the First Lady later tweeted that the American people deserve fair elections, adding every legal - not illegal - vote should be counted.

그러나 영부인은 나중에 트위터를 통해 미국 국민은 공정한 선거를 치를 자격이 있으며 불법이 아닌, 모든 합법적 투표는 개표되어야 한다고 덧붙였다.

☆deserve ~을 누릴 자격이 있다, 받을 자격이 있다

> e.g. I reckon you deserve a better man.
> 난 네가 더 나은 남자를 만날 자격이 있다고 생각해.

☆count 세다, 개표하다

Writing Exercise

1. 미국 대선결과가 마침내 주요 TV 방송국에 의해 발표된 지 하루 만인 일요일에 트럼프 대통령과 조 바이든 대통령 당선자 모두 다시 바깥으로 모습을 드러냈다.

   A day _____

   _____

2. 바이든은 가족과 함께 델라웨어 주에서 미사에 참석하며 하루를 시작했고, 그 후 바이든은 부모와 첫째 아내, 어린 딸과 아들이 묻혀 있는 묘지를 방문했다.

   Biden _____

   _____

3. 트럼프 대통령은 시위대는 물론 지지자들의 환영을 받으며 버지니아주에서 골프를 치는 모습이 목격되었다.

   President _____

   _____

4. 영부인 멜라니아 트럼프도 남편에게 패배를 받아들이라고 조언하는 동안 재러드 쿠슈너가 (사위) 대통령에게 패배를 인정하라고 접촉했다고 CNN은 보도한다.

   CNN _____

   _____

5. 그러나 영부인은 나중에 트위터를 통해 미국 국민은 공정한 선거를 치를 자격이 있으며 불법이 아닌, 모든 합법적 투표는 개표되어야 한다고 덧붙였다.

   However, _____

   _____

⊚ BRK 457/3
457/3
Today TH

영어 뉴스룸 60

English NewsRoom

BREAKING NEWS

S. Korean gov't to begin imposing fines on people who do not wear masks in public from Nov. 13. South Korea will begin imposing fines on people who do not wear face masks in public beginning Friday, as part of its latest efforts to contain the further spread of COVID-19. This comes as the 30-day grace period for the measure, announced by the government last month, comes to an end. People will be mandated to wear face masks at some 23 multi-use...

턱스크해도 과태료 10만원?

'마스크 미착용'에 대해 최대 10만원의 과태료가 부가된다는 내용입니다.

S. Korean gov't to begin imposing fines on people who do not wear masks in public from Nov. 13

South Korea will begin imposing fines on people who do not wear face masks in public beginning Friday, as part of its latest efforts to contain the further spread of COVID-19.

This comes as the 30-day grace period for the measure, announced by the government last month, comes to an end.

People will be mandated to wear face masks at some 23 multi-use facilities as well as on public transportation and at hospitals, in-door sport stadiums and demonstrations.

Violators will face a fine of up to 90 U.S. dollars.

Businesses who do not direct their users to wear face masks will also be subject to a fine of up to 27-hundred dollars.

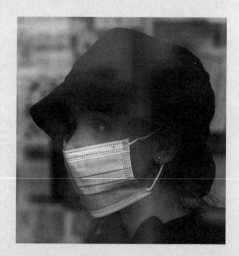

NEWS 스크립트 분석

S. Korean gov't to begin imposing fines on people who do not wear masks in public from Nov. 13
한국 정부는 11월 13일부터 공공장소에서 마스크를 착용하지 않는 사람들에게 과태료를 부과하기 시작할 것이다.

☆impose a fine 벌금을 부과하다, 과태료를 부과하다

e.g. The court imposed a fine of 100,000won on him.
법원은 그에게 10만 원의 벌금을 부과했다.

☆in public 공공장소에서 (↔in private 사적장소에서)

e.g. I'm nervous about speaking in public, but I know what they want from me.
나는 공공장소(사람들 앞)에서 말하는 게 긴장되지만, 그들이 나한테 뭘 원하는지 알아.

South Korea will begin imposing fines on people who do not wear face masks in public beginning Friday, as part of its latest efforts to contain the further spread of COVID-19.
한국은 코로나19의 추가 확산을 막기 위한 최근의 노력의 일환으로 금요일부터 공공장소에서 마스크를 착용하지 않는 사람들에게 과태료를 부과하기 시작할 것이다.

☆as part of ~의 일환으로

e.g. Moving out from your parents' house is necessary as part of learning how to be an independent person.
독립적인 사람이 되는 법을 배움의 일환으로 부모님 집에서 독립하는 것은 필요하다.

☆contain 방지하다, 억제하다

e.g. Factories have been closed off in an attempt to contain the disease.
그 병을 억제하기 위해 공장들이 문을 닫았다.

This comes as the 30-day grace period for the measure, announced by the government last month, comes to an end.
이는 지난달 정부가 발표한 이 조치를 위한 30일간의 유예기간이 끝나면서 나온 것이다.

☆grace period 유예 기간

e.g. He has a ten-day grace period until the end of the month.
그는 월말까지 10일간의 유예기간을 갖는다.

☆come to an end 끝나다, 죽다

e.g. After 2 weeks of chaos, the war finally came to an end.
2주간의 혼란 후에, 전쟁은 마침내 끝났다.

People will be mandated to wear face masks at some 23 multi-use facilities as well as on public transportation and at hospitals, in-door sport stadiums and demonstrations.
시민들은 23개 대중교통, 병원, 실내 스포츠 경기장, 시위장은 물론 다중이용시설 등에서도 마스크를 착용해야 한다.

☆mandate 명령하다, 지시하다

e.g. We have been mandated to vote yes in the referendum.
우리는 국민투표에서 찬성표를 던지도록 지시를 받았다.

☆Referendum 국민 투표, 총선거
☆multi-use facility 다중이용시설
☆in-door 실내의, 실내용의 (↔outdoor)

Violators will face a fine of up to 90 U.S. dollars.
위반자는 최대 90달러의 과태료를 물게 된다.

☆face a fine 벌금형에 처하다, 과태료를 부과받다

e.g. People will face a fine of up to 10,000 won if they smoke here.
만약 사람들이 여기서 담배를 피우면 최대 10,000원의 과태료가 부과됩니다.

Businesses who do not direct their users to wear face masks will also be subject to a fine of up to 27-hundred dollars.
이용자에게 마스크 착용을 지시하지 않은 시설운영자들도 최고 2700달러의 과태료가 부과된다.

☆be subject to ~의 대상이다

Writing Exercise

1. 한국은 코로나19의 추가 확산을 막기 위한 최근의 노력의 일환으로 금요일부터 공공장소에서 마스크를 착용하지 않는 사람들에게 과태료를 부과하기 시작할 것이다.

   South

---

2. 이는 지난달 정부가 발표한 이 조치를 위한 30일간의 유예기간이 끝나면서 나온 것이다.

   This

---

3. 시민들은 23개 대중교통, 병원, 실내 스포츠 경기장, 시위장은 물론 다중이용시설 등에서도 마스크를 착용해야 한다.

   People

---

4. 위반자는 최대 90달러의 과태료를 물게 된다.

   Violators

---

5. 이용자에게 마스크 착용을 지시하지 않은 시설운영자들도 최고 2700달러의 과태료가 부과된다.

   Businesses

◎ BRK 457/3
457/3
Today TH

영어 뉴스룸 61

English NewsRoom

BREAKING NEWS

'Lockdown' declared 'word of year' by Collins Dictionary amid COVID-19 pandemic. 'Lockdown' has been declared 'word of the year' by Collins Dictionary, following a sharp rise in its usage during the COVID-19 pandemic. Collins says it encapsulates the shared experience of billions of people around the world. It registered more than 250-thousand usages of 'lockdown' during 2020, up from just 4-thousand last year.

먹방(Mukbang)이 영국 콜린스 사전에 포함되었다고?

영국 콜린스사전 올해의 단어에 록다운, 먹방 등이 포함되었다는 내용입니다.

'Lockdown' declared 'word of year' by Collins Dictionary amid COVID-19 pandemic

'Lockdown' has been declared 'word of the year' by Collins Dictionary, following a sharp rise in its usage during the COVID-19 pandemic.

Collins says it encapsulates the shared experience of billions of people around the world.

It registered more than 250-thousand usages of 'lockdown' during 2020, up from just 4-thousand last year.

Other pandemic-linked terms on the list include 'self-isolate', 'social distancing' and 'coronavirus'.

'Mukbang', originating from South Korea which describes a host who broadcasts videos of themselves eating large quantities of food, was also newly added.

 스크립트 분석

'Lockdown' declared 'word of year' by Collins Dictionary amid COVID-19 pandemic
'록다운(lockdown)'이 COVID-19 대유행 가운데 콜린스사전의 '올해의 단어'로 선정되었다

　☆lockdown 봉쇄, 제재

　☆declare 선언하다, 공표하다, 선정하다

'Lockdown' has been declared 'word of the year' by Collins Dictionary, following a sharp rise in its usage during the COVID-19 pandemic.
'록다운(lockdown)'이 COVID-19 대유행 동안 사용이 급증한 이후 콜린스 사전의 '올해의 단어'로 선정되었다.

　☆a sharp rise 급격한 증가

> e.g. There is a sharp rise in crime in this area.
> 이 지역에서 범죄가 급증하고 있다.

　☆usage 사용, 사용량

> e.g. A decrease in its usage would indicate financial difficulties.
> 그것의 사용 감소는 재정적인 어려움을 나타낼 것이다.

Collins says it encapsulates the shared experience of billions of people around the world.
콜린스는 그것이 전 세계 수십억 명의 사람들의 공유된 경험을 압축하는 단어라고 말한다.

　☆encapsulate (몇 마디 말이나 하나의 글 속에) 요약하다, 압축하다

> e.g. His article encapsulated the ideas of the book.
> 그의 글은 그 책의 사상을 요약하고 있다.

　☆billions of people 수십억 명 (millions of people 수백만 명)

It registered more than 250-thousand usages of 'lockdown' during 2020, up from just 4-thousand last year.
콜린스는 'lockdown(봉쇄)'라는 단어가 지난 해 4천건에서 2020년 동안 25만건 이상 사용량이 증가됐다고 밝혔다.

　☆register 등록하다, (견해를) 표명하다

> e.g. Pakistan has registered a protest with the Dutch ambassador over the matter.
> 파키스탄은 그 문제에 대해 네덜란드 대사에게 항의를 표명했다.

Other pandemic-linked terms on the list include 'self-isolate,' 'social distancing' and 'coronavirus'.

이 목록에 있는 다른 유행병 관련 용어로는 '자가격리', '사회적 거리두기', '코로나바이러스' 등이 포함된다.

　☆-linked ~와 관련된, 연결된

> e.g. The government is figuring out pandemic-linked losses in the country.
> 정부는 그 나라에서 유행병과 관련된 손실을 파악하고 있다.

　☆on the list 명단에 있는, 목록에 있는

> e.g. Make sure your name is on the list.
> 명단에 당신의 이름이 있는지 확인하세요.

'Mukbang', originating from South Korea which describes a host who broadcasts videos of themselves eating large quantities of food, was also newly added.

대량의 음식을 먹는 자신의 영상들을 방송하는 진행자를 설명하는 한국에서 유래한 단어인 '먹방'도 새롭게 추가 됐다.

　☆originate from ~에서 유래하다

> e.g. Many know that it is originated from Korea.
> 많은 사람들은 그것이 한국에서 유래되었다는 것을 알고 있다.

　☆newly 최근에, 새로

Writing Exercise

1. '록다운'(lockdown)이 COVID - 19 대유행 동안 사용이 급증한 이후 콜린스 사전의 '올해의 단어'로 선정되었다.

   'Lockdown'
   _____
   _____

2. 콜린스는 그것이 전 세계 수십억 명의 사람들의 공유된 경험을 압축하는 단어라고 말한다.

   Collins
   _____
   _____

3. 콜린스는 'lockdown (봉쇄)'라는 단어가 지난 해 4천 건에서 2020년 동안 25만건 이상 사용량이 증가됐다고 밝혔다.

   It registered
   _____
   _____

4. 이 목록에 있는 다른 유행병 관련 용어로는 '자가격리', '사회적 거리두기', '코로나바이러스' 등이 포함된다.

   Other
   _____
   _____

5. 대량의 음식을 먹는 자신의 영상들을 방송하는 진행자를 설명하는 한국에서 유래한 단어인 '먹방'도 새롭게 추가됐다.

   'Mukbang,'
   _____
   _____

영어 뉴스룸 62

English NewsRoom

BREAKING NEWS

S. Korea's Lantern Lighting Festival to be added to UNESCO's Intangible Cultural Heritage list. South Korea's Lantern Lighting Festival may be added to UNESCO's Intangible Cultural Heritage list. The Cultural Heritage Administration said Tuesday that it has completed the necessary submission procedures. The 2020 nominations will be discussed by the Committee during its 15th session next month, which runs from December 14th to 19th.

연등회, 유네스코에 등재 확실시

유네스코에서 한국의 전통유산인 '연등회'를 유네스코 인류무형유산으로 등재하도록 권고했다는 내용입니다.

전체 스크립트

S. Korea's Lantern Lighting Festival to be added to UNESCO's Intangible Cultural Heritage list

South Korea's Lantern Lighting Festival may be added to UNESCO's Intangible Cultural Heritage list.

The Cultural Heritage Administration said Tuesday that it has completed the necessary submission procedures.

The 2020 nominations will be discussed by the Committee during its 15th session next month, which runs from December 14th to 19th.

If added, South Korea will have a total of 21 items of cultural heritage listed by UNESCO, including traditional Korean wrestling, 'Ssirum', and the lyrical folk song 'Arirang'.

 스크립트 분석

S. Korea's Lantern Lighting Festival to be added to UNESCO's Intangible Cultural Heritage list
유네스코 무형문화유산목록에 추가될 한국의 등불 축제(연등회)

  ☆lantern 랜턴, 손전등, 등
  ☆intangible 무형의

> e.g. Intangible assets, including patents, are very important in our life.
> 특허를 포함한 무형자산은 우리 삶에서 매우 중요하다.

  ☆heritage (국가·사회의) 유산

> e.g. These temples are a part of the cultural heritage in South Korea.
> 이 사찰들은 한국의 문화유산의 일부이다.

  ☆add 추가하다

> e.g. Two new parks will be added to the list in 2021.
> 2021년에 두 개의 새로운 공원이 추가될 것이다.

South Korea's Lantern Lighting Festival may be added to UNESCO's Intangible Cultural Heritage list.
한국의 등불 축제(연등회)가 유네스코 무형문화유산 목록에 추가될 수 있다.

The Cultural Heritage Administration said Tuesday that it has completed the necessary submission procedures.
문화재청은 이에 필요한 제출 절차를 마쳤다고 화요일에 밝혔다.

  ☆necessary 필요한

> e.g. She lacks the necessary skills for the position.
> 그녀는 그 보직에 필요한 기술이 부족하다.

  ☆submission (서류·제안서 등의) 제출

> e.g. An early deadline has been set for the submission of applications.
> 신청서 제출에 대한 조기마감일이 정해졌다.

The 2020 nominations will be discussed by the Committee during its 15th session next month, which runs from December 14th to 19th.
2020년 후보작들은(후보작들의 등재 여부는) 12월 14일부터 19일까지 열리는 다음 달 15차 회의에서 위원회가 논의한다.

☆nomination 지명, 임명, 후보작

e.g. Here is a list of nominations for 2020 best artist.
다음은 2020년 베스트 아티스트 후보 목록이다.

☆committee 위원회

☆run *(얼마의 기간 동안)* 유효하다, 계속되다

e.g. This year, the special festival runs from the 23rd to 30th.
올해, 이 특별한 축제는 23일부터 30일까지 열린다.

If added, South Korea will have a total of 21 items of cultural heritage listed by UNESCO, including traditional Korean wrestling, 'Ssirum', and the lyrical folk song 'Arirang'.

추가되면 한국은 전통 씨름 '씨름'과 서정적인 민요 '아리랑' 등 유네스코가 등재한 총 21개의 문화유산을 갖게 된다.

☆If *(it is)* added

☆lyrical 서정적인, *(표현이)* 아름답고 열정적인 =expressive

☆folk song 민요

Writing Exercise

1. 한국의 등불 축제(연등회)가 유네스코 무형문화유산 목록에 추가될 수 있다.

South

2. 문화재청은 이에 필요한 제출 절차를 마쳤다고 화요일에 밝혔다.

The Cultural

3. 2020년 후보작들은 (그러니까 후보작들의 등재 여부는) 12월 14일부터 19일까지 열리는 다음 달 15차 회의에서 위원회가 논의한다.

The 2020

4. 추가되면 한국은 전통 씨름 '씨름'과 서정적인 민요 '아리랑' 등 유네스코가 등재한 총 21개의 문화유산을 갖게 된다.

If added,

BRK 457/3
457/3
Today TH

영어 뉴스룸 63

English NewsRoom

BREAKING NEWS

Seoul city designs "silent" safety rule book for foreign construction workers. The City of Seoul has published a safety book for the city's non-Korean construction workers. Comprised only of pictures and no words, the 88-paged, pocket-sized, carry-around book, is designed to break down language barriers and maintain a safe work environment. Also available in PDF format on the city government's website, the material includes 73 guidelines...

안전교육 지침서를 그림책으로

서울시가 외국인 건설근로자들을 위해 안전교육 그림책을 발행했다는 내용입니다.

Seoul city designs "silent" safety rule book for foreign construction workers

The City of Seoul has published a safety book for the city's non-Korean construction workers.

Comprised only of pictures and no words, the 88-paged, pocket-sized, carry-around book, is designed to break down language barriers and maintain a safe work environment.

Also available in PDF format on the city government's website, the material includes 73 guidelines on how to use dangerous equipment safely.

Foreign workers make up about 18-percent of all those working at public construction sites managed by the city.

Seoul city designs "silent" safety rule book for foreign construction workers
서울시가 외국인 건설 노동자들을 위한 "그림책" 안전 규칙서를 만든다.

☆silent book 그림책 =wordless picture books

☆construction worker 공사현장 인부

The City of Seoul has published a safety book for the city's non-Korean construction workers.
서울시가 비한국인 건설근로자를 위한 안전책을 발간했다.

☆publish 출판하다

e.g. He began publishing a monthly book and became very sensitive.
그는 월간 책을 출판하기 시작했고 매우 예민해졌다.

☆non-Korean 외국인

·non-fiction 논픽션, 실화
·non profit 비영리적인
·non-professorial 정통적이지 않는
·non-prescription (약제 따위가) 처방전 없이 합법적으로 팔리는

Comprised only of pictures and no words, the 88-paged, pocket-sized, carry-around book, is designed to break down language barriers and maintain a safe work environment.
그림으로만 구성되고 글 하나 없는 88페이지의 포켓 크기의 휴대용 책은 언어 장벽을 허물고 안전한 작업 환경을 유지하기 위해 만들어졌다.

☆comprise of ~으로 구성된

e.g. My subscribers are comprised of people who live in Korea and abroad.
나의 구독자들은 극내외에 사는 사람들로 구성되어 있다.

☆pocket-sized 포켓 크기의, 소형의

e.g. I used to bring a pocket-sized dictionary, but not anymore.
예전에는 주머니 크기의 사전을 가지고 다녔는데, 더 이상은 아니다.

☆carry-around book 휴대하고 다니는 책
☆break down 허물다
☆barrier (어떤 일에 대한) 장애물

e.g. The program aims to break down the barriers between the rich and poor.
그 프로그램은 빈부 간의 장벽을 허물기 위한 것이다.

Also available in PDF format on the city government's website, the material includes 73 guidelines on how to use dangerous equipment safely.

또한 시 정부 웹사이트에서 PDF 형식으로 이용할 수 있는(즉 제공되는) 이 자료에는 위험 장비를 안전하게 사용하는 방법에 대한 73가지 지침이 포함되어 있다.

☆available 이용할 수 있는

> e.g. This car is available in 5 different colours.
> 이 차는 5가지 다른 색상으로 판매된다.

Foreign workers make up about 18-percent of all those working at public construction sites managed by the city.

시에 의해 관리되는 공공건설현장에서 일하는 외국인 근로자는 전체의 18%를 차지한다.

☆make up ~차지하다

> e.g. Advertising makes up almost 50 percent of the business.
> 광고는 사업의 거의 50%를 차지한다.

☆site 현장

☆managed by ~에 의해 관리되는

Writing Exercise

1. 서울시가 비한국인 건설근로자를 위한 안전책을 발간했다.

The City

2. 그림으로만 구성되고 글 하나 없는 88페이지의 포켓 크기의 휴대용 책은 언어 장벽을 허물고 안전한 작업 환경을 유지하기 위해 만들어 졌다.

Comprised

3. 또한 시 정부 웹사이트에서 PDF 형식으로 이용할 수 있는(즉 제공되는) 이 자료에는 위험 장비를 안전하게 사용하는 방법에 대한 73가지 지침이 포함되어 있다.

Also

4. 시에 의해 관리되는 공공건설현장에서 일하는 외국인 근로자는 전체의 18%를 차지한다.

Foreign

BRK 457/3
457/3
Today TH

영어 뉴스룸 64

English NewsRoom

BREAKING NEWS

Foreign-invested companies in S. Korea holding 5-day virtual job fair. Foreign-invested companies in South Korea are holding a five-day virtual job fair starting today. Hosted by the Ministry of Trade, Industry and Energy, 105 companies are taking part, including 15 companies on the Fortune Global 500 such as DHL Korea and BMW Korea. The ministry says it's expecting some 10-thousand jobseekers to take part, and the companies are planning to hire...

취업박람회도 비대면으로

외국인 투자기업 채용박람회가 닷새간 비대면으로 열린다는 내용입니다.

Foreign-invested companies in S. Korea holding 5-day virtual job fair

Foreign-invested companies in South Korea are holding a five-day virtual job fair starting today.

Hosted by the Ministry of Trade, Industry and Energy, 105 companies are taking part, including 15 companies on the Fortune Global 500 such as DHL Korea and BMW Korea.

The ministry says it's expecting some 10-thousand jobseekers to take part, and the companies are planning to hire around 800 people.

Many companies will be doing the entire recruitment process, from applications to final interviews, online with no in-person contact.

NEWS 스크립트 분석

Foreign-invested companies in S. Korea holding 5-day virtual job fair
닷새간 가상취업박람회를 개최하는 한국의 외국인 외투기업

- ☆foreign-invested company 외국인 투자기업
- ☆hold 개최하다

> e.g. The Prime Minister will hold a meeting to discuss the issue.
> 국무총리는 그 문제를 논의하기 위해 회의를 열 것이다.

- ☆virtual *(컴퓨터를 이용한)* 가상의

> e.g. The leader will take part in a virtual conference this Saturday to discuss varies issues.
> 그 지도자는 이번 주 토요일에 다양한 문제들을 논의하기 위해 가상 회의에 참석할 예정입니다.

- ☆job fair 공개 취직 설명회 =a job expo or career fair or career expo

Foreign-invested companies in South Korea are holding a five-day virtual job fair starting today.
한국의 외국인투자기업들이 오늘부터 5일간 가상 취업박람회를 열고 있다.

Hosted by the Ministry of Trade, Industry and Energy, 105 companies are taking part, including 15 companies on the Fortune Global 500 such as DHL Korea and BMW Korea.
산업통상자원부가 주최하는 이번 행사에는 DHL코리아, BMW코리아 등 포춘 글로벌 500대 기업 15곳을 포함해 105개 기업이 참여하고 있다.

- ☆hosted by 주최하는

> e.g. The party hosted by the government continues to highlight the importance of AI.
> 정부가 주최하는 파티는 AI의 중요성을 계속 강조하고 있다.

- ☆take part in 참여하다 =participate in

> e.g. This year he is taking part in the project to get a promotion.
> 올해 그는 승진을 위한 프로젝트에 참여할 것이다.

- ☆fortune *(특히 사람의 삶에 영향을 미치는)* 운, 재산

The ministry says it's expecting some 10-thousand jobseekers to take part, and the companies are planning to hire around 800 people.

산업통상자원부는 약 1만 명의 구직자들이 참여할 것으로 예상하고 있으며, 이 회사들은 약 800명을 채용할 계획이다.

☆expect 예상하다

☆jobseeker 구직자

> e.g. The company says they aren't sure how many jobseekers will come this year.
> 그 회사는 올해 얼마나 많은 구직자들이 올지 확신할 수 없다라고 말한다.

Many companies will be doing the entire recruitment process, from applications to final interviews, online with no in-person contact.

많은 기업들이 지원부터 최종 면접까지 채용 전 과정을 직접 접촉하지 않는 온라인으로 진행할 예정이다.

☆entire 전체의

☆recruitment 채용

☆from A to B A에서부터 B까지

> e.g. Using this map, drivers can find the fastest route from the city to the countryside.
> 이 지도를 사용하여 운전자들은 도시에서 시골로 가는 가장 빠른 경로를 찾을 수 있다.

☆application 지원

☆in-person 직접

> e.g. The hospital is interested in replacing in-person visits with video conferences due to the safety issues.
> 병원 측은 안전 문제 때문에 직접 방문하는 것을 화상 회의로 대체하는 데 관심이 많다.

Writing Exercise

1. 한국의 외국인투자기업들이 오늘부터 5일간 가상 취업박람회를 열고 있다.

   Foreign - invested
   _____

   _____

2. 산업통상자원부가 주최하는 이번 행사에는 DHL코리아, BMW코리아 등 포춘 글로벌 500대 기업 15곳을 포함해 105개 기업이 참여하고 있다.

   Hosted
   _____

   _____

3. 산업통상자원부는 약 1만 명의 구직자들이 참여할 것으로 예상하고 있으며, 이 회사들은 약 800명을 채용할 계획이다.

   The ministry
   _____

   _____

4. 많은 기업들이 지원부터 최종 면접까지 채용 전 과정을 직접 접촉하지 않는 온라인으로 진행할 예정이다.

   Many
   _____

   _____

◉ BRK 457/3
457/3
Today TH

영어 뉴스룸 65

English NewsRoom

BREAKING NEWS

Seoul's subway system reduces service during tightened COVID-19 measures. Starting today, services on some of the capital region's subway lines will be adjusted to lessen movement within the city in response to the recent surge in COVID-19 cases. As part of the "standstill for 10 million Seoulites" campaign, Lines 1, 4, the Gyeong-ui Jungang and the Gyeongchun line, will terminate before 12：30 at night, at their final stations.

전철 막차시간이 단축된다?

코로나19의 확산세를 막기 위해 수도권 전철 일부 노선의 막차시간이 0시 30분으로 단축된다는 내용입니다.

NEWS 전체 스크립트

Seoul's subway system reduces service during tightened COVID-19 measures

Starting today, services on some of the capital region's subway lines will be adjusted to lessen movement within the city in response to the recent surge in COVID-19 cases.

As part of the "standstill for 10 million Seoulites" campaign, Lines 1, 4, the Gyeong-ui Jungang and the Gyeongchun line, will terminate before 12：30 at night, at their final stations.

This will affect their regular schedule after 8 P.M.

In addition, other lines, including Line 3, will run at 80-percent usual levels after 10 P.M.

 스크립트 분석

Seoul's subway system reduces service during tightened COVID-19 measures
서울 지하철은 강화된 COVID-19 조치 동안 운행시간을 단축한다

☆reduce 줄이다, 단축하다

☆tightened 강화된

> e.g. The city government came up with tightened regulations on apartment prices.
> 서울시는 아파트 가격에 대한 강화된 규제를 내놓았다.

Starting today, services on some of the capital region's subway lines will be adjusted to lessen movement within the city in response to the recent surge in COVID-19 cases.
오늘부터 수도권 전철 일부 노선의 운행이 최근 급증하는 COVID-19 사례에 대응해 도심 내 이동을 줄이는 방향으로 조정된다.

☆adjust 조정하다, 조절하다, 적응하다

> e.g. Timetables will be adjusted to better suit online classes for the young.
> 시간표는 젊은이들을 위한 온라인 수업에 더 적합하도록 조정될 것이다.

☆lessen 크기·강도·중요도 등을 줄이다 =diminish

> e.g. Brown bread can lessen the risk of cancer.
> 갈색 빵은 암의 위험을 줄일 수 있다.

☆in response to ~에 응하여

> e.g. Many office workers will stay at home in response to the Covid-19 pandemic.
> 코로나19 팬데믹 시대에 대응하여 많은 직장인들이 집에 머물 것이다.

☆surge 급등하다, 급증하다

> e.g. Average salt prices surged 10% from July.
> 평균 소금 가격은 7월에 비해 10% 급등했다.

As part of the "standstill for 10 million Seoulites" campaign, Lines 1, 4, the Gyeong-ui Jungang and the Gyeongchun line, will terminate before 12 : 30 at night, at their final stations.
'1천만 서울시민 스탠드스틸' 캠페인의 일환으로 수도권 전철 1호선, 4호선, 경의중앙선, 경춘선이 종착역 기준으로 0시 30분 전까지 운행을 종료한다.

☆as part of ~의 일환으로

☆standstill 정지, 멈춤 =halt

e.g. The traffic came to a standstill due to the horses in the street.
거리의 말들 때문에 교통이 마비되었다.
☆ come to a standstill 정지하다

☆Seoulite 서울 시민, 서울라이트

☆terminate 끝나다, 종료되다, 종점에 닿다

e.g. This train will terminate at the next stop so passengers should change trains.
이 기차는 다음 정거장에서 종착할 것이니 승객들은 열차를 갈아타야 한다.

This will affect their regular schedule after 8 P.M.
이것이 오후 8시 이후 운행하는 열차의 정규 운행시간에 영향을 미칠 것이다.

In addition, other lines, including Line 3, will run at 80-percent usual levels after 10P.M.
또 오후 10시 이후에는 3호선 등 다른 노선은 평소의 80% 수준으로 운행된다.
☆usual 평상시의, 보통의

Writing Exercise

1. 오늘부터 수도권 전철 일부 노선의 운행이 최근 급증하는 COVID-19 사례에 대응해 도심 내 이동을 줄이는 방향으로 조정된다.

Starting _____

_____

2. '1천만 서울시민 스탠드스틸' 캠페인의 일환으로 수도권 전철 1호선, 4호선, 경의중앙선, 경춘선이 종착역 기준으로 0시 30분 전까지 운행을 종료한다.

As part _____

_____

3. 이것이 오후 8시 이후 운행하는 열차의 정규 운행시간에 영향을 미칠 것이다.

This _____

_____

4. 또 오후 10시 이후에는 3호선 등 다른 노선은 평소의 80% 수준으로 운행된다.

In addition, _____

_____

◎ BRK 457/3
457/3
Today TH

영어 뉴스룸 66

English NewsRoom

BREAKING NEWS

Life expectancy for S. Korean babies born in 2019 increases. South Korean babies born last year are expected to live on average eight years longer than those born 20 years ago, two years more than the OECD average. Due to improved public health awareness and better medical care, babies born in Korea in 2019 are expected to live for an average of 83.3 years. According to Statistics Korea, boys are expected to live for 80.3 years while girls have a life...

기대수명이 8년 늘어났다고?

작년에 태어난 한국아기의 기대수명이 20년 전보다 8년이 늘어났다는 내용입니다.

 NEWS 전체 스크립트

Life expectancy for S. Korean babies born in 2019 increases

South Korean babies born last year are expected to live on average eight years longer than those born 20 years ago, two years more than the OECD average.

Due to improved public health awareness and better medical care, babies born in Korea in 2019 are expected to live for an average of 83.3 years.

According to Statistics Korea, boys are expected to live for 80.3 years while girls have a life expectancy of 86.3 years.

The gender gap in life expectancy remains unchanged at six years for the second year in a row.

Meanwhile, the statistics agency picked cancer as the number one cause of death in the future for babies born in 2019, followed by heart disease and pneumonia.

Life expectancy for S. Korean babies born in 2019 increases

2019년생 한국 아기의 기대수명이 늘어난다

☆expectancy *(특히 좋거나 신나는 일에 대한)* 기대

☆life expectancy 기대 수명

> e.g. I'm not sure but Korea has the longest life expectancy.
> 확실하지는 않지만 한국이 기대수명이 가장 길다.

South Korean babies born last year are expected to live on average eight years longer than those born 20 years ago, two years more than the OECD average.

작년에 태어난 한국 아기들은 20년 전에 태어난 아기들보다 평균 8년 더 오래 살 것으로 예상되는데, 이는 경제협력개발기구(OECD) 평균보다 2년 이상 많은 수치이다.

☆be expected to 기대되다

> e.g. She is expected to return to power after the Presidential election.
> 그녀는 대통령 선거 후에 다시 정권을 잡을 것으로 예상된다.
>
> ☆ return to power 또다시 정권을 잡다

☆on average 평균적으로

> e.g. The man says he investigates, on average, 100 people each day.
> 그 남자는 하루 평균 100명을 조사한다고 말한다.

Due to improved public health awareness and better medical care, babies born in Korea in 2019 are expected to live for an average of 83.3 years.

공중보건의식과 의료의 질 향상으로 2019년 한국에서 태어난 아기는 평균 83.3년을 살 것으로 예상된다.

☆public health 공중보건

☆awareness *(무엇의 중요성에 대한)* 의식, 관심

> e.g. People's political awareness has increased due to the media.
> 국민들의 정치적 인식이 언론 때문에 높아졌다.

☆medical care 의료, 건강 관리

e.g. Thanks to the great medical care in Korea, I was able to recover from an injury as soon as possible.
한국의 훌륭한 의료 서비스를 받은 덕분에, 저는 하루빨리 부상에서 회복될 수 있었습니다.

☆for an average of 평균적으로

According to Statistics Korea, boys are expected to live for 80.3 years while girls have a life expectancy of 86.3 years.
통계청에 따르면 여자아이의 기대수명은 86.3세인 반면 남자아이는 80.3세라고 한다.

The gender gap in life expectancy remains unchanged at six years for the second year in a row.
기대수명의 성별 격차는 2년 연속 6년으로 변함이 없다.

☆gender gap 성별격차

e.g. The country has the largest gender gap between male and female's earnings.
그 나라는 남녀 소득간 격차가 가장 크다.

☆remain unchanged 변하지 않다

e.g. Coffee prices remain unchanged due to the weather.
날씨 때문에 커피 가격은 변동이 없다.

☆in a row 연속으로

Meanwhile, the statistics agency picked cancer as the number one cause of death in the future for babies born in 2019, followed by heart disease and pneumonia.
한편 통계청은 2019년 출생아 사망원인 1위로 암을 꼽았고 심장질환과 폐렴이 뒤를 이었다.

☆followed by 잇달아, 뒤이어
☆pneumonia 폐렴

1. 작년에 태어난 한국 아기들은 20년 전에 태어난 아기들보다 평균 8년 더 오래 살 것으로 예상되는데, 이는 경제협력개발기구(OECD) 평균보다 2년 이상 많은 수치이다.

   South

2. 공중보건의식과 의료의 질 향상으로 2019년 한국에서 태어난 아기는 평균 83.3년을 살 것으로 예상된다.

   Due to

3. 통계청에 따르면 여자아이의 기대수명은 86.3세인 반면 남자아이는 80.3세라고 한다.

   According to

4. 기대수명의 성별 격차는 2년 연속 6년으로 변함이 없다.

   The gender

5. 한편 통계청은 2019년 출생아 사망원인 1위로 암을 꼽았고 심장질환과 폐렴이 뒤를 이었다.

   Meanwhile,

BRK 457/3
457/3
Today TH

영어 뉴스룸 67

English NewsRoom

BREAKING NEWS

Virus prevention guidelines top YouTube ranking in S. Korea in 2020. YouTube has announced this year's most popular videos in South Korea in various categories. Among non-entertainment videos, the one with the most views is from the Korea Disease Control and Prevention Agency explaining its guidelines for preventing COVID-19. The music video with the most views is "Dynamite" by BTS. When it came out earlier this year, it became the fastest...

올해 유튜브 최대 조회수 영상은?

올해 가장 많은 조회수를 기록한 유튜브 영상은 '신종 코로나 바이러스 감염증 국민행동수칙'인 것으로 조사됐다는 내용입니다.

NEWS 전체 스크립트

Virus prevention guidelines top YouTube ranking in S. Korea in 2020

YouTube has announced this year's most popular videos in South Korea in various categories.

Among non-entertainment videos, the one with the most views is from the Korea Disease Control and Prevention Agency explaining its guidelines for preventing COVID-19.

The music video with the most views is "Dynamite" by BTS.

When it came out earlier this year, it became the fastest video in YouTube's history to reach 100 million views, doing so in less than 24 hours.

According to a survey by IGA-Works, eight out of ten South Koreans spend around 30 hours on YouTube per month.

Virus prevention guidelines top YouTube ranking in S. Korea in 2020

바이러스 예방 행동수칙이 2020년 한국 유튜브 순위 1위를 하다

☆guideline *(공공 기관이 제시한)* 가이드라인, 행동수칙

☆top 1위를 하다, 최고이다

> e.g. The rookie girl group topped the charts for seven weeks with their first album.
> 그 신인 걸그룹은 첫 앨범으로 7주 동안 차트 1위를 차지했다.

YouTube has announced this year's most popular videos in South Korea in various categories.

유튜브가 올해 한국에서 가장 인기 있는 영상들을 다양한 카테고리로 발표했다.

☆various 다양한 =diverse

Among non-entertainment videos, the one with the most views is from the Korea Disease Control and Prevention Agency explaining its guidelines for preventing COVID-19.

비예능 영상 중 가장 많은 조회수를 기록한 것은 COVID-19 예방 지침을 설명하는 질병관리본부의 영상이다.

☆non-entertainment 비예능

· non-profit 비영리적인

· nontoxic 무독성의

· nonlinear 직선 모양이 아닌

☆the one with the most views 가장 많은 조회수를 가진 것은

· the one with the most stress 가장 스트레스 많이 주는 것은

· the one with the most famous name 가장 유명한 이름을 가진 사람은

· the one with the most kids 가장 많은 아이들을 가진 사람은

The music video with the most views is "Dynamite" by BTS.

조회수가 가장 많은 뮤직비디오는 방탄소년단의 '다이나마이트'이다.

When it came out earlier this year, it became the fastest video in YouTube's history to reach 100 million views, doing so in less than 24 hours.

올해 초 그 뮤직비디오가 나왔을 때(즉 발표 되었을 때) 유튜브 역사상 24시간 이내에 1억 조회수를 돌파한 가장 빠른 영상이 되었다.

☆come out *(책, 음반, 영화 등이)* 나오다

> e.g. She couldn't sleep the night the song came out.
> 그 노래가 나오던 날 밤에 그녀는 잠을 잘 수가 없었다.

According to a survey by IGA-Works, eight out of ten South Koreans spend around 30 hours on YouTube per month.

IGA-Works(빅데이터 플랫폼 기업) 의 조사에 따르면, 대한민국 국민 10명 중 8명이 한 달에 30시간을 유튜브를 보는데 소비한다고 한다.

☆A out of B B명 중 A명

e.g. 3 out of 10 companies in the city are suffering from financial difficulties.
시내 기업 10곳 중 3곳이 경영난을 겪고 있는 것으로 나타났다.

Writing Exercise

1. 유튜브가 올해 한국에서 가장 인기 있는 영상들을 다양한 카테고리로 발표했다.

YouTube

2. 비예능 영상 중 가장 많은 조회수를 기록한 것은 COVID-19 예방 지침을 설명하는 질병관리본부의 영상이다.

Among

3. 조회수가 가장 많은 뮤직비디오는 방탄소년단의 '다이나마이트'이다.

The music

4. 올해 초 그 뮤직비디오가 나왔을 때 (즉 발표 되었을 때) 유튜브 역사상 24시간 이내에 1억 조회수를 돌파한 가장 빠른 영상이 되었다.

When

5. IGA-Works(빅데이터 플랫폼 기업) 의 조사에 따르면, 대한민국 국민 10명 중 8명이 한 달에 30시간을 유튜브를 보는데 소비한다고 한다.

According to

BRK 457/3
457/3
Today TH

영어 뉴스룸 68

English
NewsRoom

BREAKING NEWS

S. Korea to crack down on drunk driving on highways. From tomorrow through the end of January, the South Korean police will be conducting a mass crackdown on drunk driving on the nation's highways, stopping drivers at the main on and off-ramps across the country and at toll booths. The checks will be conducted twice a week. To mitigate the risk of infection with COVID-19, the breathalyzer device will sample air about 30 centimeters from the driver's face.

고속도로에서도 음주운전을 단속한다?

경찰청이 연말연시 음주운전에 강력히 대응하고자 전국 고속도로 주요 진출입로에서 음주단속을 실시한다는 내용입니다.

 전체 스크립트

S. Korea to crack down on drunk driving on highways

From tomorrow through the end of January, the South Korean police will be conducting a mass crackdown on drunk driving on the nation's highways, stopping drivers at the main on and off-ramps across the country and at toll booths.

The checks will be conducted twice a week.

To mitigate the risk of infection with COVID-19, the breathalyzer device will sample air about 30 centimeters from the driver's face.

South Korea enacted tougher rules on drunk driving last year, lowering the blood alcohol limit to just zero.zero-3 percent--effectively meaning even a single drink is too many.

Violators are subject to a year in jail or a fine of about 46-hundred dollars and a suspension of their license.

NEWS 스크립트 분석

S. Korea to crack down on drunk driving on highways
고속도로의 음주운전을 단속하는 한국

☆crack down 단속하다 (명사형은 crackdown 엄중 단속, 강력 탄압)

e.g. The country is going to crack down on illicit liquor.
그 나라는 불법 주류를 단속할 것이다.

☆illicit 불법의 =illegal

☆drunk driving 음주운전 | ⑬ drink driving =driving under the influence 음주 운전하다

e.g. Drunk driving is a serious problem in every society.
음주운전은 모든 사회에서 심각한 문제이다.

☆highway 고속도로 | ⑬ motorway

From tomorrow through the end of January, the South Korean police will be conducting a mass crackdown on drunk driving on the nation's highways, stopping drivers at the main on and off-ramps across the country and at toll booths.
내일부터 1월 말까지, 한국 경찰은 전국 고속도로의 주요 진출입로와 요금소 등에서 대규모 음주 운전 단속을 실시할 예정이다.

☆mass 대량의, 대규모로

☆crackdown 엄중 단속

☆conduct a crackdown 단속을 실시하다

e.g. The city conducted a crackdown on illegal construction.
그 시는 불법 건축물에 대한 단속을 실시했다.

☆on-ramp 진입 차선 (off-ramp 진출 차선)

☆toll booth 통행료 받는 곳, 도로 요금소 | ⑬ tollgate

The checks will be conducted twice a week.
단속은 일주일에 두 번 실시될 것이다.

To mitigate the risk of infection with COVID-19, the breathalyzer device will sample air about 30 centimeters from the driver's face.

COVID-19 감염 위험을 줄이기 위해 음주측정기는 운전자의 얼굴로부터 약 30cm 떨어진 곳에서 공기를 채취할 것이다.

☆mitigate 완화시키다, 경감시키다

☆breathalyzer 음주측정기

☆sample *(정보를 얻기 위해 소량을)* 채취하다

South Korea enacted tougher rules on drunk driving last year, lowering the blood alcohol limit to just zero.zero-3 percent--effectively meaning even a single drink is too many.

한국은 작년에 혈중 알코올 농도수치 제한을 0.03%로 낮춘 음주 운전에 대한 더 엄격한 법률을 제정했는데 이는 사실상 단 한 잔의 음주도 너무 많다는 것을 의미한다.

☆tougher 더 강한

☆enact *(법률을)* 제정하다

Violators are subject to a year in jail or a fine of about 46-hundred dollars and a suspension of their license.

위반자는 징역 1년 또는 약 4600달러의 벌금과 면허 정지 처분의 대상이 된다.

☆be subject to something ~의 대상이 되다

e.g. Some airlines could be subject to additional inspections at the airport
일부 항공사는 미국 공항에서 추가 검사를 받을 수 있다.

Writing Exercise

1. 내일부터 1월 말까지, 한국 경찰은 전국 고속도로의 주요 진출입로와 요금소 등에서 대규모 음주 운전 단속을 실시할 예정이다.

   From _____

   _____

2. 단속은 일주일에 두 번 실시될 것이다.

   The checks _____

   _____

3. COVID - 19 감염 위험을 줄이기 위해 음주측정기는 운전자의 얼굴로부터 약 30cm 떨어진 곳에서 공기를 채취할 것이다.

   To mitigate _____

   _____

4. 한국은 작년에 혈중 알코올 농도수치 제한을 0.03%로 낮춘 음주 운전에 대한 더 엄격한 법률을 제정했는데 이는 사실상 단 한 잔의 음주도 너무 많다는 것을 의미한다.

   South _____

   _____

5. 위반자는 징역 1년 또는 약 4600달러의 벌금과 면허 정지 처분의 대상이 된다.

   Violators _____

   _____

◎ BRK 457/3
457/3
Today TH

영어 뉴스룸 69

English NewsRoom

BREAKING NEWS

S. Korea to allow e-scooters on bike roads at Han River parks. From Thursday, e-scooters will be allowed on bike roads at Seoul's Han River parks. The Han River Business Headquarters signed an MOU last week with 15 personal mobility services to foster a safe driving culture at the parks. Under the revised regulations, users of kickboards and other personal mobility equipment must abide by rules like driving under 20 kilometers an hour and wearing a...

한강 자전거도로에 킥보드 등장?

한강공원 자전거도로에서 전동 킥보드 이용이 가능해 졌다는 내용입니다.

S. Korea to allow e-scooters on bike roads at Han River parks

From Thursday, e-scooters will be allowed on bike roads at Seoul's Han River parks.

The Han River Business Headquarters signed an MOU last week with 15 personal mobility services to foster a safe driving culture at the parks.

Under the revised regulations, users of kickboards and other personal mobility equipment must abide by rules like driving under 20 kilometers an hour and wearing a helmet.

The parks have also been designated as 'non-returnable' zones to prevent unauthorized parking.

Users driving outside the paths will be fined 50-thousand Korean won or 46 U.S. dollars.

NEWS 스크립트 분석

S. Korea to allow e-scooters on bike roads at Han River parks
한강공원 자전거도로에서 e-스쿠터(전동킥보드) 이용을 허락하는 한국(정부)

☆bike roads 자전거도로

From Thursday, e-scooters will be allowed on bike roads at Seoul's Han River parks.
목요일부터 서울 한강공원 자전거도로에서 전동 킥보드가 허용된다.

The Han River Business Headquarters signed an MOU last week with 15 personal mobility services to foster a safe driving culture at the parks.
한강사업본부는 지난 주 공원 내 안전 운전 문화 조성을 위해 15개 개인형 이동장치사업자와 업무협약(MOU)을 체결했다.

☆personal mobility 개인형 이동장치 (전동킥보드)

☆sign an MOU (MOU : memorandum of understanding) 양해 각서를 체결하다

> e.g. The school signed an MOU with the local University to improve language programs.
> 그 학교는 어학 프로그램 개선을 위해서 지역 대학과 양해각서를 체결했다.

☆foster 조성하다, 발전시키다, (수양부모로서) 아이를 맡아 기르다

> e.g. The goal of the city is to foster learning opportunities to all people.
> 그 도시의 목표는 모든 사람들에게 배움의 기회를 조성하는 것이다.

Under the revised regulations, users of kickboards and other personal mobility equipment must abide by rules like driving under 20 kilometers an hour and wearing a helmet.
개정된 규정에 따르면, 킥보드와 기타 개인 이동장비의 사용자는 시속 20킬로미터 이하로 운전하고 헬멧을 착용하는 것 등과 같은 규칙을 준수해야 한다.

☆revised 개정된, 수정된

> e.g. Under the revised law, people aged 18 or older can drive from July next year.
> 개정법에 따르면, 만 18세 이상은 내년 7월부터 운전할 수 있다.

☆abide by 준수하다, 지키다

> e.g. The participants of the competition must abide by the judge's decision.
> 그 경기 참가자들은 심판의 결정에 따라야 한다.

The parks have also been designated as 'non-returnable' zones to prevent unauthorized parking.
이 공원들은 또한 무단 주차를 막기 위해 '반납 불가' 구역으로 지정되었다.

☆non-returnable 반환 불가능한

> e.g. These plastic bags are non-returnable so think twice before buying.
> 이 비닐 봉지들은 반환 불가하니 사기 전에 다시 한번 생각해 보세요.

☆unauthorized parking 무단 주차

> e.g. The institute prohibits unauthorized parking on private property without permission.
> 그 연구소는 사유재산에 허락없이 무단으로 주차하는 것을 금지하고 있다.

Users driving outside the paths will be fined 50-thousand Korean won or 46 U.S. dollars.
도로 밖에서 운전하는 이용자에게는 5만 원 또는 46달러의 과태료가 부과될 것이다.

☆path 길, 방향
☆fine 벌금 또는 과태료를 부과하다

Writing Exercise

1. 목요일부터 서울 한강공원 자전거도로에서 전동 킥보드가 허용된다.

   From _____

   _____

2. 한강사업본부는 지난 주 공원 내 안전 운전 문화 조성을 위해 15개 개인형 이동장치사업자와 업무협약(MOU)을 체결했다.

   The Han River _____

   _____

3. 개정된 규정에 따르면, 킥보드와 기타 개인 이동장비의 사용자는 시속 20킬로미터 이하로 운전하고 헬멧을 착용하는 것 등과 같은 규칙을 준수해야 한다.

   Under _____

   _____

4. 이 공원들은 또한 무단 주차를 막기 위해 '반납 불가' 구역으로 지정되었다.

   The parks _____

   _____

5. 도로 밖에서 운전하는 이용자에게는 5만 원 또는 46달러의 과태료가 부과될 것이다.

   Users _____

   _____

영어 뉴스룸 70

English NewsRoom

BREAKING NEWS

Foreigners choose drive-thru/walk-thru screening as Seoul's best anti-virus policy. Seoul's drive-thru and walk-thru Covid-19 testing centers have been selected as the city's best anti-virus policy by non-Koreans. A poll of some 96-hundred foreigners conducted online from November 30th through December 9th showed that drive and walk thru Covid testing sites ranked as the South Korean capital's best anti-Covid response followed by help centers for...

외국인이 뽑은 서울의 우수정책 1위는?

코로나 시대, 외국인이 선정한 서울의 우수정책 1위는 '드라이브스루, 워킹스루 선별진료소'가 차지했다는 내용입니다.

전체 스크립트

Foreigners choose drive-thru/walk-thru screening as Seoul's best anti-virus policy

Seoul's drive-thru and walk-thru Covid-19 testing centers have been selected as the city's best anti-virus policy by non-Koreans.

A poll of some 96-hundred foreigners conducted online from November 30th through December 9th showed that drive and walk thru Covid testing sites ranked as the South Korean capital's best anti-Covid response followed by help centers for foreigners that offer counseling and interpretations in eight languages, including English, Vietnamese and Filipino.

Also chosen as one of the city's best policies was the use of 'clean zone stickers' which shows that a facility has been disinfected.

NEWS 스크립트 분석

Foreigners choose drive-thru/walk-thru screening as Seoul's best anti-virus policy

외국인들은 드라이브스루/워크스루 검사를 서울 최고의 바이러스 퇴치 정책으로 선택하다

☆ **drive-thru** =drive-through (walk-thru=walk-through)

☆ **screening** *(질병·결격 사유 등을 찾기 위한)* 검사

Seoul's drive-thru and walk-thru Covid-19 testing centers have been selected as the city's best anti-virus policy by non-Koreans.

서울의 드라이브스루와 워크스루 코로나19 테스트 센터(선별진료소)가 외국인들에 의해 서울 최고의 안티바이러스 정책으로 선정되었다.

☆ **be selected as** ~로 선정되다, 선택되다

> e.g. The song was selected as the theme song for the New Year.
> 그 노래는 새해 주제곡으로 선정되었다.

A poll of some 96-hundred foreigners conducted online from November 30th through December 9th showed that drive and walk thru Covid testing sites ranked as the South Korean capital's best anti-Covid response followed by help centers for foreigners that offer counseling and interpretations in eight languages, including English, Vietnamese and Filipino.

11월 30일부터 12월 9일까지 온라인 상에서 행해진 약 9600명의 외국인들을 대상으로 실시된 여론조사에서 드라이브스루, 워크스루 코로나검사 선별진료소가 한국 수도 서울의 가장 좋은 코로나 방역 대응으로 꼽혔으며 영어, 베트남어, 필리핀어 등 8개 언어로 상담과 해석을 제공하는 외국인들을 위한 지원 센터가 그 뒤를 이었다.

☆ **poll** 여론조사

☆ **be conducted online** 온라인으로 실시되다

> e.g. The survey was conducted online due to the virus.
> 그 조사는 바이러스로 인해 온라인으로 실시되었다.

☆ **30th** ['θɜ:.ti.əθ] *발음주의!*

☆ **from A through B** *(특히 요일)* A에서 B까지 =from A to B *(주로 시간, 장소)*

> e.g. The bookstore is open Monday through Friday from 8 a.m. to 2 p.m.
> 그 서점은 월요일부터 금요일까지 오전 8시부터 오후 2시까지 영업한다.

☆anti-Covid response 코로나 방역 대응

> e.g. The President praised the neighboring country's anti-Covid response.
> 대통령은 이웃 나라의 반코로나 대응을 칭찬했다.

☆followed by 뒤이어, 잇달아

> e.g. The local schools are still the most popular school, followed by foreign language schools.
> 지역 학교들은 여전히 가장 인기 있는 학교이고, 외국어 학교들이 그 뒤를 잇고 있다.

Also chosen as one of the city's best policies was the use of 'clean zone stickers' which shows that a facility has been disinfected.

또한 서울시의 가장 좋은 정책 중 하나로 선정된 것은 시설이 소독되었다는 것을 보여주는 '클린 존 스티커'의 사용이었다.

☆use 사용 [juːs] | 사용하다 [juːz]
명사, 동사 발음 다름 주의

☆disinfect 소독하다 살균하다

> e.g. The spray kills the virus living on the surface in the disinfected area.
> 그 스프레이는 소독된 구역의 표면에 살고 있는 바이러스를 죽인다.

Writing Exercise

1. 서울의 드라이브스루와 워크스루 코로나19 테스트 센터(선별진료소)가 외국인들에 의해 서울 최고의 안티바이러스 정책으로 선정되었다.

   Seoul's
   _____

   _____

2. 11월 30일부터 12월 9일까지 온라인 상에서 행해진 약 9600명의 외국인들을 대상으로 실시된 여론조사에서 드라이브스루, 워크스루 코로나검사 선별진료소가 한국 수도 서울의 가장 좋은 코로나 방역 대응으로 꼽혔으며 영어, 베트남어, 필리핀어 등 8개 언어로 상담과 해석을 제공하는 외국인들을 위한 지원 센터가 그 뒤를 이었다.

   A poll of
   _____

   _____

3. 또한 서울시의 가장 좋은 정책 중 하나로 선정된 것은 시설이 소독되었다는 것을 보여주는 '클린 존 스티커'의 사용이었다.

   Also
   _____

   _____

BRK 457/3
457/3
Today TH

영어 뉴스룸 71

English NewsRoom

BREAKING NEWS

Seoul installs new 'I SEOUL U' displays at city landmarks. The city of Seoul has installed new pieces of public artwork to promote the city and cheer people up. There's a new sculpture at Gimpo International Airport reading "I SEOUL U," the city's tourism slogan. It's on the road in front of the domestic terminal, welcoming people to the city. Also on Nodeul Island, in the middle of the Han River, there's another one celebrating the one-year anniversary of...

I·SEOUL·U 조형물을 공항에도 설치한다

서울브랜드 I·SEOUL·U 조형물을 김포공항과 한강 노들섬에 신규로 설치했다는 내용입니다.

Seoul installs new 'I SEOUL U' displays at city landmarks

The city of Seoul has installed new pieces of public artwork to promote the city and cheer people up.

There's a new sculpture at Gimpo International Airport reading "I SEOUL U," the city's tourism slogan.

It's on the road in front of the domestic terminal, welcoming people to the city.

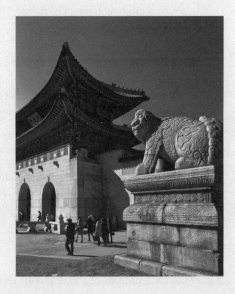

Also on Nodeul Island, in the middle of the Han River, there's another one celebrating the one-year anniversary of the island's renovation as a cultural space.

And at Yeouido Hangang Park, the 'I SEOUL U' sculpture depicts a snowy Seoul.

It'll be there until February.

Seoul installs new 'I SEOUL U' displays at city landmarks
서울시가 도심 랜드마크에 새로운 'I SEOUL U' 조형물들을 설치하다

☆install *(장비·가구를)* 설치하다

e.g. The engineer is coming to install the new machine.
그 기술자는 새 기계를 설치하러 오고 있다.

☆display 전시, 진열, 전시물
☆landmark 지형지물, 랜드마크

The city of Seoul has installed new pieces of public artwork to promote the city and cheer people up.
서울시는 서울을 홍보하고 시민들을 격려하기 위해 새로운 공공 예술 작품들을 설치했다.

☆piece 조각, 작품

e.g. It was a charming piece of music.
그것은 매력적인 음악 작품이었다.

☆cheer someone up ~의 기운을 북돋다

e.g. Tell me some creative ways to cheer the employees up.
직원들의 기분을 북돋울 수 있는 창의적인 방법을 알려주세요.

There's a new sculpture at Gimpo International Airport reading "I SEOUL U," the city's tourism slogan.
김포국제공항에는 서울의 관광 슬로건인 "I SEOUL U(너와 나의 서울)"라고 쓰인 새로운 조형물이 있다.

☆sculpture 조각품, 조형물

It's on the road in front of the domestic terminal, welcoming people to the city.
그것은 서울로 오는 사람들을 환영하며 국내선 청사 앞 도로가에 있다.

☆on the road 도로가에

e.g. We live on a busy road right now because we had no choice.
우리는 선택의 여지가 없었기 때문에 지금 바쁜 도로가에서 살고 있다.

Also on Nodeul Island, in the middle of the Han River, there's another one celebrating the one-year anniversary of the island's renovation as a cultural space.

또한 한강 한가운데에 있는 노들섬에는 문화공간으로서 섬의 개보수 1주년을 기념하는 또 다른 조형물이 있다.

☆in the middle of ~의 도중에, ~의 중앙에, 중간 무렵에

e.g. The building is in the middle of a shopping district.
그 건물은 상점가 한복판에 있다.

☆renovation 수선, 수리; 혁신, 원기 회복

And at Yeouido Hangang Park, the 'I SEOUL U' sculpture depicts a snowy Seoul.

그리고 여의도 한강 공원에는 'I SEOUL U' 조각상이 눈 덮인 서울을 묘사하고 있다.

☆depict 묘사하다, 그리다

e.g. These paintings depict the lives of the people who resided in the caves.
이 그림들은 동굴에 살던 사람들의 삶을 묘사하고 있다.

☆snowy 눈에 덮인, 눈이 많이 내리는

e.g.We had a very snowy winter last year.

It'll be there until February.

그것은 2월까지 전시될 것이다.

1. 서울시는 서울을 홍보하고 시민들을 격려하기 위해 새로운 공공 예술 작품들을 설치했다.

   The city

2. 김포국제공항에는 서울의 관광 슬로건인 "I SEOUL U(너와 나의 서울)"라고 쓰인 새로운 조형물이 있다.

   There's

3. 그것은 서울로 오는 사람들을 환영하며 국내선 청사 앞 도로가에 있다.

   It's

4. 또한 한강 한가운데에 있는 노들섬에는 문화공간으로서 섬의 개보수 1주년을 기념하는 또 다른 조형물이 있다.

   Also

5. 그리고 여의도 한강 공원에는 'I SEOUL U' 조각상이 눈 덮인 서울을 묘사하고 있다.

   And at

6. 그것은 2월까지 전시될 것이다.

   It'll

⊙ BRK 457/3
457/3
Today TH

영어 뉴스룸 72

English NewsRoom

BREAKING NEWS

S. Korea to allow usage of spending coupons around Christmas time. The South Korean government is going to resume its coupon program for restaurants to encourage consumer spending, but this time it'll only be for food delivery apps, not dining out. The coupon program had been suspended because of the third wave of the virus, but officials said it'll start again around Christmas time once they've made the necessary preparations.

음식 배달 앱을 위한 소비쿠폰 재개

코로나19 3차 확산으로 중단된 소비쿠폰을 성탄절 전후부터 순차적으로 다시 사용할 수 있다는 내용입니다.

 전체 스크립트

S. Korea to allow usage of spending coupons around Christmas time

The South Korean government is going to resume its coupon program for restaurants to encourage consumer spending, but this time it'll only be for food delivery apps, not dining out.

The coupon program had been suspended because of the third wave of the virus, but officials said it'll start again around Christmas time once they've made the necessary preparations.

Also, officials said, there will be more coupons issued in the new year if the virus situation gets under control.

These will be not just for food, but for sports, performances and more, and they'll be given to some 23 million people.

 스크립트 분석

S. Korea to allow usage of spending coupons around Christmas time
크리스마스 즈음에 소비쿠폰 사용을 허용하는 한국정부

☆usage 사용

e.g. Experts urged the public to reduce the usage of electricity.
전문가들은 국민들에게 전기 사용을 줄일 것을 촉구했다.

☆around 약, ~쯤

e.g. I think I bought this book around two months ago.
나는 이 책을 약 두 달 전 쯤에 산 것 같아.

The South Korean government is going to resume its coupon program for restaurants to encourage consumer spending, but this time it'll only be for food delivery apps, not dining out.
한국 정부는 소비자 지출을 장려하기 위해 음식점 쿠폰 프로그램(소비쿠폰)을 재개할 예정이지만, 이번에는 외식을 위한 것이 아니라 음식 배달 앱을 위한 것이다.

☆resume 재개하다, 다시 시작하다
☆consumer spending 소비자 지출

e.g. Consumer spending has fallen during 2001 due to the lack of investors.
2001년 동안 투자자들의 부족으로 인해 소비 지출이 감소했다.

☆dine out 외식하다

e.g. I love dining out with my family every Saturday.
나는 토요일마다 가족들과 외식하는 것을 좋아해.

The coupon program had been suspended because of the third wave of the virus, but officials said it'll start again around Christmas time once they've made the necessary preparations.
쿠폰 프로그램은 바이러스의 3차 확산 때문에 중단되었지만 관계자들은 필요한 준비를 마치면 크리스마스 무렵에 다시 시작할 것이라고 말했다.

☆suspend (공식적으로) 중단하다, 연기하다

e.g. The service has been suspended for a week because of the heavy snow.
그 서비스는 폭설로 인해 일주일 동안 중단되었다.

☆wave *(특정한 활동의)* 급증, 확산

> e.g. The second wave of Covid - 19 has hit local hospitals.
> 코로나19의 2차 확산이 국내 병원을 강타했다.

Also, officials said, there will be more coupons issued in the new year if the virus situation gets under control.

또한, 관계자들은 만약 바이러스 상황이 통제된다면 새해에는 더 많은 쿠폰이 발행될 것이라고 말했다.

☆get under control ~을 제어하게 되다, 통제되다

> e.g. Until the virus gets under control, we're in trouble.
> 바이러스가 통제될 때까지 우린 곤경에 처해 있어.

These will be not just for food, but for sports, performances and more, and they'll be given to some 23 million people.

이 쿠폰들은 음식에만 적용되는게 아니라 스포츠, 공연 등을 위한 것이 될 것이고 약 2300만 명을 대상으로 배포될 것이다.

Writing Exercise

1. 한국 정부는 소비자 지출을 장려하기 위해 음식점 쿠폰 프로그램(소비쿠폰)을 재개할 예정이지만, 이번에는 외식을 위한 것이 아니라 음식 배달 앱을 위한 것이다.

The South

2. 쿠폰 프로그램은 바이러스의 3차 확산 때문에 중단되었지만 관계자들은 필요한 준비를 마치면 크리스마스 무렵에 다시 시작할 것이라고 말했다.

The coupon

3. 또한, 관계자들은 만약 바이러스 상황이 통제된다면 새해에는 더 많은 쿠폰이 발행될 것이라고 말했다.

Also,

4. 이 쿠폰들은 음식에만 적용되는게 아니라 스포츠, 공연 등을 위한 것이 될 것이고 약 2300만 명을 대상으로 배포될 것이다.

These

영어 뉴스룸 73

English NewsRoom

BREAKING NEWS

Seoul city gov't donates funds raised from promotional flea market. The city of Seoul opened a pop-up store last month selling all kinds of products branded with the city's logo 'I SEOUL U.' And now they've donated the proceeds. Products on sale were items ranging from I SEOUL U coffee cups to stationery and even clothes. They made a little over 16-hundred U.S. dollars which has now been donated to the Seoul Council on Social Welfare, which will use it...

서울브랜드 I·SEOUL·U 벼룩시장 수익금 기부

서울브랜드 I·SEOUL·U가 벼룩시장 수익금을 전액 기부했다는 내용입니다.

Seoul city gov't donates funds raised from promotional flea market

The city of Seoul opened a pop-up store last month selling all kinds of products branded with the city's logo 'I SEOUL U.'

And now they've donated the proceeds.

Products on sale were items ranging from I SEOUL U coffee cups to stationery and even clothes.

They made a little over 16-hundred U.S. dollars which has now been donated to the Seoul Council on Social Welfare, which will use it to help the underprivileged.

The donation was delivered by the city's mascot 'Haechi,' and you can see the ceremony on the city's YouTube channel 'Haechi TV'.

NEWS 스크립트 분석

Seoul city gov't donates funds raised from promotional flea market
서울시에서 홍보 벼룩시장에서 모금된 수익금을 기부한다

☆promotional 홍보의, 판촉의

☆flea market 벼룩 시장

The city of Seoul opened a pop-up store last month selling all kinds of products branded with the city's logo 'I SEOUL U.'
서울시는 지난 달 'I SEOUL U' 로고가 새겨진 모든 종류의 제품을 파는 팝업 스토어를 열었다.

☆pop-up store 일시적으로 운영되는 상점 (pop-up retailer 로도 표기함)

> e.g. Many companies opened a pop-up store in Seoul as a response to the covid-19 crisis.
> 많은 기업들이 코로나19 위기에 대한 대응책으로 서울에 팝업스토어를 열었다.

☆branded 회사의 상표의, 유명 상표의

> e.g. They only buy branded goods which are typically more expensive.
> 그들은 일반적으로 더 비싼 브랜드 상품만 산다.

And now they've donated the proceeds.
그리고 현재 그들은(서울시는) 수익금을 기부했다.

☆proceeds (물건 판매·행사 등을 하여 받는) 돈, 수익금 (proceed 진행하다)

> e.g. The proceeds of yesterday's festival will go to a charity in Seoul.
> 어제 축제의 수익금은 서울의 한 자선단체에 기부될 것이다.

Products on sale were items ranging from I SEOUL U coffee cups to stationery and even clothes.
판매되고 있는 물건들은 아이서울유 커피잔부터 문구류, 심지어 옷까지 범위에 이르는 다양한 품목들이었다.

☆on sale 1. 판매되고 있는 | 2. 할인 중인 (for sale 팔려고 내놓은)

☆range from A to B A부터 B까지 범위에 이르다

> e.g. This jacket sizes range from extra-small to extra-large.
> 이 재킷의 크기는 엑스 스몰부터 엑스 라지까지 있다.

They made a little over 16-hundred U.S. dollars which has now been donated to the Seoul Council on Social Welfare, which will use it to help the underprivileged.

그들은 현재 서울시 사회복지협의회에 기부되었고 소외계층을 돕기 위해 사용될 1600달러가 조금 넘는 돈을 모금하였다.

☆underprivileged *(사회·경제적으로)* 혜택을 못 받는

☆the underprivileged 혜택을 못 받는 사람, 그룹

> e.g. Although he came from an underprivileged family background, he graduated from a university in Seoul.
> 그는 불우한 집안 출신이지만, 서울의 한 대학을 졸업했다.

The donation was delivered by the city's mascot 'Haechi', and you can see the ceremony on the city's YouTube channel 'Haechi TV'.

기부금은 서울시 마스코트 '해치'에 의해 전달되었고, 기념식을 서울시 유튜브 채널 '해치 TV'에서 볼 수 있다.

☆be delivered by~ 에 의해 전달되다

> e.g. She still believes that the surprise gift was delivered by Santa.
> 그녀는 그 깜짝 선물이 산타에 의해 전달되었다고 여전히 믿고 있다.

Writing Exercise

1. 서울시는 지난 달 'I SEOUL U' 로고가 새겨진 모든 종류의 제품을 파는 팝업 스토어를 열었다.

   The city
   _____
   _____

2. 그리고 현재 그들은 (서울시는) 수익금을 기부했다.

   And now
   _____
   _____

3. 판매되고 있는 물건들은 아이서울유 커피잔부터 문구류, 심지어 옷까지 범위에 이르는 다양한 품목들이었다.

   Products
   _____
   _____

4. 그들은 현재 서울시 사회복지협의회에 기부되었고 소외계층을 돕기 위해 사용될 1600달러가 조금 넘는 돈을 모금하였다.

   They
   _____
   _____

5. 기부금은 서울시 마스코트 '해치'에 의해 전달되었고, 기념식을 서울시 유튜브 채널 '해치 TV'에서 볼 수 있다

   The donation
   _____
   _____

⊚ BRK 457/3
457/3
Today TH

영어 뉴스룸 74

English NewsRoom

BREAKING NEWS

24 more historical sites selected as Seoul's Future Heritage. The city of Seoul has selected 24 more sites to add to its list of Seoul's Future Heritage, a designation for modern places in the city to be preserved for future generations. New to the list is 'Ggum-maru' at Seoul Children's Grand Park. It used to be a clubhouse, and was going to be demolished in 2011, but it was renovated to suit its surroundings in the park.

24개 장소를 미래유산으로 선정한 서울시

서울시가 24개 장소를 올해 새롭게 서울 미래유산으로 선정했다는 내용입니다.

24 more historical sites selected as Seoul's Future Heritage

The city of Seoul has selected 24 more sites to add to its list of Seoul's Future Heritage, a designation for modern places in the city to be preserved for future generations.

New to the list is 'Ggum-maru' at Seoul Children's Grand Park.

It used to be a clubhouse, and was going to be demolished in 2011, but it was renovated to suit its surroundings in the park.

Also added to the list is Hongreung Arboretum, Korea's first arboretum which is an iconic structure for children.

And in the neighborhood near Hongik University is Homi Art Shop, a famous place for Korean artists, especially those who attended the university.

There are now 488 places on the list of Future Heritage.

NEWS 스크립트 분석

24 more historical sites selected as Seoul's Future Heritage
서울 미래유산으로(추가로) 선정된 24개의 유적지

☆historical sites 유적지

☆selected as ~로 선택되다, 선정되다

> e.g. She was selected as one of the top singers in the competition.
> 그녀는 그 대회에서 최고의 가수 중 한 명으로 뽑혔다.

The city of Seoul has selected 24 more sites to add to its list of Seoul's Future Heritage, a designation for modern places in the city to be preserved for future generations.
서울시는 미래 세대를 위해 보존될 서울의 현대적인 장소를 지정하는 서울 미래 유산 목록에 추가할 24개의 장소를 선정했다.

☆add 추가하다

> e.g. Please add my name to the list of donors.
> 기부자 명단에 제 이름을 추가해 주세요.

☆designation 지명, 지정

☆preserve for ~을 위해 지키다, 보존하다

> e.g. The castle will be preserved for the public.
> 그 성은 대중을 위해 보존될 것이다.

☆future generations 후대, 후세, 자손

> e.g. Please save the world for future generations.
> 후세를 위해 세상을 구해주세요.

New to the list is 'Ggum-maru' at Seoul Children's Grand Park.
이 목록에 처음 오른 것은 서울 어린이대공원 '꿈마루'이다.

It used to be a clubhouse, and was going to be demolished in 2011, but it was renovated to suit its surroundings in the park.

이곳은 원래 클럽하우스였고 2011년에 철거될 예정이었으나 공원 주변 환경에 맞게 개조되었다.

☆used to ~하곤 했다, 과거 한때는 ~였다

> e.g. This place used to be a school.
> 이곳은 원래 학교였다.

☆demolish (건물을) 철거하다

☆renovate (낡은 건물·가구 등을) 개조하다, 보수하다

☆surroundings 환경 =environment

Also added to the list is Hongreung Arboretum, Korea's first arboretum which is an iconic structure for children.

또한 추가된 것은 어린이들에게는 상징적인 건축물이기도 한 한국 최초의 수목원인 홍릉숲이다.

☆iconic 상징적인

☆arboretum 수목원

And in the neighborhood near Hongik University is Homi Art Shop, a famous place for Korean artists, especially those who attended the university.

그리고 홍익대학교 근처에는 호미화방이 있는데, 호미화방은 한국 예술가들, 특히 그 대학에 다녔던 사람들에게 유명한 장소이다.

☆neighborhood 근처, 인근

There are now 488 places on the list of Future Heritage.

현재 488개의 미래유산 목록에 등재되어 있다.

Writing Exercise

1. 서울시는 미래 세대를 위해 보존될 서울의 현대적인 장소를 지정하는 서울 미래 유산 목록에 추가할 24개의 장소를 선정했다.

The city

2. 이 목록에 처음 오른 것은 서울 어린이대공원 '꿈마루'이다.

New to

3. 이곳은 원래 클럽하우스였고 2011년에 철거될 예정이었으나 공원 주변 환경에 맞게 개조되었다.

It used

4. 또한 추가된 것은 어린이들에게는 상징적인 건축물이기도 한 한국 최초의 수목원인 홍릉숲이다.

Also

5. 그리고 홍익대학교 근처에는 호미화방이 있는데, 호미화방은 한국 예술가들, 특히 그 대학에 다녔던 사람들에게 유명한 장소이다.

And in

6. 현재 488개의 미래유산 목록에 등재되어 있다.

There

◉ BRK 457/3
457/3
Today TH

영어 뉴스룸 75

English NewsRoom

BREAKING NEWS

S. Korea's wine imports in 2020 reached all-time high due to pandemic. South Korea's wine imports reached an all-time high last year, as more people enjoyed drinking at home and threw more house parties due to the COVID-19 pandemic. According to data from the Korea Customs Service on Monday, South Korea imported nearly 39-thousand tons from January to November. This is equal to nearly 240 million U.S. dollars worth of wine.

작년 와인 수입량 사상 최고치 경신

신종 코로나바이러스 여파로 지난해 와인 수입 물량이 사상 최고치를 경신했다는 내용입니다.

 NEWS 전체 스크립트

S. Korea's wine imports in 2020 reached all-time high due to pandemic

South Korea's wine imports reached an all-time high last year, as more people enjoyed drinking at home and threw more house parties due to the COVID-19 pandemic.

According to data from the Korea Customs Service on Monday, South Korea imported nearly 39-thousand tons from January to November.

This is equal to nearly 240 million U.S. dollars worth of wine.

Wine import volumes have also more than doubled compared to ten years ago.

Wines from Chile, France, Italy, and the U.S. made up the largest portion of imports.

NEWS 스크립트 분석

S. Korea's wine imports in 2020 reached all-time high due to pandemic
한국의 2020년 와인 수입량이 코로나19 대유행으로 사상 최고치를 기록했다

　☆import 1. 수입 [ˈɪm.pɔːt] | 2. 수입하다 [ɪmˈpɔːt]
　　명사와 동사일 때 강세 차이 주의!

　☆reach ~에 이르다, 닿다, 도달하다

　☆all-time high 사상 최고치 (↔all-time low 사상 최저치)

> e.g. The company's stock reached an all-time high on Monday.
> 　　　그 회사의 주가는 월요일에 사상 최고치를 기록했다.

South Korea's wine imports reached an all-time high last year, as more people enjoyed drinking at home and threw more house parties due to the COVID-19 pandemic.
코로나19 전염병으로 더 많은 사람들이 집에서 술을 즐기고 하우스 파티를 함으로써 한국의 와인 수입(물량)은 작년에 사상 최고치를 기록했다.

　☆throw a party 파티를 열다 (= to have a party ; to hold a party ; to arrange a party ; to organize a party)

> e.g. Let's throw a lunch party for the newly-born baby.
> 　　　새로 태어난 아기를 위해 점심 파티를 열자.

According to data from the Korea Customs Service on Monday, South Korea imported nearly 39-thousand tons from January to November.
월요일 관세청의 자료에 따르면, 한국은 1월부터 11월까지 거의 3만 9천 톤을 수입했다.

　☆ton 톤 [tʌn] '톤'이 아니라 '턴'으로 발음한다. 복수는 tons or ton 둘다 씀

This is equal to nearly 240 million U.S. dollars worth of wine.
이것은 거의 2억 4천만 달러치의 와인과 맞먹는다.

　☆equal to ~와 같은

> e.g. They received a bonus of 400,000 won equal to 10% of their salary.
> 　　　그들은 월급의 10%에 해당하는 40만 원의 보너스를 받았다.

☆worth of ~의 가치의

> e.g. 2 million won worth of presents have been produced for her birthday party.
> 그녀의 생일 파티를 위해 200만 원 상당의 선물이 제작되었다.

Wine import volumes have also more than doubled compared to ten years ago.
와인 수입량도 10년 전에 비해 두 배 이상 늘었다.

☆volume 양

> e.g. In October retail sales volumes increased by 3.5%.
> 10월에 소매 판매량은 3.5% 증가했다.

☆compared to ~와 비교하여

> e.g. This snow is nothing compared to what we got the day before yesterday.
> 이번 눈은 그저께 내린 것에 비하면 아무것도 아니다.

Wines from Chile, France, Italy, and the U.S. made up the largest portion of imports.
칠레, 프랑스, 이탈리아, 미국산 와인이 수입의 가장 큰 부분을 차지했다.

Writing Exercise

1. 코로나19 전염병으로 더 많은 사람들이 집에서 술을 즐기고 하우스 파티를 함으로서 한국의 와인 수입(물량)은 작년에 사상 최고치를 기록했다.

   South

2. 월요일 관세청의 자료에 따르면, 한국은 1월부터 11월까지 거의 3만 9천 톤을 수입했다.

   According to

3. 이것은 거의 2억 4천만 달러치의 와인과 맞먹는다.

   This is

4. 와인 수입량도 10년 전에 비해 두 배 이상 늘었다.

   Wine

5. 칠레, 프랑스, 이탈리아, 미국산 와인이 수입의 가장 큰 부분을 차지했다.

   Wines

BRK 457/3
457/3
Today TH

영어 뉴스룸 76

English NewsRoom

BREAKING NEWS

Seoul city to introduce new artistic attraction 'Nodeul under the moonlight'. Nodeulseom, an artificial island in the Han River in Seoul, now has its own moon. "Nodeul under the moonlight" is an art installation shaped like a giant moon and aims to bring out the island's charms. It's made of two circular metal structures, each 12 meters in diameter, with 45 - thousand holes which reflect sunlight. It opens to public on February 26th.

인공달이 노들섬에?

서울시가 오는 정월대보름에 인공달인 달빛노들 개장식을 연다는 내용입니다.

Seoul city to introduce new artistic attraction 'Nodeul under the moonlight'

Nodeulseom, an artificial island in the Han River in Seoul, now has its own moon.

'Nodeul under the moonlight' is an art installation shaped like a giant moon and aims to bring out the island's charms.

It's made of two circular metal structures, each 12 meters in diameter, with 45 - thousand holes which reflect sunlight.

It opens to public on February 26th.

NEWS 스크립트 분석

Seoul city to introduce new artistic attraction 'Nodeul under the moonlight'
새로운 예술명소 '달빛노들'을 소개할 예정인 서울시

☆artistic 예술의, 예술적인, 예술적 감각이 있는

> e.g. Her artistic ability is second to none.
> 그녀의 예술적 재능은 누구에게도 뒤지지 않는다.

☆attraction *(사람을 끄는)* 명소, 명물

> e.g. This museum is one of the major tourist attractions of the city.
> 이 박물관은 그 도시의 주요 관광 명소 중 하나이다.

Nodeulseom, an artificial island in the Han River in Seoul, now has its own moon.
서울 한강에 있는 인공섬인 노들섬에는 이제 달이 있다.

☆artificial 인공의

> e.g. This is an artificial lake designed by famous young artists.
> 이것은 유명한 젊은 예술가들이 디자인한 인공 호수입니다.

'Nodeul under the moonlight' is an art installation shaped like a giant moon and aims to bring out the island's charms.
'달빛 아래 노들('달빛노들')은 거대한 달 모양의 설치 미술품으로 섬의 매력을 끌어내는 것을 목표로 한다.

☆installation 설치 미술품

> e.g. I reckon people love his installation but for me it's hard to understand.
> 나는 사람들이 그의 설치물을 좋아한다고 생각하지만 나에게는 이해하기 어렵다.

☆aim to ~하는 것을 목표로 하다

> e.g. We aim to help the poorest families.
> 우리는 가장 가난한 가정을 돕는 것을 목표로 한다.

☆charm 매력

> e.g. He is a man of charm and cultivation.
> 그는 매력적이고 교양이 있는 사람이다.

It's made of two circular metal structures, each 12 meters in diameter, with 45-thousand holes which reflect sunlight.

그것은 두 개의 원형 금속 구조물로 만들어졌고, 각각 지름이 12미터이고, 햇빛을 반사하는 4만 5천 개의 구멍을 가지고 있습니다.

☆circular 원형의, 둥근

☆in diameter 직경이 얼마인

· diameter 직경 (지름)

e.g. The pond is 16 metres in diameter.(US meter)
그 연못의 지름은 16미터이다.

☆reflect (빛·열·음을) 반사하다, 반향을 일으키다

e.g. It reflects sunlight, which lowers temperatures.
그것은 햇빛을 반사해서 온도를 낮춥니다.

It opens to public on February 26th.

그것은(달빛노들) 2월 26일에 대중에게 공개된다.

☆public 대중

e.g. I've got to say we have to increase public awareness of the virus.
나는 우리가 바이러스에 대한 대중의 인식을 높여야 한다고 말하고 싶어.

Writing Exercise

1. 서울 한강에 있는 인공섬인 노들섬에는 이제 달이 있다.

   Nodeulseom, _____

   _____

2. '달빛 아래 노들('달빛노들')'은 거대한 달 모양의 설치 미술품으로 섬의 매력을 끌어내는 것을 목표로 한다.

   "Nodeul _____

   _____

3. 그것은 두 개의 원형 금속 구조물로 만들어졌고, 각각 지름이 12미터이고, 햇빛을 반사하는 4만 5천 개의 구멍을 가지고 있습니다.

   It's _____

   _____

4. 그것은(달빛노들) 2월 26일에 대중에게 공개된다.

   It opens _____

   _____

ⓒ BRK 457/3
457/3
Today TH

영어 뉴스룸 77

English NewsRoom

BREAKING NEWS

Youn Yuh-jeong seeks Oscar nod after NSFC runner-up spot. South Korean actress Youn Yuh-jeong, who is receiving praise from critics for her role in the movie 'Minari', is inching closer to an Oscar nomination. Youn, recently runner-up at the National Society Of Film Critics' Awards, has won her 8th U.S. film award for 'Best Supporting Actress' at the Columbus Critics Association. With the win, hopes are high Youn could get an Oscar nod...

윤여정, 오스카 후보 지명 가능성이 높아졌다

배우 윤여정이 전미 비평가협회 여우조연상에서 RUNNERS-UP에 선정되었다는 내용입니다.

 전체 스크립트

Youn Yuh-jeong seeks Oscar nod after NSFC runner-up spot

South Korean actress Youn Yuh-jeong, who is receiving praise from critics for her role in the movie 'Minari', is inching closer to an Oscar nomination.

Youn, recently runner-up at the National Society Of Film Critics' Awards, has won her 8th U.S. film award for 'Best Supporting Actress' at the Columbus Critics Association.

With the win, hopes are high Youn could get an Oscar nod this year.

Minari' depicts first-generation immigrants from South Korea in pursuit of the American dream.

If nominated for an Academy Award in April, it will be a first in the category for a South Korean actress or actor.

NEWS 스크립트 분석

Youn Yuh-jeong seeks Oscar nod after NSFC runner-up spot

윤여정, 전미 비평가협회 여우조연상 두 번째 자리를 차지한 뒤 오스카 후보 지명 노려

☆seek 노리다, 찾다, 추구하다

> e.g. Eventually, she decided to seek revenge.
> 결국, 그녀는 복수를 하기로 결심했습니다.

☆nod 1. 고개를 끄덕이다 (동사) | 2. 후보지명 (명사)

> e.g. He received the Oscar nod this year.
> 그는 올해 오스카 후보지명을 받았다.

☆runner-up 2위 입상자, 2위의 선수나 팀 a person who comes second in a race or competition

> e.g. He was runner-up in the 2020 championship.
> 그는 2020년 대회에서 준우승을 차지했다.

☆spot 자리

☆NSFC National Society Of Film Critics 전미 비평가협회

South Korean actress Youn Yuh-jeong, who is receiving praise from critics for her role in the movie 'Minari', is inching closer to an Oscar nomination.

영화 '미나리'에서의 역할로 비평가들로부터 찬사를 받고 있는 한국 여배우 윤여정이 오스카상 후보에 가까워지고 있다.

☆receive praise 칭찬을 받다, 찬사를 받다

> e.g. He received praised for the performance in the leading role.
> 그는 주연 연기로 찬사를 받았다.

☆critics 비평가들

☆inch closer to ~에 조금씩 가까워지다

> e.g. The actor has revealed he is inching closer and closer to his goal of 70kg.
> 그 배우는 자신의 목표인 70kg에 점점 더 가까워지고 있다고 밝혔다.

☆nomination 지명, 추천, 임명

Youn, recently runner-up at the National Society Of Film Critics' Awards, has won her 8th U.S. film award for 'Best Supporting Actress' at the Columbus Critics Association.

최근 전미 비평가 협회 여우조연상 2위를 차지했던 윤씨는 콜럼버스 비평가협회에서 '여우조연상'으로 8번째 미국 영화상을 수상했다.

☆supporting actor 조연

· supporting role 조연 역할 (↔leading actor 주연 배우)

With the win, hopes are high Youn could get an Oscar nod this year.

이번 수상으로 올해 오스카 후보지명을 받을 수 있을 것이라는 기대가 높다.

☆hopes are high 기대가 높다

e.g. Hopes are high for 2021 because a lot of people had a bad year in 2020.
많은 분들이 2020년에 흉년을 겪었기 때문에 2021년에 대한 기대가 크다.

'Minari' depicts first-generation immigrants from South Korea in pursuit of the American dream.

'미나리'는 아메리칸 드림을 위해 한국에서 온 1세대 이민자들을 묘사하고 있다.

☆depict 묘사하다

☆first-generation 1세대의

☆immigrant 이민자

☆in pursuit of ~을 (추구하기) 위해

e.g. During an interview, the student said she would do anything in pursuit of fame.
인터뷰 도중, 그 학생은 명성을 위해 무엇이든 할 것이라고 말했다.

If nominated for an Academy Award in April, it will be a first in the category for a South Korean actress or actor.

4월에 아카데미상 후보에 오른다면 그것은 한국 여배우나 배우로서는 첫 번째가 될 것이다.

Writing Exercise

1. 영화 '미나리'에서의 역할로 비평가들로로부터 찬사를 받고 있는 한국 여배우 윤여정이 오스카상 후보에 가까워지고 있다.

   South

2. 최근 전미 비평가 협회 여우조연상 2위를 차지했던 윤씨는 콜럼버스 비평가협회에서 '여우조연상'으로 8번째 미국 영화상을 수상했다.

   Youn,

3. 이번 수상으로 올해 오스카 후보지명을 받을 수 있을 것이라는 기대가 높다.

   With

4. '미나리'는 아메리칸 드림을 위해 한국에서 온 1세대 이민자들을 묘사하고 있다.

   'Minari'

5. 4월에 아카데미상 후보에 오른다면 그것은 한국 여배우나 배우로서는 첫번째가 될 것이다.

   If nominated

BRK 457/3
457/3
Today TH

영어 뉴스룸 78

English NewsRoom

Year-end tax adjustment service to begin on Friday. For South Korea's full-time, salaried workers, it'll be time to file taxes next month. And so this Friday, the National Tax Service is going to start providing the data you'll need to report your income and do your deductions. Just log in to the NTS website at hometax.go.kr. It'll be open on the 15th of February, until the filing deadline on the 28th. To prevent the system from crashing, each user can only log...

연말정산 서비스 시즌

국세청이 15일부터 연말정산 간소화 서비스를 개통한다는 내용입니다.

Year-end tax adjustment service to begin on Friday

For South Korea's full-time, salaried workers, it'll be time to file taxes next month.

And so this Friday, the National Tax Service is going to start providing the data you'll need to report your income and do your deductions.

Just log in to the NTS website at hometax.go.kr.

It'll be open on the 15th of February, until the filing deadline on the 28th.

To prevent the system from crashing, each user can only log in for 30 minutes at a time.

Taxpayers could save some money this year because the government is raising the percentage of your credit card spending that you can deduct from your income to as high as 80 percent in the months when the pandemic started to take its toll.

NEWS 스크립트 분석

Year-end tax adjustment service to begin on Friday
금요일부터 시작되는 연말정산 서비스

　　☆year-end 연말의

　　☆tax adjustment 세무조정

　　☆year-end tax adjustment 연말 정산

For South Korea's full-time, salaried workers, it'll be time to file taxes next month.
한국의 정규직, 봉급 생활자들은 다음 달에 세금을 신고할 때가 되었다.

　　☆salaried worker 임금근로자

　　☆file taxes 세금을 신고하다

　　　· file a complaint 항의서를 제출하다

　　　· file a lawsuit 소송을 제기하다

> e.g. You should file taxes to avoid penalties.
> 당신은 처벌을 피하기 위해 세금을 신고해야 한다.

And so this Friday, the National Tax Service is going to start providing the data you'll need to report your income and do your deductions.
그래서 이번 주 금요일에 국세청이 소득과 (세액)공제에 필요한 자료를 제공하기 시작할 예정이다.

　　☆deduction 공제(액) | 영 stoppage

> e.g. After deductions, his taxable income is less than 1,000,000 won.
> 공제 후 그의 과세 소득은 100만 원 미만이다.

Just log in to the NTS website at hometax.go.kr.
NTS 웹사이트 hometax.go.kr에 로그인하기만 하면 된다.

It'll be open on the 15th of February, until the filing deadline on the 28th.
이 서비스는 2월 15일에 개통해서 신청 마감일인 28일까지 운영된다.

　　☆filing deadline 제출 기한

> e.g. Because of my birthday party, I missed the filing deadline.
> 내 생일 파티 때문에 서류 제출 기한을 넘겼어요.

To prevent the system from crashing, each user can only log in for 30 minutes at a time.
시스템 충돌을 방지하기 위해(시스템 과부하를 막기 위해) 각 사용자는 한 번에 30분 동안만 로그인할 수 있다.

☆prevent A from B A가 B하는 것을 막다

e.g. Some people believe that wearing sunscreen will prevent your skin from tanning.
어떤 사람들은 자외선 차단제를 바르면 피부가 그을리는 것을 막을 수 있다고 믿습니다.

☆at a time 한 번에

e.g. He can only do one thing at a time.
그는 한 번에 한 가지 일만 할 수 있다.

Taxpayers could save some money this year because the government is raising the percentage of your credit card spending that you can deduct from your income to as high as 80 percent in the months when the pandemic started to take its toll.
납세자들은 올해 약간의 돈을 절약할 수 있을 것이다. 왜냐하면 정부는 코로나19 대유행병 피해를 입기 시작한 몇 달 동안 소득에서 공제할 수 있는 신용카드 지출의 비율을 80%까지 높이고 있기 때문이다.

☆take its toll ~에 큰 피해를 주다

e.g. The economic recession has taken its toll in the country.
경제 불황으로 그 나라에 큰 피해를 주었다.

Writing Exercise

1. 한국의 정규직, 봉급 생활자들은 다음 달에 세금을 신고할 때가 되었다.

   For South

2. 그래서 이번 주 금요일에 국세청이 소득과 (세액)공제에 필요한 자료를 제공하기 시작할 예정이다.

   And so

3. NTS 웹사이트 hometax.go.kr에 로그인하기만 하면 된다.

   Just

4. 이 서비스는 2월 15일에 개통해서 신청 마감일인 28일까지 운영된다.

   It'll

5. 시스템 충돌을 방지하기 위해(시스템 과부하를 막기 위해) 각 사용자는 한 번에 30분 동안만 로그인할 수 있다.

   To prevent

6. 납세자들은 올해 약간의 돈을 절약할 수 있을 것이다. 왜냐하면 정부는 코로나19 대유행병 피해를 입기 시작한 몇 달 동안 소득에서 공제할 수 있는 신용카드 지출의 비율을 80%까지 높이고 있기 때문이다.

   Taxpayers

영어 뉴스룸 79

English NewsRoom

BREAKING NEWS

S. Korea ranks 6th among 138 countries for military strength; N. Korea at 28th. South Korea's military power remained among the top ten in the world this year, while North Korea was down three notches from last year. According to the '2021 Military Strength Ranking' by Global Firepower, South Korea was ranked in 6th place among 138 countries, and North Korea was 28th. But North Korea had relatively higher rankings in some sectors,...

한국 군사력 세계 6위, 북한 28위

2021년 한국의 군사력은 세계 6위이고 북한은 28위로 세 단계 하락했다는 내용입니다.

S. Korea ranks 6th among 138 countries for military strength; N. Korea at 28th

South Korea's military power remained among the top ten in the world this year, while North Korea was down three notches from last year.

According to the '2021 Military Strength Ranking' by Global Firepower, South Korea was ranked in 6th place among 138 countries, and North Korea was 28th.

But North Korea had relatively higher rankings in some sectors, including active military manpower and tanks.

The U.S. was ranked in the top place, followed by Russia and China.

The analytics take into account around 50 factors, including military might, funding, and logistical capability, to determine the score.

S. Korea ranks 6th among 138 countries for military strength ; N. Korea at 28th
한국의 군사력 138개국 중 6위, 북한은 28위를 차지하다

☆rank *(등급, 순위를)* 차지하다, 평가하다

e.g. Last year it ranked 10th in service quality.
작년에 그것은 서비스 품질에서 10위를 차지했다.

South Korea's military power remained among the top ten in the world this year, while North Korea was down three notches from last year.
북한 군사력은 작년보다 3계단 떨어진 반면 올해 한국의 군사력은 세계 10위권 안에 들었다.

☆notch *(질·성취 정도를 나타내는)* 등급, 단계

e.g. The country's GDP ranked 23rd in the world in 2009, down two notches from the previous year.
2009년 그 나라의 GDP는 전년에 비해 두 단계 하락한 23위를 기록했다.

According to the '2021 Military Strength Ranking' by Global Firepower, South Korea was ranked in 6th place among 138 countries, and North Korea was 28th.
'글로벌파이어파워(GFP)'의 2021년 군사력 평가기관에 따르면 한국은 138개국 중 6위, 북한은 28위였다.

But North Korea had relatively higher rankings in some sectors, including active military manpower and tanks.
그러나 북한은 병력 규모과 탱크 등 일부 부문에서 상대적으로 높은 순위를 기록했다.

☆relatively 비교적

e.g. This is relatively easy compared to other things.
이것은 다른 것에 비해 비교적 쉽다.

☆manpower 인력, 병력

e.g. It was reported that the fashion industry has suffered from a lack of manpower.
패션업계가 인력 부족으로 어려움을 겪고 있는 것으로 알려졌다.

The U.S. was ranked in the top place, followed by Russia and China.
미국이 1위를 차지했고, 러시아와 중국이 그 뒤를 이었다.

The analytics take into account around 50 factors, including military might, funding, and logistical capability, to determine the score.

그 분석은(군사력) 지수를 산출하기 위해 군사력, 국방예산 및 병참 능력을 포함한 약 50개의 요인을 고려한다.

☆analytics 분석, 분석 정보

☆take into account ~을 고려하다

e.g. I hope my manager will take into account the fact that I was ill before the presentation.
발표 전에 내가 아팠던 사실을 내 매니저가 고려해 주길 바란다.

☆military might 군사력

☆might 힘 =power or strength

e.g. She tried with all her might to push the door open.
그녀는 힘껏 문을 밀어서 열려고 했다.

☆logistical 병참의, 수송의

Writing Exercise

1. 북한 군사력은 작년보다 3계단 떨어진 반면 올해 한국의 군사력은 세계 10위권 안에 들었다.

   South _____

   _____

2. '글로벌파이어파워'(GFP)의 2021년 군사력 평가기관에 따르면 한국은 138개국 중 6위, 북한은 28위였다.

   According to _____

   _____

3. 그러나 북한은 병력 규모과 탱크 등 일부 부문에서 상대적으로 높은 순위를 기록했다.

   But North _____

   _____

4. 미국이 1위를 차지했고, 러시아와 중국이 그 뒤를 이었다.

   The U.S. _____

   _____

5. 그 분석은 (군사력) 지수를 산출하기 위해 군사력, 국방예산 및 병참 능력을 포함한 약 50개의 요인을 고려한다.

   The analytics _____

   _____

영어 뉴스룸 80

English NewsRoom

BREAKING NEWS

Google launches fund to fight 'misinformation' about COVID‑19 vaccines. The Google News Initiative has launched a multimillion‑dollar global fund to fight misinformation about COVID‑19 vaccines. Dubbed the 'COVID‑19 Vaccine Counter Misinformation Open Fund', it aims to support journalism that fact‑checks false information about COVID‑19 vaccines. Google will fund up to one million dollars for each selected project.

구글이 코로나 백신 '가짜뉴스'를 잡는다

구글이 코로나 백신 '가짜뉴스'를 잡는 프로젝트에 300만달러를 지원한다는 내용입니다.

 전체 스크립트

Google launches fund to fight 'misinformation' about COVID‑19 vaccines

The Google News Initiative has launched a multimillion‑dollar global fund to fight misinformation about COVID‑19 vaccines.

Dubbed the 'COVID‑19 Vaccine Counter Misinformation Open Fund', it aims to support journalism that fact‑checks false information about COVID‑19 vaccines.

Google will fund up to one million dollars for each selected project.

Priority will be given to collaborative projects of multiple news organizations, and projects that may involve journalists working alongside medical experts.

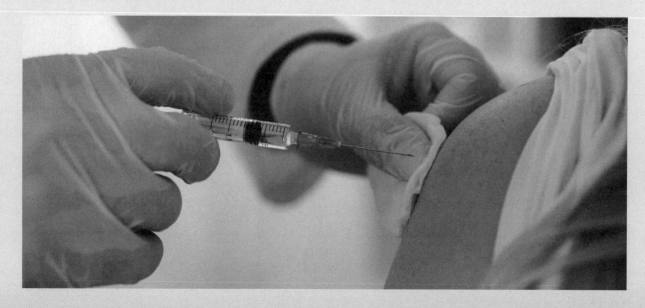

 스크립트 분석

Google launches fund to fight 'misinformation' about COVID-19 vaccines
구글이 COVID-19 백신에 대한 '오보' 퇴치를 위한 기금을 지원한다

☆launch 시작하다, 출시하다
☆misinformation 허위 정보, 오보

The Google News Initiative has launched a multimillion-dollar global fund to fight misinformation about COVID-19 vaccines.
구글 뉴스 이니셔티브는 COVID-19 백신에 대한 잘못된 정보와 싸우기 위해 수백만 달러의 글로벌 펀드를 출시했다.

☆Initiative 계획

e.g. The initiative was welcomed by supporters.
그 계획은 지지자들에게 환영을 받았다.

☆multimillion-dollar 수백만 달러

e.g. I reckon it's a multimillion-dollar lawsuit so give up.
수백만 달러 짜리 소송인 것 같으니 포기하세요.

Dubbed the 'COVID-19 Vaccine Counter Misinformation Open Fund', it aims to support journalism that fact-checks false information about COVID-19 vaccines.
'COVID-19 백신 카운터 오보 공개 기금(open fund)'로 불리는 이(프로젝트는) COVID-19 백신에 대한 허위 정보를 팩트로 확인하는 저널리즘을 지원하는 것을 목표로 한다.

☆open fund 공개 기금
☆dubbed ~로 불리는

e.g. Dubbed the 'Prince of events', the project picks the most handsome man.
'이벤트의 왕자'라고 불리는 이 프로젝트는 가장 잘생긴 남자를 뽑는다.

☆fact-check 사실 확인

e.g. Reporters should fact-check their stories before they publish them.
기자들은 그들의 기사를 올리기 전에 사실 확인을 해야 한다.

Google will fund up to one million dollars for each selected project.
구글은 선정된 프로젝트마다 최대 100만 달러(11억원)를 지원할 것이다.

☆up to 최대 ~까지

☆selected 선택된 =chosen, 선발된

e.g. All of your selected pictures will be on sale at the market.
모든 당신의 선택된 사진들이 시장에서 판매될 것입니다.

Priority will be given to collaborative projects of multiple news organizations, and projects that may involve journalists working alongside medical experts.
여러 뉴스 기관의 협력 프로젝트와 의료 전문가와 함께 일하는 기자들이 참여할 수 있는 프로젝트에 우선순위가 주어질 것이다

☆collaborative 공동의

☆Priority 우선권

☆Priority will be given 우선순위가 주어지다

e.g. Priority will be given to those who have previously participated.
이전에 참여하신 분들에게 우선권이 주어질 것입니다.

☆work alongside ~와 함께 일하다

e.g. Construction workers worked alongside professional builders.
건설 노동자들은 전문 건설업자들과 함께 일했다.

Writing Exercise

1. 구글 뉴스 이니셔티브는 COVID - 19 백신에 대한 잘못된 정보와 싸우기 위해 수백만 달러의 글로벌 펀드를 출시했다.

The Google
_____
_____

2. 'COVID - 19 백신 카운터 오보 공개 기금(open fund)'로 불리는 이 (프로젝트는) COVID - 19 백신에 대한 허위 정보를 팩트로 확인하는 저널리즘을 지원하는 것을 목표로 한다.

Dubbed
_____
_____

3. 구글은 선정된 프로젝트마다 최대 100만 달러(11억원)를 지원할 것이다.

Google
_____
_____

4. 여러 뉴스 기관의 협력 프로젝트와 의료 전문가와 함께 일하는 기자들이 참여할 수 있는 프로젝트에 우선순위가 주어질 것이다.

Priority
_____
_____

영어 뉴스룸 *81*

English NewsRoom

BREAKING NEWS

S. Korean NGO leading mask-wearing campaign online to fight COVID-19. A non-governmental organization in South Korea is leading a global online campaign to encourage people to wear masks to protect themselves and others from COVID-19. Led by a professor from Hanyang University, the Sunfull Foundation has come up with the 'Wear A Mask 4 All Challenge'. The campaign encourages people to upload videos of themselves wearing masks...

마스크 쓰기 글로벌 챌린지

한 NGO가 코로나 극복을 위해 네티즌들이 참여하는 '코로나 극복 글로벌 챌린지'를 시작했다는 내용입니다.

NEWS 전체 스크립트

S. Korean NGO leading mask-wearing campaign online to fight COVID-19

A non-governmental organization in South Korea is leading a global online campaign to encourage people to wear masks to protect themselves and others from COVID-19.

Led by a professor from Hanyang University, the Sunfull Foundation has come up with the 'Wear A Mask 4 All Challenge'.

The campaign encourages people to upload videos of themselves wearing masks onto social media with the hashtag 'WearAMask4All' and send the links to the foundation's email address.

The project was inspired by President Biden who, as president-elect last November, urged all Americans to wear masks.

NEWS 스크립트 분석

S. Korean NGO leading mask-wearing campaign online to fight COVID-19
코로나19 퇴치를 위해 온라인에서 마스크 착용 캠페인을 주도하고 있는 한국의 NGO

　　☆leading 이끄는, 선도하는, 주도하는

> e.g. The company is leading a campaign to help the SMEs hit hard by COVID-19.
> 그 회사는 코로나 19로 큰 타격을 입은 중소기업을 돕기 위한 캠페인을 주도하고 있다.

A non-governmental organization in South Korea is leading a global online campaign to encourage people to wear masks to protect themselves and others from COVID-19.
한국의 한 비정부 기구는 사람들이 COVID-19로부터 자신과 다른 사람들을 보호하기 위해 마스크를 착용하도록 장려하기 위한 세계적인 온라인 캠페인을 이끌고 있다.

　　☆non-governmental 민간, 비정부 non-profit 비영리의
　　☆encourage A to B A가 B하도록 격려하다, 장려하다

> e.g. Investors actively encouraged people to borrow money.
> 투자자들은 적극적으로 사람들이 돈을 빌리도록 장려했다.

Led by a professor from Hanyang University, the Sunfull Foundation has come up with the 'Wear A Mask 4 All Challenge'
한양대 교수가 이끄는 선플재단은 '코로나 극복, 모두를 위한 마스크 쓰기 글로벌 챌린지(#WearAMask4All global challenge)'를 제안했다.

　　☆come up with 제안하다

> e.g. She's come up with some amazing ideas for the students.
> 그녀는 학생들을 위한 몇 가지 놀라운 아이디어를 생각해 냈다.

The campaign encourages people to upload videos of themselves wearing masks onto social media with the hashtag 'WearAMask4All' and send the links to the foundation's email address.
이 캠페인은 사람들이 'WearAMask4All' 해시태그와 함께 마스크를 쓴 동영상을 SNS에 올리고 그 링크를 재단의 이메일 주소로 보내도록 독려한다.

　　☆social media 소셜 미디어 영어에서는 SNS라고 하지 않음

> e.g. Many use social media to promote the name of their business.
> 많은 사람들은 그들의 사업의 이름을 홍보하기 위해 소셜 미디어를 사용한다.

The project was inspired by President Biden who, as president-elect last November, urged all Americans to wear masks.

이 프로젝트는 바이든 대통령이 작년 11월 대통령 당선자로서 모든 미국인들에게 마스크를 착용하라고 호소한 것에서 영감을 받았다.

☆inspired by 영감을 받다

> e.g. He was inspired by his grandson to start a youtube channel.
> 그는 손자에게 영감을 받아 유튜브 채널을 시작했다.

☆president-elect 대통령 당선자

> e.g. The president-elect doesn't have any legal authority because he has not yet taken office.
> 대통령 당선자는 아직 취임하지 않았기 때문에 어떠한 법적 권한이 없다.

Writing Exercise

1. 한국의 한 비정부 기구는 사람들이 COVID-19로부터 자신과 다른 사람들을 보호하기 위해 마스크를 착용하도록 장려하기 위한 세계적인 온라인 캠페인을 이끌고 있다.

   A non-governmental
   _____
   _____

2. 한양대 교수가 이끄는 선플재단은 '코로나 극복, 모두를 위한 마스크 쓰기 글로벌 챌린지(#WearAMask4All global challenge)'를 제안했다.

   Led by
   _____
   _____

3. 이 캠페인은 사람들이 'WearAMask4All' 해시태그와 함께 마스크를 쓴 동영상을 SNS에 올리고 그 링크를 재단의 이메일 주소로 보내도록 독려한다.

   The campaign
   _____
   _____

4. 이 프로젝트는 바이든 대통령이 작년 11월 대통령 당선자로서 모든 미국인들에게 마스크를 착용하라고 호소한 것에서 영감을 받았다.

   The project
   _____
   _____

BRK 457/3
457/3
Today TH

영어 뉴스룸 82

English NewsRoom

BREAKING NEWS

Demand for mental health care rose in first half of 2020 amid COVID-19 pandemic. Demand for mental health care services in South Korea rose during the first wave of the COVID-19 pandemic with visits to mental health clinics increasing by nearly 10-percent on-year and payments for these visits by 18-percent in the first half of 2019. According to the Korea Insurance Research Institute today, there were significantly more people who suffered...

코로나 블루

코로나바이러스로 인해 정신 건강 관리에 대한 수요가 증가했다는 내용입니다.

 NEWS 전체 스크립트

Demand for mental health care rose in first half of 2020 amid COVID-19 pandemic

Demand for mental health care services in South Korea rose during the first wave of the COVID-19 pandemic with visits to mental health clinics increasing by nearly 10-percent on-year and payments for these visits by 18-percent in the first half of 2020.

According to the Korea Insurance Research Institute today, there were significantly more people who suffered from sleep disorder or depression during this time with the number of patients rising the most in February.

The most visits were made by those in their 20s and their 30s.

Demand for mental health care rose in first half of 2020 amid COVID-19 pandemic
2020년 상반기에 코로나바이러스로 인해 정신 건강 관리에 대한 수요가 증가했다

☆demand for ~에 대한 요구, ~에 대한 수요

e.g. Demand for the new model is outrunning supply.
새 모델에 대한 수요가 공급을 웃돌고 있다.

☆the first half of 상반기 | the latter half of 하반기

e.g. Over 100 people lost their job in the first half of this year.
올해 상반기에 100명이 넘는 사람들이 일자리를 잃었다.

Demand for mental health care services in South Korea rose during the first wave of the COVID-19 pandemic with visits to mental health clinics increasing by nearly 10-percent on-year and payments for these visits by 18-percent in the first half of 2020.
정신건강클리닉(정신의료기관)의 방문이 전년 동월 대비 거의 10%가 늘었고 진료비는 2020년 상반기에 18% 증가하는 등 한국의 정신 건강 관리 서비스에 대한 수요는 1차 COVID-19 대유행 기간 동안 증가했다.

☆(year-) on-year 전년 동월대비, 전년 동기대비 =compared to the same period of the previous year.

e.g. Companies in the city saw revenue drop by 10 percent on-year.
그 도시의 회사들은 전년 대비 수입이 10퍼센트 감소했다.

According to the Korea Insurance Research Institute today, there were significantly more people who suffered from sleep disorder or depression during this time with the number of patients rising the most in February.
오늘 보험연구원에 따르면 환자수가 가장 많이 상승한 2월 시기 동안 수면장애나 우울증을 앓은 환자가 훨씬 더 많은 것으로 나타났다.

☆significantly 상당히

e.g. Just 10 minutes of exercise significantly improves brain function.
단 10분간의 운동만으로도 뇌 기능이 상당히 향상된다.

☆suffer from ~로 고통 받다

e.g. She has been suffering from fever since last Monday.
그녀는 지난 월요일부터 열병을 앓고 있습니다.

☆sleep disorder 수면장애

The most visits were made by those in their 20s and their 30s.

가장 많이 방문을 한 사람들은 20~30대였다.

☆visit was made by ~에 의해 방문이 이루어졌다

e.g. Figures revealed that more than 70 percent of gym visits were made by male users.
수치에 따르면 체육관 방문의 70퍼센트 이상이 남성 이용자들에 의해 이루어졌다고 한다.

Writing Exercise

1. 정신건강클리닉(정신의료기관)의 방문이 전년 동월 대비 거의 10%가 늘었고 진료비는 2020년 상반기에 18% 증가하는 등 한국의 정신 건강 관리 서비스에 대한 수요는 1차 COVID - 19 대유행 기간 동안 증가했다.

Demand

2. 오늘 보험연구원에 따르면 환자수가 가장 많이 상승한 2월 시기 동안 수면장애나 우울증을 앓은 환자가 훨씬 더 많은 것으로 나타났다.

According to

3. 가장 많이 방문을 한 사람들은 20~30대였다.

The most

영어 뉴스룸 *83*   English NewsRoom

BREAKING NEWS

S. Korea jumps to 33rd least corrupt country in the world. In a ranking of the least corrupt countries in the world, South Korea rose last year to 33rd place. It's risen 18 spots in the last three years. This is in the latest corruption index by Transparency international. On a scale of zero to a hundred, a hundred meaning very clean, South Korea scored 61 points. The agency highlighted that the country is an example of significant improvement.

한국, 부패가 적은 국가 33위에 오르다

한국의 국가청렴도가 100점 만점에 61점으로 측정돼 세계 180개국 중 33위를 기록했다는 내용입니다.

 NEWS 전체 스크립트

S. Korea jumps to 33rd least corrupt country in the world

In a ranking of the least corrupt countries in the world, South Korea rose last year to 33rd place.

It's risen 18 spots in the last three years.

This is in the latest corruption index by Transparency international.

On a scale of zero to a hundred, a hundred meaning very clean, South Korea scored 61 points.

The agency highlighted that the country is an example of significant improvement.

Topping the index were Denmark and New Zealand at 88 points, while the United States had its worst score since 2012 at 67.

NEWS 스크립트 분석

S. Korea jumps to 33rd least corrupt country in the world
한국이 가장 부패가 적은 국가 33위로 순위가 상승하다

☆jump to *(순위가)* 상승하다

> e.g. The country has jumped to 5th position globally in internet speed.
> 그 나라는 인터넷 속도에서 세계 5위로 뛰어올랐다.

☆least 가장 적은
☆corrupt 부패한

In a ranking of the least corrupt countries in the world, South Korea rose last year to 33rd place.
세계에서 가장 부패가 적은 국가 순위(국가청렴도순위)에서 한국은 작년에 33위로 올랐다.

☆rise-rose-risen 오르다
☆place 등위, 순위

> e.g. She finished in third place.
> 그녀는 3위로 들어왔다.

It's risen 18 spots in the last three years.
지난 3년 동안 18계단 상승했다.

☆spot 계단, 자리

> e.g. The country has risen 10 spots since the last report.
> 그 나라는 지난 보고서 이후 10계단 상승했다.

This is in the latest corruption index by Transparency international.
이것은 국제투명성기구(TI)의 최근 부패지수이다.

☆latest 최근의
☆transparency 투명성, 속이 빤히 들여다보임, 명백함

> e.g. People want transparency in government.
> 국민들은 정부의 투명성을 원한다.

On a scale of zero to a hundred, a hundred meaning very clean, South Korea scored 61 points.

0에서 100점까지 중에, 매우 청렴하다는 뜻인 100점에서 한국은 61점을 득점했다.

☆on a scale of A to B A에서 B까지 중에

e.g. On a scale of 1 to 10, I give the film a 7.
1점부터 10점까지 중에, 나는 그 영화 7점 준다.

The agency highlighted that the country is an example of significant improvement.

그 기관은 한국은 대단한 상승의 사례라고 강조했다.

☆highlight 강조하다

☆be an example of 본보기·사례·예가 되다

e.g. It's a good example of how people can help others.
이것은 사람들이 다른 사람들을 어떻게 도울 수 있는지를 보여주는 좋은 예입니다.

☆significant 중요한, 의미 있는, 대단한

Topping the index were Denmark and New Zealand at 88 points, while the United States had its worst score since 2012 at 67.

미국이 67점으로 2012년 이후 최악의 점수를 받은 반면 지수 1위는 덴마크와 뉴질랜드가 88점으로 가장 높았다.

Writing Exercise

1. 세계에서 가장 부패가 적은 국가 순위(국가청렴도순위)에서 한국은 작년에 33위로 올랐다.

   In a

2. 지난 3년 동안 18계단 상승했다.

   It's

3. 이것은 국제투명성기구(TI)의 최근 부패지수이다.

   This is

4. 0에서 100점까지 중에, 매우 청렴하다는 뜻인 100점에서 한국은 61점을 득점했다.

   On a

5. 그 기관은 한국은 대단한 상승의 사례라고 강조했다.

   The agency

6. 미국이 67점으로 2012년 이후 최악의 점수를 받은 반면 지수 1위는 덴마크와 뉴질랜드가 88점으로 가장 높았다.

   Topping

◉ BRK 457/3
457/3
Today TH

영어 뉴스룸 84

**English
NewsRoom**

**BREAKING
NEWS**

Seoul city to close five of its cemeteries during Lunar New Year to prevent cluster infections. The city of Seoul is closing five cemeteries and memorial facilities to prevent people from visiting during the Lunar New Year holidays. Seoul Facilities Corporation said today that the memorial houses it operates in Gyeonggi-do Province will be closed from February 6th to 7th and 11th through 14th to prevent Covid-19. You cannot visit cemeteries in groups larger...

설연휴 중 묘지 폐쇄?

서울시가 신종 코로나바이러스 감염증(코로나19) 확산 방지를 위해 설 연휴 기간 묘지와 납골당 등 시립 장사시설 일부를 폐쇄한다는 내용입니다.

NEWS 전체 스크립트

Seoul city to close five of its cemeteries during Lunar New Year to prevent cluster infections

The city of Seoul is closing five cemeteries and memorial facilities to prevent people from visiting during the Lunar New Year holidays.

Seoul Facilities Corporation said today that the memorial houses it operates in Gyeonggi-do Province will be closed from February 6th to 7th and 11th through 14th to prevent Covid-19.

You cannot visit cemeteries in groups larger than four and eating on-site a common holiday ritual is also banned.

The city encourages the public to use the virtual memorial service set up on its website instead.

Around 80-thousand people visited the 15 cemeteries and memorials parks run by the organization during Lunar New Year in 2020.

 **스크립트 분석**

Seoul city to close five of its cemeteries during Lunar New Year to prevent cluster infections
집단 감염 예방을 위해 설 기간 중 묘지 5곳을 폐쇄하는 서울시

☆cemetery 묘지

☆Lunar 달의

☆Lunar New Year 구정 Lunar New Year holiday 설연휴

☆cluster 무리, 집단

e.g. There was a cluster of fans around her, asking for help.
그녀의 주변에는 도움을 요청하는 팬들이 모여 있었다.

The city of Seoul is closing five cemeteries and memorial facilities to prevent people from visiting during the Lunar New Year holidays.
서울시는 설 연휴 동안 사람들이 방문하는 것을 막기 위해 5개의 묘지와 추모 시설을 폐쇄하고 있다.

☆prevent A from B A가 B하는 것을 막다

☆memorial 기념비

☆memorial facility 추모시설

Seoul Facilities Corporation said today that the memorial houses it operates in Gyeonggi-do Province will be closed from February 6th to 7th and 11th through 14th to prevent Covid-19.
서울시설공단은 코로나19를 막기 위해 경기도에 위치한 납골당이 오는 2월 6일부터 7일까지, 11일부터 14일까지 문을 닫는다고 오늘 밝혔다.

☆memorial house 납골당

You cannot visit cemeteries in groups larger than four and eating on-site a common holiday ritual is also banned.
5인 이상이 묘지를 방문할 수 없으며, 일반적인 명절 의식 현장에서(묘앞에서) 취식도 금지된다.

☆on-site 현장의, 현지의

e.g. We're scheduled to meet our client on-site tonight.
우리는 오늘 밤 현장에서 고객을 만날 예정입니다.

☆ritual (특히 종교상의) 의식 절차, 의례

e.g. Tea and the newspaper are part of my morning ritual.
차와 신문은 나의 아침 의식의 일부이다.

The city encourages the public to use the virtual memorial service set up on its website instead.

서울시는 시민들이 웹사이트에 마련된 가상 추모제(사이버 추모의 집)를 대신 사용하도록 장려하고 있다.

　　☆encourage A to B A가 B하도록 장려하다

　　e.g.It is true that music encourages shoppers to buy more.
　　　음악이 쇼핑객들에게 더 많이 사도록 부추기는 것은 사실이다.

　　☆virtual 가상의

　　☆set up 설정하다, 설립하다

Around 80-thousand people visited the 15 cemeteries and memorials parks run by the organization during Lunar New Year in 2020.

8만여 명의 사람들이 2020년 설 동안 그 기관이(즉 서울시설공단이) 운영하는 15개 묘지와 기념공원을 방문했다.

Writing Exercise

1. 서울시는 설 연휴 동안 사람들이 방문하는 것을 막기 위해 5개의 묘지와 추모 시설을 폐쇄하고 있다.

The city

2. 서울시설공단은 코로나19를 막기 위해 경기도에 위치한 납골당이 오는 2월 6일부터 7일까지, 11일부터 14일까지 문을 닫는다고 오늘 밝혔다.

Seoul

3. 5인 이상이 묘지를 방문할 수 없으며, 일반적인 명절 의식 현장에서(묘앞에서) 취식도 금지된다.

You cannot

4. 서울시는 시민들이 웹사이트에 마련된 가상 추모제(사이버 추모의 집)를 대신 사용하도록 장려하고 있다.

The city

5. 8만여명의 사람들이 2020년 설 동안 그 기관이(즉 서울시설공단이) 운영하는 15개 묘지와 기념공원을 방문했다.

Around

⌾ BRK 457/3
457/3
Today TH

영어 뉴스룸 *85*

**English
NewsRoom**

**BREAKING
NEWS**
Seoul aiming to minimize movement over Lunar New Year. For the first time during the Lunar New Year holidays, public transport in Seoul will not be running on extended hours at night. The city wants to minimize the movement of people to stop the spread of COVID-19. Also, while it's a tradition for some families to pay a visit to the graves of their ancestors to show their respect, indoor areas of local cemeteries will be closed.

설 연휴기간 고강도 방역 시행

서울시가 코로나19 재확산의 중대고비에서 맞는 올해 설 연휴기간 동안 '고강도 방역' 을 시행한다는 내용입니다.

 전체 스크립트

Seoul aiming to minimize movement over Lunar New Year

For the first time during the Lunar New Year holidays, public transport in Seoul will not be running on extended hours at night.

The city wants to minimize the movement of people to stop the spread of COVID-19.

Also, while it's a tradition for some families to pay a visit to the graves of their ancestors to show their respect, indoor areas of local cemeteries will be closed.

The city's Covid-19 screening centers will, however, remain open throughout the holidays.

Seoul aiming to minimize movement over Lunar New Year
설 연휴 동안 이동 최소화를 목표로 하는 서울시

☆aim to ~하는 것을 목표로 하다

e.g. We aim to arrive at 12 o'clock.
우리는 12시에 도착하는 것을 목표로 한다.

☆minimize 최소화하다

e.g. How can we minimize the cost of maintaining this system?
어떻게 하면 이 시스템을 유지하는 비용을 최소화할 수 있을까요?

For the first time during the Lunar New Year holidays, public transport in Seoul will not be running on extended hours at night.
설 연휴 동안 처음으로, 서울의 대중 교통은 밤에 증편 운행되지 않을 것이다.

☆public transport 대중교통
☆run 운행하다

e.g. They run extra buses during the rush hour.
그들은 혼잡시간에는 추가 버스를 운행한다.

☆extended (보통 때나 예상보다) 연장된
☆extended hours 연장시간, 증편

e.g. Some workers may be working extended hours each week because of money.
일부 근로자들은 돈 때문에 매주 연장 근무를 할 수도 있다.

The city wants to minimize the movement of people to stop the spread of COVID-19.
서울시는 COVID-19 확산을 막기 위해 사람들의 움직임을 최소화하기를 원한다.

Also, while it's a tradition for some families to pay a visit to the graves of their ancestors to show their respect, indoor areas of local cemeteries will be closed.

또한, 일부 가족들이 그들의 존경을 표하기 위해 그들 조상들의 묘소를 방문하는 것은 전통이긴 하지만, 지역 묘지의 실내 공간은 폐쇄될 것이다.

☆while 1. *(주로 문장 앞)* ~이긴 하지만, ~에도 불구하고
       2. *(주로 문장 중간)* ~하는 동안에, ~하는 반면에

☆it's a tradition ~은 전통이다

> e.g. It's a tradition to dance 'butterfly' on New Year's Eve.
> 새해 전야에 '나비' 춤을 추는 것은 전통이다.

☆pay a visit 방문하다

> e.g. He paid a visit to his parents last week.
> 그는 지난주에 부모님을 방문했다.

☆show one's respect 경의를 표하다

> e.g. You'll need to bring a gift to show your respect for her.
> 그녀에게 경의를 표하려면 선물을 가져와야 할 것이다.

The city's Covid-19 screening centers will, however, remain open throughout the holidays.

그러나 서울시의 코로나19 선별진료소는 연휴 내내 문을 열 것이다.

☆screening center 선별진료소

☆throughout ~동안 쭉, 내내

> e.g. Students should continue educational activities throughout the summer holidays.
> 학생들은 여름 방학 동안 교육 활동을 계속해야 한다.

1. 설 연휴 동안 처음으로, 서울의 대중 교통은 밤에 증편 운행되지 않을 것이다.

   For the
   _____
   _____

2. 서울시는 COVID - 19 확산을 막기 위해 사람들의 움직임을 최소화하기를 원한다.

   The city
   _____
   _____

3. 또한, 일부 가족들이 그들의 존경을 표하기 위해 그들 조상들의 묘소를 방문하는 것은 전통이긴 하지만, 지역 묘지의 실내 공간은 폐쇄될 것이다.

   Also,
   _____
   _____

4. 그러나 서울시의 코로나19 선별진료소는 연휴 내내 문을 열 것이다.

   The city's
   _____
   _____

영어 뉴스룸 86

English NewsRoom

BREAKING NEWS

S. Korean sci-fi film 'Space Sweepers' tops Netflix movie chart. South Korean sci-fi film 'Space Sweepers' has topped the Netflix rankings following its worldwide release late last week. According to Flixpatrol, which ranks video-on-demand in more than a hundred countries, South Korea's first big-budget space adventure was number one just a day after its release. 'Space Sweepers' follows the crew of The Victory, a ship that collects space debris...

승리호의 승리

한국 최초의 우주 SF 영화 '승리호'가 넷플릭스 공개 하루만에 세계 영화 순위 1위를 차지했다는 내용입니다.

 전체 스크립트

S. Korean sci-fi film 'Space Sweepers' tops Netflix movie chart

South Korean sci-fi film 'Space Sweepers' has topped the Netflix rankings following its worldwide release late last week.

According to Flixpatrol, which ranks video-on-demand in more than a hundred countries, South Korea's first big-budget space adventure was number one just a day after its release.

'Space Sweepers' follows the crew of The Victory, a ship that collects space debris in the year 2092.

The movie was originally set to hit cinemas last summer, but due to COVID-19, it was instead released on Netflix.

S. Korean sci-fi film 'Space Sweepers' tops Netflix movie chart

한국 공상 과학 영화 '스페이스 스위퍼스(승리호)'가 넷플릭스 영화 순위 1위를 차지하다.

☆sci-fi film 공상 과학 영화 =science fiction film

☆top 1위를 하다

South Korean sci-fi film 'Space Sweepers' has topped the Netflix rankings following its worldwide release late last week.

한국 공상과학 영화 '스페이스 스위퍼스(승리호)'가 지난주 전 세계 개봉에 이어 넷플릭스 랭킹 1위를 차지했다.

☆Sweeper 청소부, 청소기

☆following ~에 이어

☆release 발표, 개봉

> e.g. More than a decade after the movie's release, the actress returned to the screen.
> 영화가 개봉된 지 10여 년이 지난 후, 그 여배우는 스크린으로 돌아왔다.
> return to the screen 다시 복귀하다

According to Flixpatrol, which ranks video-on-demand in more than a hundred countries, South Korea's first big-budget space adventure was number one just a day after its release.

100여 개국의 주문형 비디오(VOD) 순위를 매기는 플릭스 패트롤에 따르면, 한국의 첫 번째 대규모 예산 우주 모험 영화가 개봉 하루 만에 1위를 차지했다고 한다.

☆video-on-demand VOD 주문형 비디오 시스템

☆big-budget 많은 예산의

> e.g. His story was made into a big-budget film in Korea.
> 그의 이야기는 한국에서 많은 예산을 들인 영화로 만들어졌다.

'Space Sweepers' follows the crew of The Victory, a ship that collects space debris in the year 2092.

'스페이스 스위퍼스'는 2092년에 우주 쓰레기를 줍는 배인 빅토리호(승리호)의 선원들을 다룬다.

☆follow (누구의 삶이나 무엇의 발달 과정을) 따라가다, 계속 다루다

> e.g. The novel follows the fortunes of two families in a small town.
> 이 소설은 작은 마을에 사는 두 가족의 운명을 추적한다.

☆debris 잔해, 쓰레기 | 🇬🇧 [dəˈbriː], 🇺🇸 [ˈdeb·riː] 둘 다 쓰임
영국, 미국 발음 다름 주의!

The movie was originally set to hit cinemas last summer, but due to COVID-19, it was instead released on Netflix.
이 영화는 원래 지난 여름 개봉될 예정이었으나 COVID-19로 인해 넷플릭스에서 개봉되었다.

☆be set to ~하기로 예정되어 있다

e.g. The price of cigarettes is set to rise again.
담뱃값이 다시 오를 예정이다.

☆hit the cinema 영화관에서 개봉하다

e.g. The movie is set to hit the cinema sooner than you expected.
그 영화는 당신이 예상했던 것보다 빨리 개봉될 예정이다.

Writing Exercise

1. 한국 공상과학 영화 '스페이스 스위퍼스(승리호)'가 지난주 전 세계 개봉에 이어 넷플릭스 랭킹 1위를 차지했다.

South

2. 100여개국의 주문형 비디오 (VOD) 순위를 매기는 플릭스 패트롤에 따르면, 한국의 첫 번째 대규모 예산 우주 모험 영화가 개봉 하루 만에 1위를 차지했다고 한다.

According to

3. '스페이스 스위퍼스'는 2092년에 우주 쓰레기를 줍는 배인 빅토리호(승리호)의 선원들을 다룬다.

'Space Sweepers'

4. 이 영화는 원래 지난 여름 개봉될 예정이었으나 COVID-19로 인해 넷플릭스에서 개봉되었다.

The movie

영어 뉴스룸 87

English NewsRoom

BREAKING NEWS

S. Korean military lifts ban on vacations, off-site trips for 2 weeks. A nationwide ban on vacations and off-site trips on nearly all South Korean military personnel has been lifted for the first time in 80 days. This comes as the military has eased distancing measures by a notch to level two the third-highest tier in its five-tier system for the next two weeks. As a precautionary measure, it'll be required for all personnel returning from leave to be tested and...

군 장병 휴가 통제 해제

코로나19확산 방지를 위해 통제됐던 군 장병의 휴가가 15일부터 가능해진다는 내용입니다.

 NEWS 전체 스크립트

S. Korean military lifts ban on vacations, off-site trips for 2 weeks

A nationwide ban on vacations and off-site trips on nearly all South Korean military personnel has been lifted for the first time in 80 days.

This comes as the military has eased distancing measures by a notch to level two the third-highest tier in its five-tier system for the next two weeks.

As a precautionary measure, it'll be required for all personnel returning from leave to be tested and quarantined.

As of Monday morning, the South Korean military has reported 558 cases.

Five of them are still receiving treatment.

 스크립트 분석

S. Korean military lifts ban on vacations, off-site trips for 2 weeks
한국군은 휴가, 외출에 대한 금지조치를 2주간 해제한다.

☆lift ban 금지를 풀다

> e.g. The government lifted ban on export of foreign snacks.
> 정부는 외국 과자의 수출 금지를 해제했다.

☆off-site *(어느 특정한 장소에서)* 떨어진, 부지 밖의

> e.g. It is more difficult to manage off-site employees.
> 외근직원을 관리하는 것은 더 어렵습니다.

A nationwide ban on vacations and off-site trips on nearly all South Korean military personnel has been lifted for the first time in 80 days.
거의 모든 한국군의 전국적인 휴가 및 외출 금지가 80일 만에 처음으로 해제되었다.

☆nationwide 전국적인

☆nearly 거의

> e.g. It's been nearly two months since the death of my cat.
> 내 고양이가 죽은 지 거의 두 달이 되었다.

☆personnel *(조직·군대의)* 인원들, 직원들

> e.g. The country is importing a broad range of skilled personnel.
> 그 나라는 광범위한 숙련된 인력을 해외에서 충원하고 있다.

This comes as the military has eased distancing measures by a notch to level two the third-highest tier in its five-tier system for the next two weeks.
이는 군이 향후 2주 동안 5단계에서 3번째로 높은 2단계로 사회적 거리두기 조치를 완화한 데 따른 것이다.

☆eased 완화된

> e.g. One of the eased regulations is the reopening of parks.
> 규제 완화 중 하나는 공원 재개장이다.

☆notch 단계, 급수

☆tier 줄, 단, 단계

> e.g. I remember my wedding cake had six tiers.
> 내 웨딩 케이크는 6단이었던 것으로 기억한다.

As a precautionary measure, it'll be required for all personnel returning from leave to be tested and quarantined.
예방 조치로, 휴가에서 돌아오는 모든 군인은 검사 및 격리되어야 한다.

☆precautionary 예방의
☆return from leave 귀대하다, 복귀하다

As of Monday morning, the South Korean military has reported 558 cases.
월요일 아침기준으로 현재 한국군은 558건의 확진자를 보고했다.

Five of them are still receiving treatment.
이 중 5명은 아직 치료를 받고 있다.

☆receive treatment 치료를 받다

> e.g. I insist you receive medical treatment right now.
> 지금 당장 치료를 받으셔야 합니다.

Writing Exercise

1. 거의 모든 한국군의 전국적인 휴가 및 외출 금지가 80일 만에 처음으로 해제되었다.

   A nationwide
   _____

   _____

2. 이는 군이 향후 2주 동안 5단계에서 3번째로 높은 2단계로 사회적 거리두기 조치를 완화한 데 따른 것이다.

   This comes
   _____

   _____

3. 예방 조치로, 휴가에서 돌아오는 모든 군인은 검사 및 격리되어야 한다.

   As a
   _____

   _____

4. 월요일 아침기준으로 현재 한국군은 558건의 확진자를 보고했다.

   As of
   _____

   _____

5. 이 중 5명은 아직 치료를 받고 있다.

   Five of
   _____

   _____

◎ BRK 457/3
457/3
Today TH

영어 뉴스룸 *88*

**English
NewsRoom**

**BREAKING
NEWS**

N. Korea shortens mandatory military service period to deploy young labor force : NIS .North Korea has reportedly shortened its mandatory military service period in an attempt to revive its sluggish economy by deploying more young workers. Seoul's National Intelligence Service said Tuesday the term for men has been reduced to around eight years from ten years and five years from eight years for women. It explained that Pyeongyang is putting....

북한군 의무복무기간이 줄어든다?

북한이 군복무를 줄여 젊은 노동력을 생산현장에 투입한다는 내용입니다.

 전체 스크립트

N. Korea shortens mandatory military service period to deploy young labor force : NIS

North Korea has reportedly shortened its mandatory military service period in an attempt to revive its sluggish economy by deploying more young workers.

Seoul's National Intelligence Service said Tuesday the term for men has been reduced to around eight years from ten years and five years from eight years for women.

It explained that Pyeongyang is putting more youth into the work force in a bid to make its new five-year economic development plan a success.

South Korea's defense ministry estimates there are around 1.3 million North Korean troops, but that number is expected to drop as a result of the shortened military term.

NEWS 스크립트 분석

N. Korea shortens mandatory military service period to deploy young labor force : NIS
국가정보원에 따르면 북한이 젊은 노동력을 효율적으로 활용하기 위해 의무 군복무 기간을 단축한다.

☆shorten 단축하다, 짧아지다

e.g. His injury probably shortened his football career.
그의 부상은 아마도 그의 축구 경력을 단축시켰을 것이다.

☆mandatory 법에 정해진, 의무적인
☆mandatory military service 의무 군복무
☆deploy 효율적으로 사용하다, (군대·무기를) 배치하다
☆NIS National Intelligence Service 국가정보원

North Korea has reportedly shortened its mandatory military service period in an attempt to revive its sluggish economy by deploying more young workers.
보도에 따르면 북한은 젊은 노동력을 효율적으로 사용하여 침체된 경제를 되살리기 위해 군 복무 기간을 단축했다.

☆reportedly 보도에 따르면, 전하는 바에 따르면
☆in an attempt to ~하기 위하여, ~하려는 시도로

e.g. The city closed the road in an attempt to reduce traffic in morning rush hours.
그 도시는 아침 출근 혼잡 시간대에 교통 혼잡을 줄이기 위해 도로를 폐쇄했다.

☆revive 되살리다, 회복시키다
☆sluggish 부진한

e.g. The stock market has been very sluggish.
주식 시장이 매우 침체되어 있다.

Seoul's National Intelligence Service said Tuesday the term for men has been reduced to around eight years from ten years and five years from eight years for women.
국가정보원은 남성의 군 복무기간 경우10년에서 8년, 여성의 경우 8년에서 5년으로 단축됐다고 화요일에 밝혔다.

☆term 기간

It explained that Pyeongyang is putting more youth into the work force in a bid to make its new five-year economic development plan a success.

국가정보원은 평양이 새로운 경제개발 5개년 계획을 성공시키기 위해 더 많은 젊은이들을 노동력으로 투입하고 있다고 설명했다.

☆put A into B A를 B로 넣다 *(투입하다)*

☆work force 노동력

☆in a bid to do something ~을 하기 위한 노력의 일환으로, ~을 하기 위해

e.g. We need to be more careful in a bid to prevent further infections.
우리는 더 이상의 감염을 막기 위해 좀 더 조심할 필요가 있다.

☆make A B A를 B하게 만들다

South Korea's defense ministry estimates there are around 1.3 million North Korean troops, but that number is expected to drop as a result of the shortened military term.

국방부는 북한군 병력이 130만 명 정도로 추정하고 있지만, 군 복무기간 단축에 따라 그 숫자는 감소할 것으로 예상된다.

☆estimate 추정하다, 추산하다

e.g. Police said it was difficult to estimate how many vehicles had been destroyed.
경찰은 얼마나 많은 차량이 파괴되었는지 추정하기 어렵다고 말했다.

☆be expected to 예상되다, 기대되다

Writing Exercise

1. 보도에 따르면 북한은 젊은 노동력을 효율적으로 사용하여 침체된 경제를 되살리기 위해 군 복무 기간을 단축했다.

North _____

_____

2. 국가정보원은 남성의 군 복무기간 경우10년에서 8년, 여성의 경우 8년에서 5년으로 단축됐다고 화요일에 밝혔다.

Seoul's _____

_____

3. 국가정보원은 평양이 새로운 경제개발 5개년 계획을 성공시키기 위해 더 많은 젊은이들을 노동력으로 투입하고 있다고 설명했다.

It explained _____

_____

4. 국방부는 북한군 병력이 130만 명 정도로 추정하고 있지만, 군 복무기간 단축에 따라 그 숫자는 감소할 것으로 예상된다.

South _____

_____

BRK 457/3
457/3
Today TH

영어 뉴스룸 *89*

English
NewsRoom

**BREAKING
NEWS**

S. Korea aims to extend healthy life expectancy to 73.3 yrs by 2030. South Korean government announced its plans to extend the nation's healthy life expectancy by 2.9 years, to 73.3 by 2030. Healthy life expectancy is the average life of people in good health with no illness or disease. It's been 70.4 years since 2018, which is 12 years shorter than the total life expectancy. Also in Wednesday's announcement, the health ministry proposed reducing the nation's...

담뱃값 또 인상?

정부가 2030년까지 국민 건강수명을 73.3세로 연장하겠다는 정책 목표를 제시했다는 내용입니다.

 **전체 스크립트**

S. Korea aims to extend healthy life expectancy to 73.3 yrs by 2030

South Korean government announced its plans to extend the nation's healthy life expectancy by 2.9 years, to 73.3 by 2030.

Healthy life expectancy is the average life of people in good health with no illness or disease.

It's been 70.4 years since 2018, which is 12 years shorter than the total life expectancy.

Also in Wednesday's announcement, the health ministry proposed reducing the nation's smoking and drinking prevalence.

For that, it plans to raise the prices of cigarettes and liquors by charging consumers with public health contribution fees, and enhancing related restrictions.

 스크립트 분석

S. Korea aims to extend healthy life expectancy to 73.3 yrs by 2030
한국은 2030년까지 건강 수명을 73.3세로 연장하는 것을 목표로 한다

☆aim to ~하는 것을 목표로 하다

☆extend 연장하다

e.g. The club has extended its opening hours.
그 클럽은 영업시간을 연장했다.

☆life expectancy 기대 수명

☆healthy life expectancy 건강 수명

South Korean government announced its plans to extend the nation's healthy life expectancy by 2.9 years, to 73.3 by 2030.
한국 정부는 2030년까지 한국의 건강 수명을 73.3세로 2.9세 연장할 계획을 발표했다.

Healthy life expectancy is the average life of people in good health with no illness or disease.
건강 수명은 병이나 질환이 없는 건강한 사람들의 평균 수명이다.

☆average 평균의

☆in good health 건강한 ↔ in bad health

e.g. She is in good health for her age.
그녀는 나이에 비해 건강하다.

It's been 70.4 years since 2018, which is 12 years shorter than the total life expectancy.
2018년 이후 건강 수명은 70.4세로 전체 기대수명 보다 12년 짧다.

Also in Wednesday's announcement, the health ministry proposed reducing the nation's smoking and drinking prevalence.
또한 수요일 발표에서 보건복지부는 흡연율과 음주율을 줄이는 것을 제시했다.

☆propose 제안하다, 제시하다

☆prevalence 널리 퍼짐, 유행, 보급, 유병률

e.g. The prevalence of smoking among the students was 25% for the boys and 28% of the girls.
학생들의 흡연율은 남학생이 25%, 여학생이 28%였다.

For that, it plans to raise the prices of cigarettes and liquors by charging consumers with public health contribution fees, and enhancing related restrictions.

이를 위해 소비자에게 국민건강증진기금 부담금을 부과하고 관련 규제를 강화하는 등 담뱃값과 주류 가격을 인상할 계획이다.

☆charge 부과하다, 청구하다

e.g. How much do you charge for a haircut?
머리 자르는데 얼마예요?

☆enhance 향상시키다

e.g. You've got to enhance the quality of life for yourself.
넌 자신을 위해서 삶의 질을 높여야 해.

Writing Exercise

1. 한국 정부는 2030년까지 한국의 건강 수명을 73.3세로 2.9세 연장할 계획을 발표했다.

South

2. 건강 수명은 병이나 질환이 없는 건강한 사람들의 평균 수명이다.

Healthy

3. 2018년 이후 건강 수명은 70.4세로 전체 기대수명 보다 12년 짧다.

It's

4. 또한 수요일 발표에서 보건복지부는 흡연율과 음주율을 줄이는 것을 제시했다.

Also

5. 이를 위해 소비자에게 국민건강증진기금 부담금을 부과하고 관련 규제를 강화하는 등 담뱃값과 주류 가격을 인상할 계획이다.

For that,

BRK 457/3
457/3
Today TH

영어 뉴스룸 90

English NewsRoom

BREAKING NEWS

South Koreans must pay 20% tax when Bitcoin trading profit exceeds US$ 2,260 beginning 2022. Starting next year in South Korea, the cryptocurrency, Bitcoin, will no longer be tax-free. According to the Ministry of Economy and Finance on Monday, income gained from trading the digital currency will be subject to tax. South Koreans will have to pay a 20-percent tax, when trading profits exceed 2.5 million won, equal to 2-thousand 260 U.S. dollars.

내년부터 비트코인으로 1천만원 벌면 세금이 150만원?

내년부터 비트코인 수익의 20퍼센트를 세금으로 낸다는 내용입니다.

 **전체 스크립트**

South Koreans must pay 20% tax when Bitcoin trading profit exceeds US$ 2,260 beginning 2022

Starting next year in South Korea, the cryptocurrency, Bitcoin, will no longer be tax-free.

According to the Ministry of Economy and Finance on Monday, income gained from trading the digital currency will be subject to tax.

South Koreans will have to pay a 20-percent tax, when trading profits exceed 2.5 million won, equal to 2-thousand 260 U.S. dollars.

The new measure comes after the government recognized Bitcoin as a financial asset, categorized under "other income".

Profits will have to be reported on income statements with taxes to be paid every year in May.

South Koreans must pay 20% tax when Bitcoin trading profit exceeds US $ 2,260 beginning 2022
2022년부터 비트코인 거래소득이 2,260달러를 넘으면 20%의 세금을 내야 한다.

　☆trading profit 거래소득

　☆exceed *(특정한 수·양을)* 넘다, 초과하다

　e.g. The cost should not exceed 10,000 won.
　　　그 비용은 10,000원을 초과해서는 안 된다.

Starting next year in South Korea, the cryptocurrency, Bitcoin, will no longer be tax-free.
내년부터 한국에서 가상화폐인 비트코인은 더 이상 비과세가 되지 않는다.

　☆no longer 더 이상 ~가 아니다

　e.g. You have no right to say this because you don't work here any longer.
　　　넌 더 이상 여기서 일하지 않기 때문에 이런 말을 할 권리가 없어.

　☆tax-free 비과세

　e.g. All of this is tax-free, so you can buy things at special low prices.
　　　이 모든 것은 비과세이기 때문에 당신은 특별 저가로 물건을 살 수 있다.

According to the Ministry of Economy and Finance on Monday, income gained from trading the digital currency will be subject to tax.
월요일 기획재정부에 따르면 디지털화폐를 거래해 얻은 소득은 과세 대상이 된다.

　☆gain 얻다

　e.g. Some English language learners from the class gained confidence over the last couple of weeks.
　　　그 수업의 일부 영어 학습자들은 지난 몇 주 동안 자신감을 얻었습니다.

　☆digital currency 전자 화폐

　☆be subject to ~의 대상이다

　e.g. Large boats are subject to a high domestic tax.
　　　대형 선박은 높은 내국세의 대상이다.

South Koreans will have to pay a 20-percent tax, when trading profits exceed 2.5 million won, equal to 2-thousand 260 U.S. dollars.

한국인은 거래소득이 2천 260달러, 즉 250만 원을 넘을 때는 20퍼센트의 세금을 내야 한다.

☆equal to ~와 같은

The new measure comes after the government recognized Bitcoin as a financial asset, categorized under "other income".

이 새로운 조치는 정부가 비트코인을 '기타소득'으로 분류한 금융자산으로 인정한 데에 따른 것이다.

☆recognize 인정하다, 인식하다

e.g. We must recognize that we have been defeated.
우리는 우리가 패배했다는 것을 인정해야 한다.

☆categorized under ~로 분류한

e.g. This material is categorized under essential commodities.
이 물질은 필수 상품으로 분류된다.

☆other income 기타소득

Profits will have to be reported on income statements with taxes to be paid every year in May

소득은 매년 5월에 납부해야 할 세금과 함께 소득명세서에 신고되어야 한다.

☆income statement 소득명세서

1. 내년부터 한국에서 가상화폐인 비트코인은 더 이상 비과세가 되지 않는다.

   Starting
   _____

   _____

2. 월요일 기획재정부에 따르면 디지털화폐를 거래해 얻은 소득은 과세 대상이 된다.

   According to
   _____

   _____

3. 한국인은 거래소득이 2천 260 달러, 즉 .250만 원을 넘을 때는 20 퍼센트의 세금을 내야 한다.

   South
   _____

   _____

4. 이 새로운 조치는 정부가 비트코인을 '기타소득'으로 분류한 금융자산으로 인정한 데에 따른 것이다.

   The new
   _____

   _____

5. 소득은 매년 5월에 납부해야 할 세금과 함께 소득명세서에 신고되어야 한다.

   Profits
   _____

   _____

영어 뉴스룸 91

English NewsRoom

BREAKING NEWS

'Minari' wins best foreign language film at Golden Globes. The Golden Globes has awarded the 2021 Best Motion Pictures in the foreign language category to Lee Isaac Chung's American drama "Minari." The Arkansas-set tale about a Korean American immigrant family that moves to a rural farm in the 1980s is based on Chung's own childhood and stars Steven Yeun, Han Yeri, and veteran Korean actress Youn Yuh-jung.

영화 '미나리', 골든글로브 최우수 외국어영화상 수상

영화 '미나리'가 미국 양대 영화상인 골든글로브에서 최우수 외국어영화상을 수여받았다는 내용입니다.

 NEWS 전체 스크립트

'Minari' wins best foreign language film at Golden Globes

The Golden Globes has awarded the 2021 Best Motion Pictures in the foreign language category to Lee Isaac Chung's American drama "Minari."

The Arkansas-set tale about a Korean American immigrant family that moves to a rural farm in the 1980s is based on Chung's own childhood and stars Steven Yeun, Han Yeri, and veteran Korean actress Youn Yuh-jung.

Written by Korean-American Chung and co-produced by A24 and Brad Pitt's Plan B Entertainment, "Minari" is in both English and Korean but was ineligible for entry into the best picture race, per Hollywood foreign Press Association rules for films more than 50-percent in a language other than English.

Chung accepted the award Sunday evening thanking his cast and collaborators as his young daughter clung to his neck.

'Minari' wins best foreign language film at Golden Globes

'미나리' 골든글로브 외국어 영화상을 수상하다

　☆foreign 외국의 ['fɒr.ən] *발음 주의*

....

The Golden Globes has awarded the 2021 Best Motion Pictures in the foreign language category to Lee Isaac Chung's American drama "Minari."

골든글로브가 아이삭 정 감독의 미국 영화 '미나리'에게 외국어 부문 2021년 외국어영화상을 수여했다.

　☆award 수여하다

> e.g. The company has awarded its employees who worked hard.
> 　　그 회사는 열심히 일한 직원들에게 상을 주었다.

....

The Arkansas-set tale about a Korean American immigrant family that moves to a rural farm in the 1980s is based on Chung's own childhood and stars Steven Yeun, Han Yeri, and veteran Korean actress Youn Yuh-jung.

1980년대에 시골 농장으로 이주한 한국계 미국인 이민자 가족에 대한 아칸소 주 배경의 이야기는 정감독의 어린 시절을 바탕으로 하며 스티븐 연, 한예리, 그리고 한국의 베테랑 여배우 윤여정이 출연한다.

　☆-set ~를 배경으로 한

　☆tale 이야기

> e.g. They told some interesting tales about their life in the city.
> 　　그들은 도시 생활에 관한 그들의 몇 가지 재미있는 이야기를 들려주었다.

　☆immigrant 이민자

> e.g. Many of the immigrants have come from Russia.
> 　　많은 이민자들은 러시아에서 왔다.

　☆veteran 베테랑, 노련한

> e.g. He's a veteran speaker for human rights.
> 　　그는 인권에 대한 노련한 연설가이다.

　☆star 출연하다

Written by Korean-American Chung and co-produced by A24 and Brad Pitt's Plan B Entertainment, "Minari" is in both English and Korean but was ineligible for entry into the best picture race, per Hollywood foreign Press Association rules for films more than 50-percent in a language other than English.

한국계 미국인 정감독이 쓰고 A24와 브래드 피트의 플랜B 엔터테인먼트가 공동 제작한 '미나리'는 영어와 한국어를 둘 다 사용하지만 영어 이외 언어 비율이 50프로 이상인 영화에 대한 헐리우드 외신기자협회(HFPA)의 규정에 따라 최우수 작품 경쟁에 참가할 자격이 없었다.

☆(as) per ~에 따라

☆rule for ~에 대한 규정

☆ineligible 자격이 없는, 부적격의

Chung accepted the award Sunday evening thanking his cast and collaborators as his young daughter clung to his neck.

정감독은 일요일 저녁 그의 어린 딸이 그의 목에 매달리는 동안 출연자들과 동료들에게 감사하며 이 상을 받았다.

☆cling 매달리다 cling to one's neck ~의 목에 매달리다

Writing Exercise

1. 골든글로브가 아이삭 정 감독의 미국 영화 '미나리'에게 외국어 부문 2021년 외국어영화상을 수여했다.

   The Golden

2. 1980년대에 시골 농장으로 이주한 한국계 미국인 이민자 가족에 대한 아칸소 주 배경의 이야기는 정감독의 어린 시절을 바탕으로 하며 스티븐 연, 한예리, 그리고 한국의 베테랑 여배우 윤여정이 출연한다.

   The Arkansas-set

3. 한국계 미국인 정감독이 쓰고 A24와 브래드 피트의 플랜B엔터테인먼트가 공동 제작한 '미나리'는 영어와 한국어를 둘 다 사용하지만 영어 이외 언어 비율이 50프로 이상인 영화에 대한 헐리우드 외신기자협회(HFPA)의 규정에 따라 최우수 작품 경쟁에 참가할 자격이 없었다.

   Written

4. 정감독은 일요일 저녁 그의 어린 딸이 그의 목에 매달리는 동안 출연자들과 동료들에게 감사하며 이 상을 받았다.

   Chung

⊚ BRK 457/3
457/3
Today TH

영어 뉴스룸 92

English NewsRoom

BREAKING NEWS
'KSI Korean AI Tutor' offers free Korean language practice. If you want to learn Korean, you might want to consider downloading this smartphone app for free. It's from the King Sejong Institute Foundation, which operates Korean language and culture centers around the world. The app is called the 'KSI Korean AI Tutor.' It uses artificial intelligence to teach the Korean language for things in everyday life, like ordering food and shopping.

무료 회화앱을 출시한 세종학당재단

세종학당재단이 무료로 한국어 회화를 배울 수 있는 '세종학당 인공지능 모바일 애플리케이션'을 출시했다는 내용입니다.

 **전체 스크립트**

'KSI Korean AI Tutor' offers free Korean language practice

If you want to learn Korean, you might want to consider downloading this smartphone app for free.

It's from the King Sejong Institute Foundation, which operates Korean language and culture centers around the world.

The app is called the 'KSI Korean AI Tutor'.

It uses artificial intelligence to teach the Korean language for things in everyday life, like ordering food and shopping.

You can practice using dialogues for situations you might encounter at school or the office.

The AI uses voice recognition technology, to help with pronunciation and colloquial expressions.

The app only came out this morning, so it'll take some time before it appears for download, but it's for both Android and Apple.

NEWS 스크립트 분석

'KSI Korean AI Tutor' offers free Korean language practice
'세종학당 AI 선생님'이 무료 한국어 연습을 제공한다.

☆offer 제공하다, 제안하다

> e.g. The company offers free legal advice to people on low incomes.
> 그 회사는 저소득층 사람들에게 무료 법률 자문을 제공한다.

If you want to learn Korean, you might want to consider downloading this smartphone app for free.
한국어를 배우고 싶다면 이 스마트폰 앱을 무료로 다운로드 받는 것을 고려해 보는 것이 좋다.

☆consider -ing ~을 고려하다

☆for free 무료로, 공짜로

> e.g. You could get it for free if you are a member.
> 회원이시면 무료로 받으실 수 있습니다.

It's from the King Sejong Institute Foundation, which operates Korean language and culture centers around the world.
그 앱은 전 세계에 걸쳐 한국어와 문화센터를 운영하고 있는 세종학당재단이 만들었다.

☆operate 운영하다

> e.g. There are some changes to make the department operate more efficiently.
> 그 부서를 더 효율적으로 운영하기 위해 약간의 변화가 있다.

The app is called the 'KSI Korean AI Tutor.'
이 앱의 이름은 '세종학당 AI 선생님'이라고 불린다.

It uses artificial intelligence to teach the Korean language for things in everyday life, like ordering food and shopping.
이 앱은 음식을 주문하고 쇼핑하는 것과 같은 일상 생활에서 쓰는 한국어를 가르치기 위해 인공지능을 사용한다.

☆artificial intelligence 인공지능

☆everyday life 일상생활 =Daily life

> e.g. AI plays a significant role in everyday life.
> AI는 일상생활에서 중요한 역할을 한다.

You can practice using dialogues for situations you might encounter at school or in the office.

여러분은 학교나 사무실에서 마주칠 수 있는 상황에 대해 대화문을 사용해서 연습을 할 수 있다.

☆encounter 마주치다, 맞닥뜨리다

> e.g. On his way home he encountered a boy selling pens.
> 집으로 돌아오는 길에 그는 펜을 파는 소년을 마주쳤다.

The AI uses voice recognition technology, to help with pronunciation and colloquial expressions.

그 인공지능은 발음과 구어 표현을 돕기 위해 음성 인식 기술을 사용한다.

☆voice recognition technology 음성 인식 기술

☆colloquial 일상적인 대화체의

☆colloquial expressions 구어체의 표현.

The app only came out this morning, so it'll take some time before it appears for download, but it's for both Android and Apple.

그 앱은 오늘 오전에 나왔기 때문에 다운로드 받기까지는 시간이 좀 걸리겠지만, 안드로이드와 애플 둘 다 사용할 수 있다.

Writing Exercise

1. 한국어를 배우고 싶다면 이 스마트폰 앱을 무료로 다운로드 받는 것을 고려해 보는 것이 좋다.

   If you

2. 그 앱은 전 세계에 걸쳐 한국어와 문화센터를 운영하고 있는 세종학당재단이 만들었다.

   It's

3. 이 앱의 이름은 '세종학당 AI 선생님"이라고 불린다.

   The app

4. 이 앱은 음식을 주문하고 쇼핑하는 것과 같은 일상 생활에서 쓰는 한국어를 가르치기 위해 인공지능을 사용한다.

   It uses

5. 여러분은 학교나 사무실에서 마주칠 수 있는 상황에 대해 대화문을 사용해서 연습을 할 수 있다.

   You

6. 그 인공지능은 발음과 구어 표현을 돕기 위해 음성 인식 기술을 사용한다.

   The AI

7. 그 앱은 오늘 오전에 나왔기 때문에 다운로드 받기까지는 시간이 좀 걸리겠지만, 안드로이드와 애플 둘 다 사용할 수 있다.

   The app

BRK 457/3
457/3
Today TH

영어 뉴스룸 93

English NewsRoom

BREAKING NEWS

People who hinder epidemiological investigations to receive longer prison terms. Starting Tuesday, the South Korean health authorities are going to mete out harsher punishments to those who hinder efforts to track and trace virus cases and those who violate quarantine measures. Under a change to the law, those who intentionally disrupt epidemiological investigations will be sentenced to up to three years in prison or fined up to 30 million won,...

새치기하면 200만원?

앞으로 고의로 역학조사를 방해하는 사람에게 가중처벌이 가능해진다는 내용입니다.

 전체 스크립트

People who hinder epidemiological investigations to receive longer prison terms

Starting Tuesday, the South Korean health authorities are going to mete out harsher punishments to those who hinder efforts to track and trace virus cases and those who violate quarantine measures.

Under a change to the law, those who intentionally disrupt epidemiological investigations will be sentenced to up to three years in prison or fined up to 30 million won, which is around 27-thousand U.S. dollars.

The health ministry can also claim compensation from those who spread the virus on purpose.

Those who jump the queue and get vaccinated before their turn can be fined up to two million won, or about 18-hundred dollars.

NEWS 스크립트 분석

People who hinder epidemiological investigations to receive longer prison terms
더 긴 징역형을 받는 역학 조사를 방해하는 자

　☆hinder 방해하다

> e.g. Our journey was hindered by lack of money and high winds.
> 　　　우리의 여행은 자금 부족과 강풍으로 방해를 받았다.

　☆epidemiological 전염병학의
　☆epidemiological investigation 역학 조사
　☆prison term 형기

> e.g. His son served a prison term of 7 months.
> 　　　그의 아들은 징역 7개월을 복역했다.

Starting Tuesday, the South Korean health authorities are going to mete out harsher punishments to those who hinder efforts to track and trace virus cases and those who violate quarantine measures.
화요일부터 한국 보건당국은 바이러스 감염자를 추적하고 찾아내는 노력을 방해하는 자와 방역조치를 위반한 자에 대해 가중처벌을 내릴 예정이다.

　☆mete out (벌·가혹 행위 등을) 가하다, 부과하다

> e.g. Teachers meted out physical punishment to students 20 years ago.
> 　　　교사들은 20년 전에 학생들에게 체벌을 가했다.

　☆harsher 더 가혹한　harsh 가혹한
　☆track and trace 추적하고 찾아내다

Under a change to the law, those who intentionally disrupt epidemiological investigations will be sentenced to up to three years in prison or fined up to 30 million won, which is around 27-thousand U.S. dollars.
법 개정에 따라 역학조사를 고의로 방해한 사람에게는 3년 이하의 징역을 선고 받거나 3천만원 이하의 벌금(2만7천 달러)이 부과된다.

　☆intentionally 고의로
　☆disrupt 방해하다, 지장을 주다

> e.g. The conference was disrupted by a group of people who were not invited.
> 　　　그 회의는 초대받지 못한 한 무리의 사람들로 인해 방해받았다.

☆be sentenced to 형을 받다

e.g. She was sentenced to life in prison.
그녀는 종신형을 선고받았다.

☆up to 최대 ~까지

☆fine ~에게 벌금을 과하다, 과료에 처하다

e.g. Drivers who exceed the speed limit will be fined.
속도 제한을 초과한 운전자는 과태료를 물게 될 것이다.

The health ministry can also claim compensation from those who spread the virus on purpose.
보건복지부는 또한 고의로 바이러스를 퍼뜨린 사람들에게 또한 손해배상을 청구할 수 있다.

☆claim compensation 손해배상을 청구하다

e.g. It's difficult to claim compensation for workplace accidents.
직장 사고에 대한 손해배상 청구가 어렵다.

☆on purpose 고의로

e.g. Was it an accident, or did they do it on purpose?
사고였나요, 아니면 일부러 그런 건가요?

Those who jump the queue and get vaccinated before their turn can be fined up to two million won, or about 18-hundred dollars.
자기 차례가 되기 전에 새치기를 하고 예방접종을 받는 사람은 최대 200만원 또는 약 1800달러의 벌금이 부과될 수 있다.

☆jump the queue 새치기하다

e.g. We can't jump the queue in this place.
여기에서 우리는 새치기를 하면 안됩니다.

Writing Exercise

1. 화요일부터 한국 보건당국은 바이러스 감염자를 추적하고 찾아내는 노력을 방해하는 자와 방역조치를 위반한 자에 대해 가중처벌을 내릴 예정이다.

   Starting

   _____

2. 법 개정에 따라 역학조사를 고의로 방해한 사람에게는 3년 이하의 징역을 선고 받거나 3천만원 이하의 벌금(2만7천 달러)이 부과된다.

   Under

   _____

3. 보건복지부는 또한 고의로 바이러스를 퍼뜨린 사람들에게 또한 손해배상을 청구할 수 있다.

   The health

   _____

4. 자기 차례가 되기 전에 새치기를 하고 예방접종을 받는 사람은 최대 200만원 또는 약 1800달러의 벌금이 부과될 수 있다.

   Those

   _____

영어 뉴스룸 94

English NewsRoom

BREAKING NEWS

WHO advises against 'vaccine passports' The World Health Organization says there are "real, practical and ethical considerations" for countries to implement a so-called 'vaccine passport' system. The WHO advises against using them as a condition for international travel, not only because there aren't enough vaccines for the world, but also because data is still being collected on how long immunity lasts. It added that inequity and unfairness should not...

백신 여권 반대?

유럽연합 등이 '코로나19 백신 여권'을 만들려는 움직임에 대해 세계보건기구가 반대 입장을 밝혔다는 내용입니다.

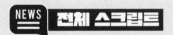

NEWS 전체 스크립트

WHO advises against 'vaccine passports'

The World Health Organization says there are "real, practical and ethical considerations" for countries to implement a so-called 'vaccine passport' system.

The WHO advises against using them as a condition for international travel, not only because there aren't enough vaccines for the world, but also because data is still being collected on how long immunity lasts.

It added that inequity and unfairness should not be branded into the system.

NEWS 스크립트 분석

WHO advises against 'vaccine passports'
WHO는 '백신 여권'에 대해 경고한다.

☆WHO World Health Organization 세계 보건 기구

☆against ~에 반대하여, ~에 맞서

e.g. More than 70 people voted against the new bill.
70명 이상의 사람들이 새 법안에 반대표를 던졌다.

The World Health Organization says there are "real, practical and ethical considerations" for countries to implement a so-called 'vaccine passport' system.
세계보건기구(WHO)는 각국이 이른바 '백신 여권' 제도를 시행하기 위해 "현실적, 실용적 그리고 윤리적인 고려사항"이 있다고 말한다.

☆ethical 윤리적인

☆consideration 고려사항

☆so-called 이른바

e.g. My so-called friend has stolen my boyfriend.
내 소위 친구가 내 남자친구를 훔쳐갔다.

☆implement 실행하다, 시행하다

e.g. The company will implement a special program for seniors.
그 회사는 노인들을 위한 특별 프로그램을 시행할 것이다.

The WHO advises against using them as a condition for international travel, not only because there aren't enough vaccines for the world, but also because data is still being collected on how long immunity lasts.
세계보건기구(WHO)는 세계에 백신이 충분하지 않을 뿐만 아니라 면역력이 얼마나 오래 지속되는 지에 대한 데이터가 여전히 수집되고 있기 때문에 백신 여권을 국제여행의 조건으로 삼지 말라고 조언한다.

☆condition 조건, 상태

e.g. This is a condition for publication.
이것은 출판을 위한 조건이다.

☆not only A but also B A뿐만 아니라 B도

e.g. The investigation is not only demanding but also stressful.
수사는 까다로울 뿐만 아니라 스트레스도 큽니다.

☆collected 수집된
☆immunity 면역력
☆last 지속되다

e.g. The reporter said the snow will last until the end of next week.
그 기자는 눈이 다음 주 말까지 계속될 것이라고 말했다.

It added that inequity and unfairness should not be branded into the system.
세계보건기구는 불평등과 불공정이 이 제도에 낙인 찍혀서는 안 된다고 덧붙였다.

☆inequity 불평등

e.g. Some professors teach gender inequity in the class.
일부 교수들은 수업에서 성 불평등을 가르친다.

☆unfairness 불공정

e.g. I cannot bear unfairness.
난 불공정을 참을 수 없어.

☆brand 1. 상표 (명사) | 2. 낙인을 찍다 (동사)

e.g. She branded him as a man without moral convictions.
그녀는 그를 도덕적 신념이 없는 남자로 낙인찍었다.

Writing Exercise

1. 세계보건기구(WHO)는 각국이 이른바 '백신 여권' 제도를 시행하기 위해 "현실적, 실용적 그리고 윤리적인 고려사항"이 있다고 말한다.

   The World

2. 세계보건기구(WHO)는 세계에 백신이 충분하지 않을 뿐만 아니라 면역력이 얼마나 오래 지속되는 지에 대한 데이터가 여전히 수집되고 있기 때문에 백신 여권을 국제여행의 조건으로 삼지 말라고 조언한다.

   The WHO

3. 세계보건기구는 불평등과 불공정이 이 제도에 낙인 찍혀서는 안 된다고 덧붙였다.

   It added

⊙ BRK 457/3
457/3
Today TH

영어 뉴스룸 95 · English NewsRoom

BREAKING NEWS | S. Korean gov't announces special measures to prevent 4th wave of COVID-19. To stop a potential fourth wave of COVID-19, the South Korean health authorities are going to be enforcing the virus prevention guidelines more proactively. Under the new measures, announced Tuesday, specifically targeting the greater Seoul area, the government will select 30 locations such as parks, department stores, and shopping areas and closely monitor...

공원과 백화점에 집중 방역 시행

코로나19 확진자가 수도권에서 집중적으로 발생함에 따라 정부가 공원, 백화점, 시장 등 30곳에 대해 특별방역을 시행한다는 내용입니다.

NEWS 전체 스크립트

S. Korean gov't announces special measures to prevent 4th wave of COVID-19

To stop a potential fourth wave of COVID-19, the South Korean health authorities are going to be enforcing the virus prevention guidelines more proactively.

Under the new measures, announced Tuesday, specifically targeting the greater Seoul area, the government will select 30 locations such as parks, department stores, and shopping areas and closely monitor them for two weeks starting Wednesday.

Due to the cluster infections reported from saunas, users in the capital area will have to check-in using QR codes on their phones rather than physically signing a visitor log.

They're also going to ramp up their inspections of workplaces with foreign workers.

 스크립트 분석

S. Korean gov't announces special measures to prevent 4th wave of COVID-19

한국 정부, 코로나 4차 확산 방지 특별조치(특별방역대책)를 발표하다

To stop a potential fourth wave of COVID-19, the South Korean health authorities are going to be enforcing the virus prevention guidelines more proactively.

잠재적 코로나 4차 확산을 막기 위해, 한국 보건 당국은 바이러스 예방 지침을 보다 적극적으로 시행할 예정이다.

☆potential ~이 될 가능성이 있는, 잠재적인

> e.g. They are potential buyers who will invest in our new development project.
> 그들은 우리의 새로운 개발 프로젝트에 투자할 잠재적 구매자들이다.

☆enforce 시행하다, 집행하다

> e.g. The government is working on a new law to enforce the curfew.
> 정부는 통행금지를 시행하기 위한 새로운 법을 마련하고 있다.

☆proactively 적극적으로

> e.g. The city is working proactively to help solve some of the country's social problems.
> 그 도시는 그 나라의 사회 문제들 중 일부를 해결하는 것을 돕기 위해 적극적으로 일하고 있다.

Under the new measures, announced Tuesday, specifically targeting the greater Seoul area, the government will select 30 locations such as parks, department stores, and shopping areas and closely monitor them for two weeks starting Wednesday.

특히 서울을 포함한 수도권 지역을 대상으로 화요일 발표된 새로운 대책에 따르면, 정부는 공원, 백화점, 쇼핑 지역 등 30곳을 지정하고 수요일부터 2주 동안 지정된 곳들을 면밀히 감시할 것이다.

☆specifically 특별히

> e.g. These jackets are designed specifically for young girls.
> 이 재킷들은 어린 소녀들을 위해 특별히 디자인되었다.

Due to the cluster infections reported from saunas, users in the capital area will have to check-in using QR codes on their phones rather than physically signing a visitor log.

사우나에서 보고된 집단 감염 때문에 수도권의 이용자들은 방문자 일지에 수기로 방문기록을 작성하는 것이 아니고 휴대전화 QR코드를 이용해 체크인해야 한다.

☆cluster 무리, 집단

e.g. A cluster of people is waiting outside of the building.
한 무리의 사람들이 건물 밖에서 기다리고 있다.

☆sauna 사우나 | 🔊 ['sɔː.nə], 🔊 ['saʊ.nə]
영국, 미국 발음 다름 주의!

☆physically 신체적으로, 육체적으로

They're also going to ramp up their inspections of workplaces with foreign workers.
정부는 또한 외국인 노동자가 있는 사업장에 대한 조사를 늘릴 예정이다.

☆ramp up ~을 늘리다, 증가시키다

e.g. The company ramped up the use of eco - friendly bags.
그 회사는 친환경 가방 사용을 늘렸다.

Writing Exercise

1. 잠재적 코로나 4차 확산을 막기 위해, 한국 보건 당국은 바이러스 예방 지침을 보다 적극적으로 시행할 예정이다.

To stop

2. 특히 서울을 포함한 수도권 지역을 대상으로 화요일 발표된 새로운 대책에 따르면, 정부는 공원, 백화점, 쇼핑 지역 등 30곳을 지정하고 수요일부터 2주 1 지정된 곳들을 면밀히 감시할 것이다.

Under

3. 사우나에서 보고된 집단 감염 때문에 수도권의 이용자들은 방문자 일지에 수기로 방문기록을 작성하는 것이 아니고 휴대전화 QR코드를 이용해 체크 인해야 한다.

Due to

4. 정부는 또한 외국인 노동자가 있는 사업장에 대한 조사를 늘릴 예정이다.

They're

영어 뉴스룸 96

English NewsRoom

BREAKING NEWS

Seoul backs down on testing all foreign workers for COVID-19. After numerous complaints about the policy, the city of Seoul is canceling plans to require all foreign workers in its jurisdiction to get tested for COVID-19. The order from earlier this week has been amended to say instead that testing is "recommended" for foreigners at high-risk workplaces. The order for mass testing, issued Wednesday, prompted the National Human Rights Commission of...

외국인 노동자는 코로나19 검사를 의무화?

서울시 등이 외국인 노동자에 대한 코로나19 검사 의무화를 철회했다는 내용입니다.

Seoul backs down on testing all foreign workers for COVID-19

After numerous complaints about the policy, the city of Seoul is canceling plans to require all foreign workers in its jurisdiction to get tested for COVID-19.

The order from earlier this week has been amended to say instead that testing is "recommended" for foreigners at high-risk workplaces.

The order for mass testing, issued Wednesday, prompted the National Human Rights Commission of Korea to launch an inquiry, saying it appeared to be discriminatory.

It also drew complaints from at least two foreign embassies -- those of Britain and France.

Another proposal has also been taken off the table by the Province of Gyeonggi-do, which would have required tests by all foreign jobseekers.

NEWS 스크립트 분석

Seoul backs down on testing all foreign workers for COVID-19
서울시가 모든 외국인 근로자들의 COVID-19 검사를 철회하다.

☆back down 철회하다, 포기하다

> e.g. The government had to back down on its plan for the future.
> 정부는 미래를 위해 계획을 철회해야만 했다.

After numerous complaints about the policy, the city of Seoul is canceling plans to require all foreign workers in its jurisdiction to get tested for COVID-19.
그 정책에 대한 수많은 불만이 나온 후에 서울시는 관할구역에 있는 모든 외국인 근로자들에게 COVID-19 검사를 받도록 요구하는 계획을 취소하고 있다.

☆numerous 많은

> e.g. The reporter has written numerous articles about love.
> 그 기자는 사랑에 대한 수많은 기사를 썼다.

☆complaint 불평, 항의
☆require A to B A에게 B하기를 요구하다
☆jurisdiction 관할 구역

The order from earlier this week has been amended to say instead that testing is "recommended" for foreigners at high-risk workplaces.
이번 주 초부터 그 행정명령은 대신 고 위험 작업장에서의 외국인들에게 코로나19 검사를 "권고"한다고 개정되었다.

☆amend (법 등을) 개정하다, 수정하다

> e.g. The special law has been amended several times.
> 그 특별법은 여러 번 개정되었다.

☆high-risk 위험성이 큰

The order for mass testing, issued Wednesday, prompted the National Human Rights Commission of Korea to launch an inquiry, saying it appeared to be discriminatory.

수요일에 발표된 대규모 코로나19 검사 명령은 국가인권위원회가 차별적인 것으로 보인다며 조사에 착수하도록 했다.

☆prompt A to B A가 B하도록 자극하다, 촉발하다

e.g. What prompted you to write a book?
책을 쓰게 된 계기가 무엇입니까?

☆launch an inquiry 조사에 착수하다

e.g. The government will launch an independent inquiry into the allegation.
정부는 그 혐의에 대한 독립적인 조사에 착수할 것이다.

☆discriminatory 차별적인

It also drew complaints from at least two foreign embassies -- those of Britain and France.

이는 또한 적어도 두 외국 대사관, 영국과 프랑스의 대사관으로부터도 불만을 샀다.

☆draw complaint 불만을 사다

Another proposal has also been taken off the table by the Province of Gyeonggi-do, which would have required tests by all foreign jobseekers.

외국인 구직자 전원에게 검사를 요구했던 경기도의 또 다른 제안도 추진 대상에서 제외됐다.

☆take off the table 철회하다, 논의대상에서 제외하다

e.g. The deal has been taken off the table.
그 거래는 취소되었다.

☆jobseeker 구직자

Writing Exercise

1. 그 정책에 대한 수많은 불만이 나온 후에 서울시는 관할구역에 있는 모든 외국인 근로자들에게 COVID - 19 검사를 받도록 요구하는 계획을 취소하고 있다.

   After

2. 이번 주 초부터 그 행정명령은 대신 고 위험 작업장에서의 외국인들에게 코로나19 검사를 "권고"한다고 개정되었다.

   The order

3. 수요일에 발표된 대규모 코로나19 검사 명령은 국가인권위원회가 차별적인 것으로 보인다며 조사에 착수하도록 했다.

   The order

4. 이는 또한 적어도 두 외국 대사관, 영국과 프랑스의 대사관으로부터도 불만을 샀다.

   It also

5. 외국인 구직자 전원에게 검사를 요구했던 경기도의 또 다른 제안도 추진 대상에서 제외됐다.

   Another

◉ BRK 457/3
457/3
Today TH

영어 뉴스룸 97

**English
NewsRoom**

**BREAKING
NEWS**

Early voting for Seoul mayoral by-election to be held next week. Early voting will be held for the Seoul mayoral election next Friday and Saturday April 2nd and 3rd. If you're eligible as a Seoul resident, you can cast a ballot at one of the 424 polling stations throughout the country. On election day, however, you can only vote at your designated site. There are options for voters in quarantine, too.

서울시장 보궐선거 사전투표 실시

서울시가 사전투표소 424곳에서 서울시장 재·보궐 선거의 사전투표를 실시한다는 내용입니다.

 NEWS 전체 스크립트

Early voting for Seoul mayoral by-election to be held next week

Early voting will be held for the Seoul mayoral election next Friday and Saturday April 2nd and 3rd.

If you're eligible as a Seoul resident, you can cast a ballot at one of the 424 polling stations throughout the country.

On election day, however, you can only vote at your designated site.

There are options for voters in quarantine, too.

Those quarantined at home can vote by mail or, if asymptomatic, go to a polling station in their own car or on foot as long as they're back home within 30 minutes.

For quarantine facilities, there'll be voting booths set up on site.

 스크립트 분석

Early voting for Seoul mayoral by-election to be held next week
다음 주 서울시장 보궐선거 사전투표 실시

☆early voting 사전투표
☆mayoral 시장의
☆by-election 보궐 선거
☆mayoral by-election 시장 보궐선거

Early voting will be held for the Seoul mayoral election next Friday and Saturday April 2nd and 3rd.
다음 주 금요일과 토요일 4월 2일과 3일에 서울시장 선거에 대한 사전투표가 실시된다.

If you're eligible as a Seoul resident, you can cast a ballot at one of the 424 polling stations throughout the country.
서울시민으로서 자격이 있다면 전국 424개 투표소 중 한 곳에서 투표할 수 있다.

☆eligible 자격이 있는

e.g. Only people over 19 are eligible to vote.
19세 이상만 투표할 수 있다.

☆cast a ballot 투표하다, 표를 던지다

e.g. Candidates should also cast a ballot for the president in the election.
후보들도 선거에서 대통령을 투표해야 한다.

☆polling station 투표소

On election day, however, you can only vote at your designated site.
그러나 선거일에는 지정된 사이트에서만 투표할 수 있다.

☆designated 지정된

e.g. Visitors should smoke at designated areas.
방문객들은 지정된 장소에서 담배를 피워야 한다.

There are options for voters in quarantine, too.
또한 격리된 유권자들을 위한 옵션들도 있다.

☆in quarantine 격리되어

e.g. He agreed to stay in quarantine for another two weeks.
그는 2주 더 격리 하기로 동의했다.

Those quarantined at home can vote by mail or, if asymptomatic, go to a polling station in their own car or on foot as long as they're back home within 30 minutes.
집에 격리된 사람들은 우편으로 투표할 수도 있고, 무증상인 경우 30분 안에 집에 돌아오는 한 자가용이나 도보로 투표소에 갈 수도 있다.

☆asymptomatic 증상이 없는

☆on foot 걸어서, 도보로

e.g. It takes about 20 minutes by car, but 2 hours on foot.
차로 20분 정도 걸리지만, 걸어서 2시간 정도 걸립니다.

For quarantine facilities, there'll be voting booths set up on site.
방역시설에는 현장에 투표소가 설치될 예정이다.

☆set up 설치하다

☆on site 현장의

Writing Exercise

1. 다음 주 금요일과 토요일 4월 2일과 3일에 서울시장 선거에 대한 사전투표가 실시된다.

   Early _____

   _____

2. 서울시민으로서 자격이 있다면 전국 424개 투표소 중 한 곳에서 투표할 수 있다.

   If you're _____

   _____

3. 그러나 선거일에는 지정된 사이트에서만 투표할 수 있다.

   On election _____

   _____

4. 또한 격리된 유권자들을 위한 옵션들도 있다.

   There _____

   _____

5. 집에 격리된 사람들은 우편으로 투표할 수도 있고, 무증상인 경우 30분 안에 집에 돌아오는 한 자가용이나 도보로 투표소에 갈 수도 있다.

   Those _____

   _____

6. 방역시설에는 현장에 투표소가 설치될 예정이다.

   For quarantine _____

   _____

◎ BRK 457/3
457/3
Today TH

영어 뉴스룸 98

English NewsRoom

BREAKING NEWS

Traffic controls in Seoul's Yeouido area to deter big crowds from viewing cherry blossoms. As most of the popular places in Seoul to see cherry blossoms are closed to the public, traffic control in the Yeouido area is being enforced a day earlier than planned, starting today. The area just behind the National Assembly building, home to the so-called cherry blossom tunnel, was originally set to be under road traffic control from April 1st to the 12th.

벚꽃관람 통제

코로나19로 인해 여의도 국회 인근 벚꽃관람을 통제한다는 내용입니다.

Traffic controls in Seoul's Yeouido area to deter big crowds from viewing cherry blossoms

As most of the popular places in Seoul to see cherry blossoms are closed to the public, traffic control in the Yeouido area is being enforced a day earlier than planned, starting today.

The area just behind the National Assembly building, home to the so-called cherry blossom tunnel, was originally set to be under road traffic control from April 1st to the 12th.

However, controls started a few hours ago in a bid to deter big gatherings of people due to the pandemic.

Traffic controls in Seoul's Yeouido area to deter big crowds from viewing cherry blossoms
상춘객들을 막기 위해 서울의 여의도 지역의 교통 통제

☆traffic control 교통 통제

☆deter 단념시키다, 그만두게 하다

> e.g. The policy was made to deter people from going abroad during the summer holiday season.
> 그 정책은 여름 휴가철에 사람들이 해외로 나가는 것을 막기 위해 만들어졌다.

☆crowd 무리, 군중

☆cherry blossom 벚꽃

As most of the popular places in Seoul to see cherry blossoms are closed to the public, traffic control in the Yeouido area is being enforced a day earlier than planned, starting today.
벚꽃을 볼 수 있는 서울의 대부분의 인기 있는 지역들이 대중들에게 출입이 금지되어 있으므로, 여의도 지역의 교통 통제는 예정보다 하루 일찍인 오늘부터 시행되고 있다.

☆the public 대중, 일반국민

> e.g. The building is open to the public.
> 그 건물은 일반인에게 개방되어 있다.

☆enforce (법률 등을) 집행하다, 시행하다

> e.g. In this case, the law is being enforced.
> 이 경우 법이 시행되고 있다.

The area just behind the National Assembly building, home to the so-called cherry blossom tunnel, was originally set to be under road traffic control from April 1st to the 12th.
소위 벚꽃 터널의 본고장인 국회의사당 건물 바로 뒤 지역은 원래 도로 교통 통제를 4월 1일부터 12일까지 시작하도록 되어 있었다.

☆home to ~의 본고장, ~의 고향

☆so-called 소위, 이른바

☆originally 원래

☆be set to ~하도록 예정되어 있다

> e.g. The group was originally set to debut this month.
> 그 그룹은 원래 이번 달에 데뷔할 예정이었다.

☆under control 통제되는

e.g. Many doctors are worried that the situation isn't under control.
많은 의사들은 상황이 통제되지 않는 것을 걱정하고 있다.

However, controls started a few hours ago in a bid to deter big gatherings of people due to the pandemic.
그러나 코로나19로 인해 사람들의 큰 모임들을 막기 위해서 통제는 몇 시간 전에 시작했다.

☆in a bid to do something ~하기 위하여, ~을 겨냥하여

e.g. The company will cut more than 100 jobs in a bid to reduce costs.
그 회사는 비용 절감을 위해 100명 이상의 일자리를 줄일 것이다.

Writing Exercise

1. 벚꽃을 볼 수 있는 서울의 대부분의 인기 있는 지역들이 대중들에게 출입이 금지되어 있으므로, 여의도 지역의 교통 통제는 예정보다 하루 일찍인 오늘부터 시행되고 있다.

   As most

2. 소위 벚꽃 터널의 본고장인 국회의사당 건물 바로 뒤 지역은 원래 도로 교통 통제를 4월 1일부터 12일까지 시작하도록 되어 있었다.

   The area

3. 그러나 코로나19로 인해 사람들의 큰 모임들을 막기 위해서 통제는 몇 시간 전에 시작했다.

   However,

◎ BRK 457/3
457/3
Today TH

영어 뉴스룸 99

English NewsRoom

BREAKING NEWS

New Jersey city proclaims October 21st 'Korean Hanbok Day' : AAYC. 'Korean Hanbok Day' has been proclaimed for the very first time outside of South Korea. The Asian American Youth Council announced on Sunday, that a city in New Jersey decided to name October 21st as the annual day for celebrating South Korea's traditional attire, 'Hanbok'. South Korean youth activists led the move to refute false claims that say South Korea's 'Hanbok' and the...

한복이 중국 전통의상?

한복이 중국 전통의상이라는 억지 주장에 분노한 미국의 한인 고교생들이 해외 최초로 '한복의 날' 제정을 이끌어 냈다는 내용입니다.

 **전체 스크립트**

New Jersey city proclaims October 21st 'Korean Hanbok Day' : AAYC

'Korean Hanbok Day' has been proclaimed for the very first time outside of South Korea.

The Asian American Youth Council announced on Sunday, that a city in New Jersey decided to name October 21st as the annual day for celebrating South Korea's traditional attire, 'Hanbok'.

South Korean youth activists led the move to refute false claims that say South Korea's 'Hanbok' and the well-known dish 'Kimchi' are Chinese.

Tenafly was the first city to pass the petition and is set to hold a proclamation ceremony on Tuesday.

The council is aiming to enact 'Korean Hanbok Day' in other cities across the U.S. as well.

New Jersey city proclaims October 21st 'Korean Hanbok Day' : AAYC

뉴저지 주 시에서 10월 21일을 '한국 한복의 날'로 선포하다 : AAYC

　　☆proclaim 선언[선포]하다

> e.g. He proclaimed that he will run for the election next year.
> 　　　그는 내년에 선거에 출마하겠다고 선언했다.

　　☆AAYC The Asian American Youth Council 재미차세대협의회

'Korean Hanbok Day' has been proclaimed for the very first time outside of South Korea.

　　☆'(한국) 한복의 날'이 해외에서 최초로 선포되었다.

　　☆for the very first time 최초로

> e.g. He has attended the award ceremony for the very first time.
> 　　　그는 그 시상식에 처음으로 참석했다.

The Asian American Youth Council announced on Sunday, that a city in New Jersey decided to name October 21st as the annual day for celebrating South Korea's traditional attire, 'Hanbok'.

재미차세대협의회는 미국 뉴저지의 한 도시가 한국의 전통의상인 '한복'을 기념하기 위해 10월 21일을 연례일로 지정하기로 결정했다고 일요일 밝혔다.

　　☆name 이름을 지어주다, 명명하다

> e.g. My parents named our cats Fodera and Zoo.
> 　　　우리 부모님은 우리 고양이들의 이름을 Fodera와 Zoo라고 지으셨어.

　　☆attire 의복, 복장 *(격식)*

> e.g. I think mini skirts are inappropriate attire for a conference.
> 　　　난 미니스커트가 회의에 부적절한 복장이라고 생각해.

South Korean youth activists led the move to refute false claims that say South Korea's 'Hanbok' and the well-known dish 'Kimchi' are Chinese.

한국의 청소년 운동가들은 한국의 '한복'과 잘 알려진 음식 '김치'가 중국의 것이라는 잘못된 주장을 반박하기 위해 이러한 움직임을 주도했다.

☆refute 논박[반박]하다; 부인하다

e.g. He had refuted the allegations, saying that the ruling party was wrong this time.
그는 이번에는 여당이 잘못했다며 주장들을 반박했었다.

☆false claim 거짓 주장, 사실이 아닌 주장

e.g. I believe that this is a false claim by the government, so be careful.
저는 이것이 정부의 거짓 주장이라고 믿으니 주의하세요.

Tenafly was the first city to pass the petition and is set to hold a proclamation ceremony on Tuesday.
테너플라이는 청원서를 통과시킨 첫 번째 도시로 화요일에 선포식을 가질 예정이다.

☆Tenafly 테너플라이 (미국, 뉴저지 주)
☆proclamation 선언서, 성명서; 선언, 선포

The council is aiming to enact 'Korean Hanbok Day' in other cities across the U.S. as well.
이 협의회는 미국 전역의 다른 도시에서도 '한국 한복의 날'을 제정하는 것을 목표로 하고 있다.

☆aim to ~을 목표로 하다
☆enact (법을) 제정하다

e.g. The immigration law is to be enacted on Tuesday.
이민법은 화요일에 제정될 예정이다.

1. '(한국)한복의 날'이 해외에서 최초로 선포되었다.

   'Korean
   _____
   _____

2. 재미차세대협의회는 미국 뉴저지의 한 도시가 한국의 전통의상인 '한복'을 기념하기 위해 10월 21일을 연례일로 지정하기로 결정했다고 일요일 밝혔다.

   The Asian
   _____
   _____

3. 한국의 청소년 운동가들은 한국의 '한복'과 잘 알려진 음식 '김치'가 중국의 것이라는 잘못된 주장을 반박하기 위해 이러한 움직임을 주도했다.

   South
   _____
   _____

4. 테너플라이는 청원서를 통과시킨 첫 번째 도시로 화요일에 선포식을 가질 예정이다.

   Tenafly
   _____
   _____

5. 이 협의회는 미국 전역의 다른 도시에서도 '한국 한복의 날'을 제정하는 것을 목표로 하고 있다.

   The council
   _____
   _____

영어 뉴스룸 100

◎ BRK 457/3
457/3
Today TH

English NewsRoom

BREAKING NEWS

Seoul awarded by UNESCO for bridging 'digital divide' among seniors. The city of Seoul has been recognized by UNESCO with an award for its innovative ways of bridging the "digital divide" among its senior citizens. Seoul is one of ten cities to be featured at a forum this week on sustainable, inclusive and smart cities. Specifically, the award for Seoul is in the education category. It got the Linking Cities award for its use of robots in the homes of senior...

로봇으로 노인들의 '디지털 격차'를 줄인다?

서울시가 유네스코가 선정하는 세계 10대 연결도시에 이름을 올렸다는 내용입니다

NEWS 전체 스크립트

Seoul awarded by UNESCO for bridging 'digital divide' among seniors

The city of Seoul has been recognized by UNESCO with an award for its innovative ways of bridging the "digital divide" among its senior citizens.

Seoul is one of ten cities to be featured at a forum this week on sustainable, inclusive and smart cities.

Specifically, the award for Seoul is in the education category.

It got the Linking Cities award for its use of robots in the homes of senior citizens to help them catch up with the kinds of technology now ubiquitous in our daily lives.

For instance, the robots help seniors use the messenger app KakaoTalk

And it helps them book train tickets and use digital kiosks at restaurants.

The award will be presented on April 15, Paris time, at the 'UNESCO Netexplo Linking Cities Forum'.

Seoul awarded by UNESCO for bridging 'digital divide' among seniors
노인들의 '디지털 격차'를 메운 공로로 유네스코로부터 상을 수여받은 서울시

☆bridge 다리를 놓다, 형성하다

e.g. He's working to bridge the gap between education and technology.
그는 교육과 기술 사이의 격차를 해소하기 위해 일하고 있다.

☆senior 노인

The city of Seoul has been recognized by UNESCO with an award for its innovative ways of bridging the "digital divide" among its senior citizens.
서울시는 노인들의 "디지털 격차"를 해소하는 혁신적인 방법으로 유네스코로부터 상을 받았다.

☆innovative 혁신적인, 획기적인 | 영 ['ɪn.ə.və.tɪv], 미 ['ɪn.ə.veɪ.tɪv]
영국, 미국 발음 다름 주의!

Seoul is one of ten cities to be featured at a forum this week on sustainable, inclusive and smart cities.
서울은 이번 주에 지속 가능하고, 포용적이며, 스마트한 도시에 관한 포럼에 소개될 10개의 도시 중 하나이다.

☆sustainable 지속 가능한

e.g. Sustainable economic growth is important not only for the country, but also for many companies.
지속 가능한 경제 성장은 국가 뿐만 아니라 많은 기업들에게도 중요하다.

☆inclusive 포용적인

Specifically, the award for Seoul is in the education category.
구체적으로, 서울시가 받은 상은 교육분야이다.

☆specifically 구체적으로, 특별히

e.g. These sunglasses are designed specifically for pets.
이 선글라스는 애완동물을 위해 특별히 디자인되었다.

It got the Linking Cities award for its use of robots in the homes of senior citizens to help them catch up with the kinds of technology now ubiquitous in our daily lives.

서울시는 현재 우리의 일상 생활에서 어디에나 있는 기술들을 노인들이 따라잡을 수 있도록 노인들의 집에서 로봇을 사용한 공로로 연결 도시 상을 받았다.

☆use 사용 | [juːs], [juːz]
명사, 동사 발음 다름 주의!

☆catch up with 따라가다, 따라잡다

> e.g. Can you slow down a little bit so that I can catch up with you?
> 제가 당신을 따라잡을 수 있도록 조금만 천천히 해주시겠어요?

☆ubiquitous 어디에나 있는, 아주 흔한

For instance, the robots help seniors use the messenger app KakaoTalk.

예를 들어, 그 로봇들은 노인들에게 메신저 앱 카카오톡을 사용하도록 도와준다.

And it helps them book train tickets and use digital kiosks at restaurants.

그리고 그것은 그들이 기차표를 예약하고 식당에서 디지털 무인단말기를 사용하는 것을 돕는다.

☆kiosk *(공공장소에 설치된)* 무인단말기

The award will be presented on April 15, Paris time, at the 'UNESCO Netexplo Linking Cities Forum'.

이 상은 파리 시간으로 4월 15일 '유네스코 넷엑스플로 연결 도시 포럼'에서 수여될 것이다.

☆present 수여하다

> e.g. The award for Best Actress will be presented at a conference with her fans.
> 여우주연상은 팬들과의 콘퍼런스에서 수여될 것이다.

1. 서울시는 노인들의 "디지털 격차"를 해소하는 혁신적인 방법으로 유네스코로부터 상을 받았다.

   The city _____

   _____

2. 서울은 이번 주에 지속 가능하고, 포용적이며, 스마트한 도시에 관한 포럼에 소개될 10개의 도시 중 하나이다.

   Seoul _____

   _____

3. 구체적으로, 서울시가 받은 상은 교육분야이다.

   Specifically, _____

   _____

4. 서울시는 현재 우리의 일상 생활에서 어디에나 있는 기술들을 노인들이 따라잡을 수 있도록 노인들의 집에서 로봇을 사용한 공로로 연결 도시 상을 받았다.

   It got _____

   _____

5. 예를 들어, 그 로봇들은 노인들에게 메신저 앱 카카오톡을 사용하도록 도와준다.

   For instance, _____

   _____

6. 그리고 그것은 그들이 기차표를 예약하고 식당에서 디지털 무인단말기를 사용하는 것을 돕는다.

   And it _____

   _____

7. 이 상은 파리 시간으로 4월 15일 '유네스코 넷엑스플로 연결 도시 포럼'에서 수여될 것이다.

   The award _____

   _____

Memo

권아나의 영어 뉴스룸 시사영어 100

발행일　2024년 1월 30일

발행인　조순자

편저자　권주현·김기성 공저

편집·표지디자인　김현수

발행처　종이향기

※ 본 교재는 공공누리 제1유형에 해당하는 아리랑 뉴스 스크립트를 활용하여 집필되었습니다.

※ 낙장이나 파본은 교환해 드립니다.

정　가　26,000원　　　　　**ISBN**　979-11-91292-74-9